Survival of Rural America

Survival of

Rural America

Small Victories and Bitter Harvests

RICHARD E. WOOD

 University Press of Kansas

Published by the University Press of Kansas (Lawrence, Kansas
66045), which was organized by the Kansas Board of Regents
and is operated and funded by Emporia State University, Fort
Hays State University, Kansas State University, Pittsburg State
University, the University of Kansas, and Wichita State
University

Library of Congress Cataloging-in-Publication Data
Wood, Richard E.
Survival of rural America : small victories and bitter harvests /
Richard E. Wood.
p. cm.
Includes bibliographical references and index.
ISBN 978-0-7006-1577-3 (cloth : alk. paper)
1. Kansas—Rural conditions. 2. Sustainable development—
Kansas. I. Title.
HN79.K23W66   2008
307.7209781—dc22
2007045599

British Library Cataloguing-in-Publication Data is available.

Printed in the United States of America

10 9 8 7 6 5 4 3 2 1

For my parents

RICHARD ARMIT WOOD AND HELEN VIRGINIA CONKLIN WOOD

Like most people born in rural America, they wasted little time getting away from their small hometowns and into a big city. As I never showed much interest in rural America when they dragged me back there to visit friends and family, I suspect they would have been surprised by this book. I hope they also would have been pleased by it.

Contents

Acknowledgments

Survival of Rural America is a book about people. From a macro perspective it is about the movement of tens of millions of people out of rural communities and into cities and metropolitan areas, and the impact that this migration is having on the world, on the places they leave behind, and on our culture.

But it is also a book that examines rural life from a micro, or personal, perspective, telling the stories of people who remain in their small towns and who are trying to make sure that their way of life will offer hope and promise to generations to come.

These people generously shared their experiences and helped bring this book to life, and I am indebted to them for their time and their willingness to help tell the story of rural America in the twenty-first century.

I am also indebted to Fred Woodward, director of the University Press of Kansas, who was supportive of the book from the start, and Susan McRory, Susan Schott, and all the others at the Press. Long before I was fortunate enough to become one of their authors, I was impressed both by the breadth and diversity of books published by them—and by their counterparts at university presses in other states—and by their dedication to their rural heritage.

Introduction

Rural America: Our Field of Dreams

If it were to happen quickly—terrorism, perhaps, or some kind of plague—then it would be headline news. I'm referring to the destruction of small-town rural America, home to about one of every nine Americans, living on two-thirds of the land, and of the threat to a culture and a way of life that in many ways still defines America. Well, it *is* happening, has been for most of a century, but it has been taking place very slowly and, for most of us, invisibly.

Today, more than ever in our history, the 83 percent of Americans who live in metropolitan areas have about as much real-life knowledge of the other 17 percent, and of rural America in general, as they do of central Africa. Worse, much of the little they think they know isn't true.

It may be best to begin with a definition. What is rural America? The most universally accepted definition is that of the U.S. Census Bureau, which says rural America is open country with small settlements of fewer than 2,500 people. In other words, while everyone would readily agree that the Hamptons and Aspen are certainly not rural, neither is Fargo, North Dakota, or Kokomo, Indiana.

When people do travel through the countryside, they usually still miss seeing rural America because they tend to cling to interstate highways and the larger cities that have grown around well-positioned interchanges. It's easy to miss rural America. It's a big country, but most of it is unoccupied. In fact, you could move every man, woman, and child in the country—some 300 million people—to Texas, give them each half an acre, and *still* the population density of Texas would be just a small fraction of the density of Chicago or Los Angeles, let alone New York City. Even though there is a lot of rural America out there (over 75 percent of the nation's land area, as the map in Figure 1 indicates), it can be surprisingly difficult to find if you're not looking for it.

As a result, most Americans don't know what a rural American town—or a rural American for that matter—looks like. If they have any

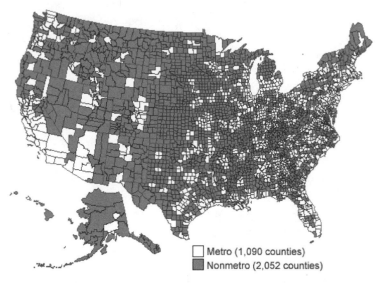

Metro (1,090 counties)
Nonmetro (2,052 counties)

Figure 1. Metropolitan and Nonmetropolitan Counties, 2003
In 2003, in an effort to achieve greater accuracy, the U.S. Census Bureau changed its nomenclature from "rural" and "urban" to "metropolitan" and "nonmetropolitan." As a result about 7 million people who lived in areas previously designated as rural were now considered to live in metropolitan areas, largely because previously rural areas were being swallowed up by suburban expansion.
Source: U.S. Department of Agriculture, Economic Research Service.

image of rural America it may come from a movie, a television show such as *Little House on the Prairie,* or perhaps the venerable *Prairie Home Companion* radio program. Their image probably includes farming and ranching, although the vast majority of rural Americans are engaged in neither pursuit. And if they were asked to imagine rural towns, they would probably picture a relatively stable little place with a church, some barns, and modest, well-tended houses with white siding and a front porch, and perhaps there would be a "downtown" cafe with people wearing overalls and John Deere baseball caps and drinking Maxwell House coffee. That's how I—as a representative of urban America—probably would have imagined rural America a couple of years ago.

Like most people living in cities, I really didn't think much about rural America and had not spent much time there since college. Food from rural farms regularly showed up on grocery store shelves, and interstate highways made it easy to get from city to city without having to venture more than a few hundred yards from the road to find a franchise motel and fast food restaurant.

I assumed rural America was getting along okay. Not growing much, perhaps, but basically stable and comfortable, enjoying rising land prices, and free from most of the problems and challenges of urban America. Rural America also seemed to be politically powerful, as evidenced by headlines such as "Failure of Global Trade Talks Is Traced to the Power of Farmers," which appeared on the first page of the *New York Times* business section on July 27, 2006. In most elections it seemed that the predominantly rural "red states" were able to hold their own against the larger and more urban "blue states."

It was, therefore, with some surprise that I read a newspaper story in 2005 that said many rural towns were so desperate for people that they actually were *giving away land* if people would only move there. The story told of massive population shifts away from rural communities, school closings, aging demographics, no jobs, and a poverty rate more than 20 percent above the national average. Perhaps because one of the towns mentioned in the story was my father's birthplace, I was intrigued. What had happened to rural America while I wasn't paying attention?

A little research uncovered the grim story: for at least the last half-century people have been fleeing most small rural towns as if they were radioactive. Family farms have given way to large-scale corporate farms requiring fewer workers per acre, many textile, furniture, and other manufacturing plants have gone offshore, highways have improved access from rural America to the shopping and other amenities of urban America, and more rural youth have gone to college and found escape from their hometowns and dead-end jobs. I thought of my own family, in which everyone had left their small rural towns long ago, and of the many rural students I had known in college who were now living in urban America.

As I learned more about what was happening to rural America, I came across Thomas Frank's best-selling book, *What's the Matter with Kansas?* in which he uses his home state as an example to examine the entire country's political division into red and blue states. Frank's description of what was happening in rural communities reinforced what I was learning. He describes the more rural parts of Kansas as being "pretty much in free fall . . . a civilization in the early stages of irreversible decay."[1] He also thinks he knows what has caused it: free-market capitalism.

Certainly the magnitude of the exodus from rural communities, as shown in Figure 2, is shocking. Much of rural America, from New York to California, is experiencing population declines—often steep declines—and those rural communities that are growing have tended to be suburbs-in-waiting near major metropolitan areas or places close to recreational attractions such as mountains, lakes, and oceans. In other words, it seems like rural America can't win. If it is relatively isolated, it is being depopulated out of existence, and if it is near a big city or a recreational amenity, it is attracting population and becoming a suburb or a city in its own right. When the U.S. Department of Agriculture (USDA) posted an article on its web site in 2003 titled "Farewell Rural America," I suspect many readers thought that even the USDA was throwing in the towel and reminding the last one out to turn off the lights. In fact, it turned out to be just an unfortunately named article announcing that the USDA was changing the name of its magazine, which had been titled *Rural America,* to *Amber Waves.*

The trend has not been limited to the United States. Rural communities throughout the world have been depopulating just as fast or faster. Stories from China have told of tens of millions of people leaving the countryside for uncertain futures in urban centers, prompting Chinese leaders to call for a new five-year plan to create a "new socialist countryside" promising more rural development and improvements in education, public services, and public health. The fact that rural depopulation is an international phenomenon made me wonder if Frank's theory was correct or if what was happening to so many rural communities wasn't perhaps being caused by a much broader and deeper dynamic than simply "free-market capitalism."

I began to consider the merits of writing about rural depopulation, its causes, and the effect it is having on both the communities that are losing people and those that are gaining them. There is certainly evidence of stress on both sides of the migration equation.

Yet as I learned more about what was going on and began to travel in rural America, I uncovered something I hadn't expected. It turns out that a lot of people in rural America—including certainly those involved

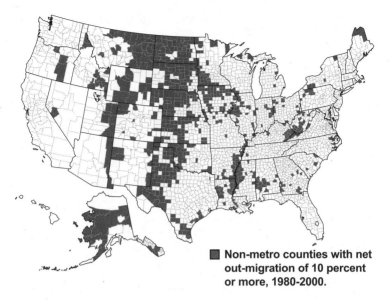

Non-metro counties with net out-migration of 10 percent or more, 1980-2000.

Figure 2. Population Loss Counties
Source: U.S. Department of Agriculture, Economic Research Service.

in the "free land" giveaways—are determined to change their destiny and try to reverse, or at least slow, the population losses they are suffering. There are still people who believe in rural America and who see a future that does not contain just a handful of surviving cities linked by interstate highways and surrounded by thousands of ghost towns.

What had been a research effort focused primarily on despair and failure began to give way to stories about hopeful and creative people who may have seen the handwriting on the wall but have chosen to ignore it. From projects as small as local school bond issues and community medical clinics to plans for vast regional buffalo grassland parks covering large parts of several states, it is clear that the frontier spirit is not dead and that the final chapter of rural America is not—yet—set in stone. After years of tending to treat rural economies as primarily agricultural, the federal government and a few states have acknowledged the changes that have taken place in rural America and are seeking better ways to address the needs of rural communities. At the dawn of the twenty-first century there are significant areas of hope and promise for rural America, including the alternative fuels industry, the trend toward natural foods derived from sustainable sources, the desire of many people for the relative safety and security of rural life, improvements in communications and transportation, and the growth of rural entrepreneurship. There is also one group of people who *are* migrating to rural America. For the last couple of decades, Latinos have been virtually the only people moving into rural areas in any meaningful numbers—although most of their migration has been for jobs in relatively large cities (by rural American standards) such as Marshalltown, Iowa, and Garden City, Kansas, both centers of the meat-packing industry.

As this book makes clear, the odds remain very much against any kind of permanent, widespread rural revival, at least in those places that are not favored by desirable climate, location, or topography. Even in places that are bucking the trend, their success stories may be just temporary upward ticks in an essentially down trending graph, or their population growth may actually signal the end of their rural existence. For example, in some places in New England, rural communities are threatened not so much by depopulation as by the onslaught of urban subdivisions and strip malls.

While there are those who talk of a broad-based rural renaissance or a natural cycle of repopulation, there is little evidence for such things. Overall, rural population trends for the last fifty years have been predominantly downward but erratic, characterized by some gains in the 1970s, followed by losses in the 1980s, small gains again in the early 1990s, followed again by losses in the late 1990s and early 2000s. Moreover, even the periods of growth can be misleading. There is not one kind of rural American community, there are many. Sharp gains in rural areas with good amenities or locations mask the fact that there have been few if any gains in large parts of the country, including most of the Great Plains, the rural South, and the rural Northeast. People born in rural America are still, on balance, leaving their communities. It is likely that as rural revivals occur they will happen one by one, town by town, and be slow, difficult, and tenuous; sadly, they will probably be offset by other communities that don't make it and that become—literally—twenty-first-century ghost towns. Unless something can be done to stabilize rural population trends it is quite likely that by the twenty-second century most of small-town rural America—and all that it connotes—will have disappeared. By the next century, rural America may survive only as a theme park along an interstate highway: Six Flags over FarmWorld, taking its place alongside Williamsburg and the Alamo as reminders of another era.

This book endeavors to shed some light on what's actually happening in small rural communities, including the causes and effects of their depopulation, and to tell about people who care about rural America and are trying to revive it with both big regional or national plans and small, local efforts. Broad public policy and planning initiatives are interesting and, in some cases, necessary, but in the end the success of most communities individually, and of rural America as a whole, will depend more on the actions and commitment of the people who live there.

The next decade will reveal a great deal about the prospects for rural America to survive. For the first time in many years there are some powerful trends that seem to be favoring rural America—trends in food, in energy, in communications, and in transportation. If, despite these trends, populations continue to shrink, rural America as we know it may all but disappear during the twenty-first century.

Will it matter? I think so. This book explores the history, the value, and the appeal of rural America as well as some of the reasons why so many urban dwellers still care about the fate of the small communities from which so many of them came yet about which they know so little.

As the North Dakota historian David Danbom wrote, "Whatever the reality of rural America, the *idea* of rural America will always be popular with major segments of our population because, in the last analysis, it is America's field of dreams."[2]

Survival of Rural America

Part 1

THE DECLINE OF
RURAL COMMUNITIES

1

Transition: The Depopulation of Rural America

The twentieth century was a time of enormous innovation and change—indeed, more and faster changes than in any century that preceded it, including the introduction of the automobile, air travel, computers, and nuclear power. As the twentieth century began, most people in the United States walked or rode horses to get around—usually on dirt roads. They had to. There were only about 8,000 cars at the time and just 150 miles of paved roads. In their homes they probably did not have telephones, and they certainly didn't have televisions, radios, or computers. A few people had typewriters and electric lighting, items that were considered "high tech." Most children were born at home, not in a hospital, and they had a life expectancy of about fifty years. Most homes were heated by wood or coal, and few of them had such luxuries as central heating or indoor plumbing.

But among all the changes that took place during the twentieth century, few were more significant than the dramatic shift of population from rural to urban areas. Most people in 1900 lived in a rural community, and many lived on farms. Indeed, in 1900 farmers accounted for about 40 percent of the total workforce in the United States, compared to 90 percent in 1790. By the year 2000 that number would be down to just 1.9 percent.[1]

By the year 2000 the balance between the rural and urban populations of the United States looked very different from a century earlier. According to the U.S. Census Bureau, in 1900 those living in rural areas accounted for more than 60 percent of the population. That picture changed dramatically. By 1950 the country's population was about evenly divided between rural and urban areas, and the trend continued so that by 2000 more than 80 percent of the population lived in urban areas.

Strangely enough, in addition to small rural towns the other type of community that has suffered population loss is the urban city core. During the second half of the twentieth century, eighteen of the twenty-five largest cities in the United States lost population—and many cities lost population at rates that rival the losses in rural towns: for example, Chicago's population declined by 25 percent, Philadelphia's by 29 percent, Cleveland's by 43 percent, and Buffalo's by 50 percent. Where were the people going? Not to rural America certainly, but to the suburbs. By 1990 the United States had more people living in suburbs than in cities and small towns *combined.*[2]

Of course, small towns and traditional cities are very different. Although New York State led the nation in out-migration from 2000 to 2005, followed by California, Illinois, Massachusetts, and New Jersey, there are cities in those states—such as Chicago and Buffalo—that will never become ghost towns.[3] But there are some striking similarities. Both small rural towns and traditional inner cities suffer from some of the same things: a declining number and quality of services, an aging population, a desire on the part of teenagers to get out and not come back, and school problems—poor schools in inner cities and the closing of schools in many rural towns. And inner cities can add high crime rates to their list of ills.

Although there is some evidence that the pace of "rural flight" in the United States abated somewhat during the decade from 1990 to 2000, the fundamental trend of the past 100 years has not changed, and this is particularly true for smaller rural communities away from urban areas. Further, this trend is not limited to the United States. According to the United Nations, the rural population of European countries fell from 207.3 million in 1985 to 192.8 million in 1995, and it is projected to fall to 128.4 million by 2025.[4] Worldwide, the numbers are equally dramatic. In 1800 only 2 percent of the planet's population lived in cities. By 1900 that number was 12 percent, by 2000 it was over 47 percent, and by 2008 the urban population of the planet will outnumber the rural for the first time.[5]

The seemingly inexorable migration of people from rural to urban areas is a primary reason why so much of the history of rural towns is a history of despair, defeat, and desertion. In Kansas alone it is estimated that about 6,000 communities have disappeared since 1854, when the state was opened for settlement.[6] Some of the communities died at birth or never got beyond the wishful stage of laying out a few streets, but many others existed and even thrived before their ultimate demise. Today Atchison, Kansas, is a relatively prosperous county-seat river town of more than 10,000 people, but in the mid-nineteenth century it was smaller than nearby Sumner and seemed to have a less promising future. Political turmoil and an 1860 tornado effectively did away with Sumner and its 2,000 residents, and today there is no trace of the town. In *Ghost Towns of Kansas,* Daniel Fitzgerald tells a hundred stories similar to that of Sumner. Joseph Snell, former executive director of the Kansas State Historical Society, notes that "the possibility of dying still haunts rural communities as businesses and residents move to nearby larger towns, thanks to the mobility provided by the automobile."[7]

Thomas Frank begins his best-selling book, *What's the Matter with Kansas?* by observing that "the poorest county in America isn't in Appalachia or the Deep South. It is on the Great Plains, a region of struggling ranchers and dying farm towns." He then describes what he sees happening in rural parts of one of those Great Plains states, his home state of Kansas. "It's pretty much in free fall," he says. "Walk down the main street of just about any farm town in the state, and you know immediately [that] this is a civilization in the early stages of irreversible decay."[8] Frank's reference to poor and decaying plains counties is quite misleading. In fact, the poverty rate in Kansas and most of the Midwest and Great Plains is *below* the national average, and while the poorest county in the country *is* in the plains, and is very poor indeed, it is not exactly a typical Great Plains county of "struggling ranchers and dying farm towns." It is Buffalo County, South Dakota, population 2,032, and most of the people in the county are Sioux Indians, living on the Crow Creek Indian Reservation.[9] As Figure 3 clearly shows, the poorest rural areas in America are in Appalachia, the South, and the East.

Moreover, what Frank considers the "early stages" of decay are in fact nothing of the sort. The early stages took place long ago, when the railroad or interstate highway bypassed the town, or a rival community became the county seat, or the school district closed the town's schools and consolidated them with schools in a neighboring town. What Frank is seeing now in many areas are the late stages of decay: the boarded-up shops, abandoned and run-down housing, broken-down cars in front

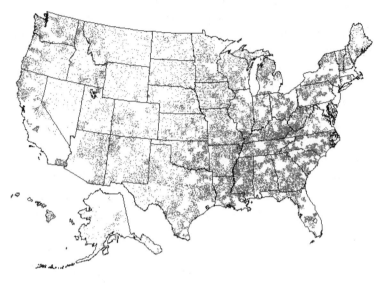

Figure 3. Location of the Nonmetropolitan Poor
Each dot represents 200 poor persons.
Source: U.S. Department of Agriculture, Economic Research Service.

yards, and streets and sewers in need of repair. These are among the last stages of decay before prairie grasses and tumbleweed reclaim the land.

Because Frank's book is essentially a political polemic, he largely ignores almost two centuries of worldwide rural decline in demographic history. Instead, he looks for an evildoer in the story of rural Kansas, and he finds one: "The villain that did this to my home state . . . is the conservatives' beloved free-market capitalism, a system that . . . has little use for small-town merchants or the agricultural system that supported the small towns in the first place."[10] And Frank goes on to mourn the passing of Kansas' early political history of liberal radicalism and populism.

A little over 100 years ago Kansas' William Allen White, one of the best-known newspaper editors of his day, wrote an editorial in his *Emporia Gazette* titled "What's the Matter with Kansas?" the very phrase Frank borrowed for his book 107 years later.

White, like Frank, was on the lookout for a villain and was determined to make a political statement. But White's villain was at the opposite end of the political spectrum from Frank's. White bemoaned the fact that Kansas was losing population and money. "Every month in every community sees someone who has a little money pack up and leave the state," he wrote, adding, "In towns where ten years ago there were three or four or half a dozen money-lending concerns, stimulating industry by furnishing capital there is now none, or one or two that are looking after the interests and principal already outstanding." Kansas, White concluded, was laughed at, cussed and forgotten: "She had traded [places] with Arkansas and Timbuctoo."[11]

White believed the problem with Kansas in 1896 was that the state was controlled by the *anticapitalists* and populists: people who demonized Wall Street and tried to "legislate to make the masses prosperous" and favor debtors over creditors. "What's the Matter with Kansas?" White asked. "She is losing wealth, population and standing . . . and the money power is afraid of her."[12]

Both White and Frank viewed Kansas from their own political perspectives: Frank as an urban liberal, White as a rural conservative. Neither really got it right, and neither approach contributes much to an understanding of what is happening in and to rural America.

Not only are the "problems" with Kansas that are identified by both Frank and White not at all limited to Kansas, but they also may better be thought of not as discrete problems but as the result of broad historical trends being played out on a much larger scale than just one state or region. In 2005 two veteran Midwestern journalists received a Patterson Foundation grant to study rural America, specifically the northern plains (western Minnesota, northern Iowa, and North and South Dakota). Writing with no evident political ax to grind, their initial report, *Sweeping out the Plains,* concludes that

the great wave of population, which swept homesteaders onto the Northern Great Plains with the promise of free land and hope for a bright future around the turn of the last century, is sweeping back out again at the beginning of this one. A culture that has been central to the history of America's westward expansion and whose virtues of simple living, honesty, hard work and religious faith became the core of how the United States came to see itself, is close to disappearing. After cresting in the 1930s and 1950s, the rural population on the Northern Great Plains has steadily decreased. Younger people moved to cities. Older people tended to stay. That process has now reached a point where, unless something is done to alter the trend, when this generation of senior citizens is gone, *the culture of the Northern Great Plains will virtually disappear, leaving a few islands of urban prosperity along its eastern edge.*[13] (emphasis added)

One factor that likely will contribute to changes in "the culture of the Northern Great Plains" and of rural America in general is that for many areas the only bright spot in terms of migration has come from Mexico and Central America, or from Latinos moving from places such as California and Texas. From 1980 to 2000 the Latino population in rural America increased from 1.5 million to 3.2 million, and between 1990 and 2000 Latino migration to Iowa increased by 90 percent and to Minnesota by 151 percent. Unfortunately for small-town rural America, most of this migration has been to midsize rural cities and to rural areas near urban centers.[14]

Most of the people interviewed for *Sweeping out the Plains* believe that the depopulation trend is irreversible. Some think it has been caused or accelerated by policy decisions. One local rural affairs official refers to "a national policy to empty the plains," and a farmer complains about "federal policies [that] have pushed people out of the Great Plains."[15] The gist of the public policy complaints seems to be the contention that federal subsidy programs favor large farmers at the expense of small ones. The complaint has merit. According to the Kellogg Foundation, "By far the largest federal rural program is the farm subsidy program."[16] The charge that most of this subsidy goes to large farmers and to corporate or industrial farms would appear to be borne out by the finding that more than 60 percent of federal farm subsidy payments go to just 7.2 percent of the farmers participating in the program. The Kellogg report points out another problem with federal priorities: although about 90 percent of rural income is derived from nonfarming sources, and agriculture only accounts for about 6 percent of rural employment, much more federal support goes to farming subsidies than to rural business and community development efforts, which would benefit the majority of people living in rural America.[17] Yet some of the proposed solutions offered by politicians and both private and public agencies meet with a mixed reception. Asked about legislation—such as the "New Homestead Act," proposed by Senator Byron Dorgan of North Dakota—

Jack Zaleski, editorial page editor of the *Forum of Fargo-Moorhead*, said, "Any effort to repopulate North Dakota is a fool's errand."[18]

Churches have long been a mainstay and focal point for small rural towns, yet the clergy, too, is pessimistic. "When you have more funerals than baptisms, you have problems," says Sandy LeBlanc, director of the Evangelical Lutheran Church of America's Rural Ministry resources program in Des Moines. Rural clergy typically ride the circuit from town to town and church to church because the congregations in most towns are too small to support a full-time clergyman. Father Frank Schuster, who serves three communities in North Dakota, thinks the depopulation of his part of rural America is "unstoppable," adding that he thinks that "what's happening is out of our control."[19]

Finally, although a common complaint of the northern plains people in *Sweeping out the Plains* is that "no one cares" and that the area and its people are "forgotten," there is abundant evidence in that study and elsewhere that a lot of people care about rural America. Many organizations, public and private, are concerned with rural communities, including the Center for Small Towns, the Aldo Leopold Center, the Center for Rural Affairs, Cornell's Rural New York Initiative, several land-grant universities, and the Federal Reserve Banks of Kansas City and Minneapolis. And the existence of a still very powerful institution in the heart of rural America, the Iowa presidential primary, ensures that aspiring politicians will at least pay lip service to rural issues. For example, in a major policy speech in 2006 at a farm in Cambria, New York (population 5,400), Senator Hillary Rodham Clinton joined the voices supporting revitalization of rural America. As usual, Clinton had done her homework, and her assessment of much of rural New York was both accurate and bleak. Most rural towns in New York lost population between 1900 and 2000.[20] She could easily have been talking, however, about rural Oklahoma or Alabama when she said, "As I travel around the state, the results are pretty plain to see. Once vibrant rural communities are facing abandoned storefronts, houses in disrepair, signs of economic distress." More than 40 percent of the counties in New York State are classified as rural and have lost almost 7 percent of their population from 1980 to 2000. Clinton proposed federal support for a cornucopia of rural initiatives, including expanding rural Internet access, promoting ethanol and other crop-based alternative fuels, funding efforts to attract doctors to rural areas, rebuilding downtowns, and creating tourist attractions. Noting that most rural Americans aren't farmers or ranchers, she also endorsed more federal support for rural economic development, not just agriculture.[21]

While Senator Clinton's proposals are nothing new, they serve to underscore that the problems facing rural America are pervasive and not confined to just one region, such as the Midwest. Indeed, in their 1993 book *Forgotten Places,* Thomas A. Lyson and William W. Falk identified nine geographically and culturally diverse rural areas with serious problems: Appalachia, the Ozarks, the southern "Black Belt," the Mississippi Delta, the Lower Rio Grande Valley, Northern New England, Michigan's Upper Peninsula, the forest-industry areas of the Pacific Northwest, and rural California.[22]

Yet despite the attention the subject is receiving, there have been no silver bullets, although there is no shortage of recommendations ranging from the kinds of things Senator Clinton proposed to starting organic niche farms and developing wind power. Still others see high tech as the answer, and there are those who figure people will move to the plains when big cities just get too crowded or to escape terrorism.[23]

It is not surprising that the results of studies such as these, and the opinions of the people of the plains, are full of contradictions and inconsistencies. And while it may be a natural reaction for those whose way of life is threatened (or for the politically motivated such as Thomas Frank and William Allen White) to seek scapegoats and sinister forces at work—venal politicians and uncaring Wall Streeters, for example—it doesn't help us to understand what is really taking place, what it means for our culture or our identity, or what might be done about it.

Rural America is deeply imbedded in our national DNA. Most of our presidents have come from rural America, and at least twelve have been ranchers or farmers. So many of the significant and enduring examples of American literature, fine arts, and music are about rural America that it is difficult to imagine what the American arts would be like without the music of composers and performers from Aaron Copland to Johnny Cash, or a long list of writers including Willa Cather and James Michener, painters such as Andrew Wyeth and Grant Wood, and humorists from Mark Twain to Andy Griffith and Jeff Foxworthy.

Rural America even has its own national publications, including the venerable *Cappers* and *Grit* magazines which began publication in the late nineteenth century. *Grit,* which calls itself "America's Rural Lifestyle Magazine," reached a high circulation of 1.5 million in 1969. There is also a relative newcomer, *Acreage,* which began publishing in 1966. It bills itself as "The Magazine for Rural Living" and calls its readers "Ruralpolitans," a term it actually has registered as a trademark. The magazines contain rural news and feature stories such as how to install a culvert, tips on raising mules, choosing the right kind of mulch, and testing well water.

And when America goes to war, rural America pays a steep price: almost half the Iraq war casualties are from rural America. As military sociologist Charles Moskos said, "Basically, who is dying in America's recent wars is small town America, the inner city and the barrio, not suburbia."[24]

Clearly, what is occurring in rural areas is a result of major, long-term trends that will not be remedied easily—if at all—and certainly won't be remedied by any single stroke of legislation or regulation. Economic and public policy realities induced millions to settle in rural America in the first place, and similar realities are now contributing to the changes taking place in such areas—and have been for decades. These kinds of changes are neither inherently good nor evil, although some of them certainly are dispiriting. It *is* sad to see an inner city decay or a small town die. Yet the fact is that nothing is permanent. Many of the bustling urban downtowns and prosperous small towns we experienced in our youths (or in our imaginations or on the movie screen) are, or soon will be, just memories.

Writing about what he saw as the closing of the frontier era, historian Walter Prescott Webb used words that might well apply to a disappearing rural America:

> The end of an age is always touched with sadness for those who lived it and those who love it. . . . The people are going to miss the frontier more than words can express. For four centuries they heard its call, listened to its promises, and bet their lives and fortunes on its outcome. It calls no more, and regardless of how they bend their ears for its faint whisper they cannot hear the suggestion of a promise.[25]

2

Prospects for a Rural Revival

Notwithstanding the well-documented and massive movement of people throughout the world from farms and small towns to cities and suburbs, there are those who see—and certainly also those who want to see—the potential for a countermigration away from the urban centers and back to the country. Indeed, there are those who believe such a trend may already be evident.[1]

In a widely quoted 1998 article in the *Wilson Quarterly*, published by the Woodrow Wilson International Center for Scholars, the authors contend that "a variety of powerful social and economic forces appears to be reversing patterns that have prevailed in the United States for a century or longer. They are pushing and pulling significant numbers of Americans into the areas beyond the metropolitan fringes."[2]

Indeed, there are data showing a gain in overall "rural population" in the 1970s and 1990s (the economy in the 1980s was depression-like for much of rural America). In addition, there is considerable evidence that the high cost of housing—and living and doing business—particularly near the coasts, has driven people to rural areas, although primarily to cities, not small rural towns.[3] There are even books about it, from Nola Kelsey's *Bitch Unleashed: The Harsh Realities of Goin' Country,* to *Country Bound: Trading Your Business Suit Blues for Blue Jean Dreams,* by Marilyn Heimberg Ross and Tom Ross.[4]

A 2006 *Wall Street Journal* op-ed article about the Great Plains by Joel Kotkin seemed to be heralding a rural revival, proclaiming that "the portraits of a dying region are increasingly dated . . . over the past five years, the fastest growth in per capita income has taken place in energy-rich Wyoming, Montana, North Dakota, New Mexico and West Virginia, while highly urbanized places like California, New York, Michigan and Illinois gather dust at the bottom of the pack."[5] Kotkin attributed much of the prosperity to energy development—coal, oil, natural gas, and ethanol—and to a strong entrepreneurial ethic in the plains.

Yet it is important to look beneath the gross numbers and the headlines to understand the confusion caused by differing interpretations of the term "rural." Kotkin's article focuses on a few growing cities that happen to be *surrounded by* rural America—Fargo, Bismarck, Iowa City, Grand Forks, Rapid City, Sioux Falls—cities with populations from 50,000 to over 150,000. He concedes that most *small* rural towns are losing population. Similarly, while the authors of the *Wilson Quarterly* article state that "the rural rebound is for real," they also recognize that it is very limited, restricted in fact to a few cities, recreational communities, and places popular with retirees: "the Sunbelt, coastal regions, parts of the West, and the Upper Great Lakes, places that offer beautiful scenery or recreational attractions, from lakes to ski slopes and golf courses."[6] Ominously, they also note that population losses continue to be the norm elsewhere, including in much of the Great Plains, the Midwest, and the South, and a substantial amount of the growth in rural counties has occurred in cities like those Kotkin identified and in places such as Douglas County, Colorado.

Douglas County was a sleepy rural community of about 10,000 people as late as the mid-1970s. The biggest retailer in the county seat of Castle Rock was a Western wear store on the main street, and the county's assessed valuation was less than $75 million. But Douglas County is adjacent to metropolitan Denver, and in the late 1970s it began growing rapidly. By 2007 the population had increased more than 2,000 percent to 280,000, and the assessed valuation had increased by 6,000 percent to over $4.5 billion. Subdivisions, strip malls, and golf courses had replaced a lot of rural Douglas County.[7]

The *Wilson Quarterly* study did find some success stories in nonmetropolitan places, including Dickinson County, Kansas, and its county seat, Abilene, which benefited greatly from the opening of a large Russell Stover factory in 1994: "What Dickinson and other growing rural counties have in common is net in-migration."[8] A *Wall Street Journal* series on successful U.S.-based manufacturers found that "many of the strongest U.S. manufacturers set up production far away from urban centers, with their high taxes, labor, and utility costs, and instead look for locations in small towns, close to major highways and railroads."[9]

The authors of *The Rural Rebound* believe they see some strong trends with the potential to help rural communities:

> Driving the revival is a potent blend of economic, social, and
> technological forces. Improvements in communications technology
> and transportation have sharply reduced the "friction of distance"
> that once hobbled rural areas in the competition with the great
> metropolitan centers for people and commerce. In practical terms,
> rural areas are now much less isolated than they were only a few
> decades ago. Satellite technology, fax machines, and the Internet are
> among the most familiar aids, rendering distance virtually irrelevant
> in the transmission of information. Other sources of change are less
> obvious. Decades of steady state and federal investment in roads and
> airports—building and widening of highways, runway paving, and
> subsidies for equipment purchases—have also made an enormous
> difference. At the same time, congestion has increasingly vexed the
> nation's large metropolitan areas. . . . [These] advances have freed
> businesses to light out for the hinterlands and all their perceived
> advantages: lower labor and land costs, the absence of unions, what
> many executives see as the superior work ethic of the rural labor
> force, and economic incentive programs offered by state and local
> governments.[10]

Another potential boon for rural communities is a trend toward tele-commuting, or telework, which allows employees and outsource providers to work from their homes or, indeed, almost anywhere. Hundreds of companies, from the largest of the Fortune 500 to small start-ups, take advantage of telecommuting, as do many government agencies. As an example, almost all JetBlue Airlines reservation agents work from home, and there may be as many as 9 million telecommuting households in the United States, according to research firm IDC. The telecommuting trend is not only a boon to rural workers, it also saves money compared to operating call centers and results in lower employee turnover.[11]

The authors of the *Wilson Quarterly* study raise questions (premature, to say the least, for most rural communities) about the ability of rural America to accommodate significant in-migration and the problem of what will happen to urban America when everyone deserts it for the boondocks. They conclude with the mildly positive observation that "the problems and challenges that await a growing rural America are bound to be daunting. But whatever they are they will almost certainly be preferable to the challenges posed by isolation, exodus, and decline."[12]

Another relatively optimistic—but highly speculative—view of the future of rural America is offered by James R. Shortridge, a professor of cultural geography at the University of Kansas, in his book *The Middle West: Its Meaning in American Culture.* Shortridge explores the possibility that communities, and even regions, may be subject to natural ebbs and flows: "The Middle West rose mercurially from an obscure to a major place designation between 1890 and 1900 because it provided a focus for America's pastoral sentiments at a time when such sentiments were highly regarded. It rose to even loftier heights, to be seen as the most American part of America, around 1915."[13] In the mid-twentieth century, America's interest in the Middle West was eclipsed by its interest in the East Coast—land of the federal government, finance, and business—and the West Coast—land of technology, glamour, and youth: "There is evidence to indicate that over the last decade [1980s] or so the image of the Middle West has risen again . . . [perhaps due to] a disillusionment with the modern urban existence of the country, with its emphasis on fast-paced technological change, ecological irresponsibility and detachment from old securities such as family, community, and a sense of place."[14]

Shortridge's thesis is echoed in the writings of the iconoclastic social commentator J. B. Jackson, who perceived a three-stage "rediscovery" pattern in which places may expect to experience "a golden age, followed by a period of neglect and then by a time of rediscovery and restoration."[15] Examples of "rediscovery" patterns would include the restoration of many urban downtown areas that had fallen into an advanced state of neglect just a few years ago.

There is some evidence for this view, and Shortridge cites the experience of New England, and particularly rural Vermont, where Woodstock is an extreme example of the kind of rural restoration that is taking place—albeit less dramatically—elsewhere in the state and region. Yet even in New England, restoration is not universal. More common is the loss of rural areas to unchecked growth, as described by the authors of a policy paper for New England Futures, a regional advocacy group:

Our meadows, fields and forests are in peril. Houses are going up all over the place. . . . We're sacrificing two centuries of rural tradition for suburban speculation. Affluent people from "down country" come in and buy land and everyone's assessment goes up. Even in poor towns, big houses are all that's coming in. Property taxes are driving people to sell farms, cut more timber when they don't want to. A chain convenience store opens on an open field beside the general store in town, which then goes out of business. The less traveled road is getting harder and harder to come by.[16]

The plight of rural New England was chronicled eloquently by the late Dartmouth professor—and Vermont farmer—Noel Perrin in several books, including *Best Person Rural*. Perrin saw large parts of rural Vermont disappear in the forty-one years he farmed there—a victim of people "killing the thing they love [while] local people are gradually taxed out of existence"—and golf courses and fancy restaurants, replace dairy farms and forests.[17] Perrin was particularly annoyed at "restoration" that resulted in a phony, overpriced, and overly precious rural New England, perhaps best illustrated by a story he told of seeing a rural shopkeeper opening boxes of store-bought cellophane-wrapped crackers and dumping them into an old barrel to be passed off as some kind of homespun "cracker barrel" product. Writing in 1978, Perrin predicted that if development went unchecked soon Vermont would look like "central New Jersey with hills."[18] His writings, and his work on behalf of land conservation, helped slow down that transformation.

Shortridge suggests, with qualifications, that the Middle West may be reemerging as "a producer of wholesome and natural food, a place in which people can still leave their doors unlocked, and in which governors will occasionally answer their own telephones . . . and . . . [as a] keeper of the nation's values."[19] As *Time* magazine observed in a cover story on Minnesota, "California is the flashy blonde you like to take out once or twice. Minnesota is the girl you want to marry."[20] Rural America also scores well in "places-rated" kinds of surveys, including the well-regarded Morgan Quitno Press study in 2006, which found that eleven of the top twenty healthiest and smartest states were rural, as were twelve of the twenty "most livable" and fourteen of the twenty safest.[21]

However, any discussion of a rural revival needs to occur in the appropriate context, notably including the observation that, for the most part, the population trends of the past are expected to continue in the future. The U.S. Census Bureau projects, for example, that over the next quarter-century the nation's population will increase by 30 percent, yet the populations of Kansas, Nebraska, Iowa, North Dakota, and South Dakota—along with New York and Ohio—will enjoy at best single-digit percentage increases, if indeed there are any increases at all.[22] And if past trends are *not* reversed, most of any population gains will occur near already-crowded urban areas.

Although both the rural South and the Great Plains are suffering from persistent out-migration, the plains states appear to have one advantage when it comes to being capable of supporting any kind of rural revival: "In the rural South, the persistence of poverty accompanied by inadequate educational, health and welfare programs, create enormous challenges . . . [while] in the Great Plains there have been greater investments in people."[23] Even in the face of diminishing resources, most plains states have continued to provide a relatively high level of education, healthcare, and social services.

Rural poverty remains a problem, but the situation has been improving, at least overall. Although rural poverty rates have declined from over 20 percent to less than 15 percent over the last three decades, rural counties still have poverty rates almost 25 percent higher than urban counties and account for almost 90 percent of all of the "persistent-poverty" counties—defined by the U.S. Department of Agriculture as counties that have experienced poverty rates above 20 percent for the past thirty years.[24] One result of this has been that rural Americans receive more federal aid, per capita, than urban Americans. However, there are those who question the poverty-level model, which does not take into account where people live or the cost-of-living differences between, for example, Mitchell, South Dakota, and New York City.

The National Research Council, responding to a request from Congress in 1990, suggested that the government should include cost of living in determining poverty levels. It turns out that when cost of living is factored into the model, rural poverty rates go from being 25 percent higher than urban rates to 12 percent lower.[25] In other words, a change in how the poverty rate is calculated could make rural America look quite a bit more prosperous than before. Yet seventeen years after Congress asked the Census Bureau to look into it, there has been no official change in how the government defines poverty. Even by federal government standards, such a delay seems unusually long, but it turns out that there are a number of complications. First, there is some debate among statisticians and academics about how best to measure the cost of living. Second, and probably most important, any change would be likely to have enormous political repercussions, as up to two million, formerly "officially poor" rural residents would lose benefits while two million newly "officially poor" urbanites would begin receiving them. The net result would be a significant loss of revenue going into rural America.

There is no question that, in some cases, "rural revivals" are taking place. Not on a macro basis—rural America as a whole is not filling up again—but on a town-by-town basis. This struggle for survival—the growth of certain rural communities and the demise of others—occupies much of the balance of this book. I profile towns that are in some cases beating the odds and defying the trends. They are attracting in-migration, or at least they are maintaining their populations better than might be expected, and as a result they are among the rural towns with a chance to survive and, perhaps, to provide examples for others to follow. But most of the potentially successful communities also are near towns that are in danger of dying, and I also profile these communities because their failure to survive often is linked to the relative success of their neighbor. Indeed, ultimately the fate of the smallest and most endangered towns may depend on their ability to create a new kind of relationship with their neighboring and relatively more successful towns, a process that involves a redefinition of what a community is.

3
Kansas: The Essence
of Rural America

I have chosen Kansas as the state for the focus of this study—and as a surrogate for the rest of rural America—for three reasons. First, Kansas is a very typical, average state. A 2006 CNN analysis of census data for all fifty states ranked Kansas third, behind Wisconsin and Missouri, and just ahead of Indiana and Ohio, in being "average . . . a microcosm of the whole country."[1] The average state is characterized by having large rural geographic areas but with the bulk of its population and commerce in a small region, which in the case of Kansas has been termed "the Kansas Industrial Triangle," a wedge from Kansas City to Wichita, west to Hays, and returning east to Kansas City, which makes up only a fifth of the state's area.[2] If we can understand Kansas, we can understand much of what is taking place elsewhere in those large parts of rural America that are not favored by an abundance of amenities. Second, although most of rural America is threatened by declining populations, the problem is more acute in the High Plains and prairie states. If efforts at rural revival can succeed in those areas, they may well be able to work in regions with less severe problems. Finally, as a "near-native" Kansan, it is the state with which I am most familiar.[3]

Kansas is in the exact geographical center of the continental United States. It has a lot in common with the other plains states, including much of Texas, Oklahoma, Nebraska, Iowa, North and South Dakota, Minnesota, eastern Colorado, Wyoming, and large parts of New Mexico and Montana. The name "Kansas" comes from the Kansa Indians, a Siouan people, who were in the area at least as long ago as 1600. "Kansa" means "South Wind People."[4]

Writing in the *Wall Street Journal* about the movie *Capote* and Truman Capote's relationship with Kansas through *In Cold Blood,* his best-selling book about the 1959 murder of the Clutter family in Holcomb, Kansas, the columnist Daniel Henniger says, "What I took away [from the movie] was how far the distance was in 1959 from New York's Upper East Side to Kansas. More than forty years later that distance remains, defined almost every day of the week by our national politics." Henniger quotes from a post-2004 election article in the *New York Times* in which a woman from the liberal blue state of New York expressed her feelings about people in Kansas and the other conservative red states: "If the heartland feels so alienated from us, then it behooves us to wrap our arms around the heartland . . . to bring [them] our way of life, which is honoring diversity and having compassion for people with different lifestyles." "By all means do," Henniger urges, adding, "Truman Capote made the trip. Like him, other pilgrims journeying into the heart of the country may find places and people more complex than they had ever imagined."[5]

Henniger may be referring to the fact that political, social, and cultural life in rural areas is by no means as narrow as the well-meaning New York woman may think, beginning with the revelation that "rural" is not always, or even mostly, "agricultural." The surprisingly diverse nature of rural communities was underscored by the oft-quoted phrase coined by Daryl Hobbs, professor emeritus of rural sociology at the University of Missouri: "When you've seen one rural community, you have seen *one* rural community."[6]

After all, Kansans elected Republican Senator Sam Brownback and Democrat Governor Kathleen Sebelius, both winning by comfortable margins, and after many years as a seemingly reliable "red" state, it was more blue than red in 2006, prompting a postelection *New York Times* editorial, "What's Right with Kansas," which labeled the state "a bastion of moderation."[7] Kansas, apparently, had finally gotten it "right," at least in the opinion of the *New York Times,* recalling George Will's observation that "when liberals' presidential nominees consistently fail to carry Kansas, liberals do not rush to read a book titled 'What's the Matter with Liberals' Nominees?' No, the book they turned into a bestseller is titled 'What's the Matter with Kansas?'"[8] There are many places in Kansas where the New York woman would feel right at home. But there also are places like Holcomb, population 2,000, and midsize cities like Salina and Hays, where Kansas' "redness" is more evident. And there is that controversy about the theory of evolution and the Kansas State Board of Education, which, beginning in 1999, favored de-emphasizing Darwin's theory and urged the teaching of "intelligent design" in science classrooms.

But even in Kansas, the evolution issue was anything but clear-cut. At the same time that the Board of Education was holding hearings about teaching "intelligent design" in science classes, the state's largest educational institution, the University of Kansas, was hosting an "Explore Evolution" exhibit at its natural history museum, and the university chancellor made it clear that "we are committed to fact-based research and teaching. . . . Creationism and intelligent design are most appropriately taught in a religion, philosophy, or sociology class, rather than a science class."[9] In 2006 Kansas voters elected a new Board of Education, which promptly returned Darwin to the science classroom.[10] In short, as Henniger says, Kansas is "more complex" than many people—particularly those who have spent their lives in the coastal blue states—seem to think.

But I suspect Henniger means more than just that there are sizable "blue" areas within "red" Kansas, or that Kansas ranks twelfth among all states in the percentage of the population with college degrees, or even that Kansas is one of only five states with a branch of Dean and DeLuca, the upscale New York specialty food store.[11] I think his real point is that even in the small towns of Kansas most people are not one-dimensional. Their values and attitudes certainly differ from those of the New York woman, but they have been shaped by the kinds of processes that are no less complex than those by which she developed her beliefs. It is common among liberal pundits to bemoan the fact that almost everyone in red Kansas usually votes for Republicans, yet curiously they seldom pause to question the equally one-sided voting habits of their neighbors in New York City. In their minds, political wisdom, it seems, is a product of blue states much as grains are a product of red states.

While it is easy to get drawn into political issues, they are outside the scope of this book—beyond one key point. To understand what is going on in rural America, it is *not* helpful for people such as Thomas Frank (or William Allen White, for that matter) to find politics to blame for the ills that affect their communities. The causes, as we have seen, are broad, well entrenched, and affecting rural communities throughout the world. Moreover, the image of Kansas in the public consciousness transcends politics.

Kansas' identity has been shaped by many things, including its dramatic birth in the midst of the free state–slave state controversy and the Bleeding Kansas era that coincided with the Civil War. As part of the "Wild West," Kansas lingers in the national consciousness, giving us the archetypes of Dodge City, Wyatt Earp, "Wild Bill" Hickok, the Chisholm Trail, and outlaws galore. Kansas burst on the national scene at a time of westward expansion, gold rushes, and transcontinental transportation, and its location put it squarely in the midst of these events. From the Pony Express to the Oregon and Santa Fe trails, Kansas' strategic central location attracted the nation's attention. Indeed, in the 1850s, Kansas even figured briefly in a remarkable proposal that would have drastically changed the shape of development and industrialization in the United States: the creation of something called the "Great Central American Water Line." It was to be a navigable system of east-to-west rivers and canals that was to stretch from the Rocky Mountains (then part of Kansas Territory) through Kansas, Missouri, Illinois, and Ohio to Norfolk, Virginia.[12] It would have rivaled, and perhaps surpassed, the Missouri-Mississippi River route, and it was not a far-fetched idea. In the 1850s steamboats were able—at least at some times of the year—to travel into Kansas on the Kaw River (also known as the Kansas River), reaching about as far as present-day Junction City. But the plan encountered stiff opposition from the railroad companies, and in 1864 the Kansas Legislature declared the state's rivers officially "nonnavigable" and allowed bridge and dam construction to begin, ending chances of establishing a major river port in central Kansas. The "nonnavigable" status was lifted in 1913, but by then the damage had been done to any hopes Kansas might have had for a commercial waterway system.[13]

The public image of Kansas also transcends geography. As Thomas Frank suggests in his book *What's the Matter with Kansas?* "As long as America loves authenticity, my home state of Kansas is going to be symbolically preeminent. . . . If it's 100 percent Americanism we're looking for, Kansas delivers 110 percent. . . . Kansas is the most middling of all possible American places . . . the vortex of the nation, in Allen Ginsberg's phrase . . . [and] the heart of the heartland."[14]

Kansas, adds Frank, is "the home of the bright boy in the mail room who wants to be a player on Wall Street. It's where Dorothy wants to return. It's where Superman grows up. It's where Bonnie and Clyde steal a car and Elmer Gantry studies the Bible and Russian ICBM's destroy everything and the overchurched antihero of *An American Tragedy* learns the sinful ways of the world." Kansas is also quintessential "fly-over" territory. In the James Bond movie *Diamonds Are Forever,* the villain Blofeld needs to demonstrate the ability of his satellite to destroy whole cities, but is thwarted because at the moment it is orbiting over the Midwest. "If I destroyed Kansas," he observed to Bond, somewhat archly, "the world might not hear about it for years."

Indeed, Frank goes on to say that Kansas "*is familiar even if you've never been there*" (emphasis added). It is the birthplace or home of many chain restaurants like Pizza Hut, Applebee's, and the first national hamburger chain, White Castle, and it is the home of that quintessential middle-American business, the Fuller Brush Company. "Kansas also supplies the nation with anchormen, comedians, and actors of wholesome visage and accent inoffensive. Kansas City is the home of Hallmark Cards and the nation's very first suburban shopping center. Thanks to its unerring sense for the middle, the state is a politician producer of the first rank, a reliable wellspring of down-home statesmen . . . the home of the unaffected common man."[15] When L. Frank Baum was looking for a drab and desolate farm location for Dorothy Gale's home in *The Wonderful Wizard of Oz,* he picked Kansas, a place he visited at most only once and then for a meeting in Lawrence—a town neither drab nor desolate.[16]

Why Kansas? Some who interpret *The Wonderful Wizard of Oz* in political terms suggest a political motive, as Kansas was then a hotbed of populism. Yet Baum himself insisted he was writing a children's book, not a political one, and it seems unlikely he had any hidden agenda when he chose Kansas. Philip Wedge and Thomas Averill, who have created a college course on Kansas literature, suggest that in fact nineteenth-century Kansas was a logical choice for Baum: "Kansas was prominent in the national consciousness. Baum picked it, no doubt, because people would recognize it, as they had all through the latter nineteenth century, for its Civil War connections; for its place in the rapid expansion into the West after the Civil War; for its place in the saga of cowboys, cavalry, and Indians; for its early experiments with Prohibition."[17] Or perhaps it is, as Thomas Frank observed, that Kansas had already become the focal point for mid-America and, "like Peoria or Muncie, Kansas figures in literature and film as a stand-in for the nation as a whole, the distilled essence of who we are."[18]

Whatever the reason, the state was immortalized in 1900 in Baum's classic book, and even more so in the subsequent 1939 MGM movie *The Wizard of Oz*, which introduced one of the most memorable and quoted lines in American cultural history. Upon landing in the bizarre and colorful land of Oz, Dorothy observed to her dog Toto, "I've a feeling we're not in Kansas anymore." That phrase has achieved universal recognition as shorthand for acknowledging that one is in a new and unusual location or situation.

Victor Fleming, director of the movie version of *The Wizard of Oz*, made a very deliberate decision to portray Dorothy's Kansas home as a bleak and barren place, just as Baum had described it: an impoverished farm in the midst of a drought. "When Dorothy stood in the doorway," Baum wrote,

> she could see nothing but the great gray prairie on every side. Not a tree nor a house broke the broad sweep of flat country that reached to the edge of the sky in all directions. The sun had baked the plowed land into a gray mass, with little cracks running through it. Even the grass was not green, for the sun had burned the tops of the long blades until they were the same gray color to be seen everywhere. Once the house had been painted, but the sun blistered the paint and the rains washed it away, and now the house was as dull and gray as everything else.[19]

To make sure the point was not missed, the beginning Kansas scenes in the movie were even filmed in black and white, in sharp contrast to the vivid, Technicolor scenes that take place later in Oz. And although the people at Dorothy's Kansas farm are nice enough, they are also a little sad and drab.

Baum describes an Aunt Em who "never smiled" and an Uncle Henry who "never laughed" and "did not know what joy was." Dorothy's home itself is run down and remote. Very remote. In the movie version, Dorothy and her family seem to live under the rule of a sinister but wealthy woman, a neighbor who apparently has the county sheriff in her hip pocket.

In contrast, Oz is—everything else! It is a combination of Las Vegas and Miami Beach and the Napa Valley. Of pageantry, and parades, and fascinating people. Of music and flowers and streets of gold. If the slogan of Kansas used to be "Land of Ahhhhhhs," (and, unfortunately, it did), the motto for Oz might well have been "It's party time!"

In short, and as Dorothy informed her dog, Oz ain't Kansas! And yet . . . there is something curious going on in *The Wizard of Oz*. Something even more curious than Oz itself. After all, what's the movie all about? *Dorothy's struggle to get back to Kansas!*

It is, of course, always possible to read too much into things. But it is interesting that few people have questioned Dorothy's passion to forsake the glamour and glitter—and remarkably familiar friends—of Oz for the drab flatness of Kansas where, for all she knows, her home and family were completely destroyed by the monster tornado that carried her away. Beyond Dorothy's heartfelt observation to Aunt Em that "there's no place like home," her obsession with Kansas is never further explained. And perhaps in a sentimental book like Baum's it doesn't require explanation, although if the history of population migration away from rural America tells us anything, it is clear that for many people there are lots of places better than their rural homes.

Perhaps the reason Dorothy's desire to return to Kansas does not strike a jarring note with readers and viewers is that they have—at some level of understanding and emotion—"adopted" Kansas as a surrogate for things they sometimes dream of: simpler times, less-complicated lives, children riding bikes or playing around a "swimming hole," swings hanging from trees, the smell of fried chicken on Sundays, and the sound of wooden screen doors opening and closing on hot summer days. In short: Home! Probably not the drought-stricken home of Dorothy's farm but more a place such as that described by William Inge, a native of Independence, Kansas, as the setting for *Picnic,* a Pulitzer Prize–winning Broadway play and a movie that won two Academy Awards. The setting is described as tidy houses in "a typical, small Midwestern town, with a church steeple, a grain elevator, a railroad station, a great silo in the center of a cattle ranch. . . . The scene has the color of luscious fruit just beginning to ripen. Dew is still on the countryside and mist rises from the earth in the distance. Far off, the whistle of a train is heard coming to town. It is a happy, promising sound. A factory whistle blows, a dog barks."[20]

Kansas is well suited to serve the role of stand-in for the kind of "good old days" and "hometowns" that we know probably don't really exist anymore—and perhaps never did—but about which we still care in some visceral way. Katherine Lee Bates wrote the song "America the Beautiful" after a journey from Massachusetts to Colorado Springs, a journey that took her through Kansas' wheat fields on July 4, 1893. She put pen to paper later that year after having climbed Pikes Peak, and her words forever commemorated Kansas and her trip west through the plains: "O beautiful for spacious skies, / For amber waves of grain, / For purple mountain majesties / Above the fruited plain!" More recently, with characteristic optimism and a little hyperbole, President Ronald Reagan, a midwesterner himself, spoke approvingly of Kansas as "a state where tall wheat and prairie grasses reach through a wide-open sky . . . [and where] people are keeping our frontier spirit alive. . . . Here in the heartland of America lies the hope of the world."[21]

Kansas, like rural America itself, is important to us. Thomas Frank's observation that Kansas is "familiar even if you've never been there" is perceptive and means, I think, that such places are part of our national collective consciousness, our "field of dreams," as David Danbom called it.[22] That's why there is concern about what is happening to rural and farming communities—those amber waves of grain—and why stories about their efforts to survive are featured prominently in national publications. We don't want those communities to die, even as we understand that the odds are against them. We care about communities that are trying to keep an important way of life—and our hopes and memories—alive.

4
Rural Communities at Risk

Lake Wobegon: "The town that time forgot and that decades cannot improve."

Garrison Keillor's ten-word description of a small rural town in Minnesota, created for the long-running *Prairie Home Companion* show on National Public Radio, aptly sums up what's happened to a lot of rural America. Most of the changes can be attributed to two primary factors: improved transportation and the industrialization of agriculture. Most rural communities reached their population peak between 1900 and 1950, before the interstate highway system was built and before large-scale farming entered the picture. The changes in transportation and agriculture that began to affect rural America significantly by the mid-twentieth century touched off an era of decline and depopulation that continues to this day—and that decades have not been able to improve.

No community ever started out to become a small, dying town. Each of the thousands of new settlements in rural America began with high hopes. In the mid-nineteenth century, rural towns were located based on how far a person could walk or ride his horse in a few hours, which meant that towns sprang up every few miles. Later, towns developed around rivers, then railroads, then eventually highways, which in turn influenced town growth and survival.

It was the advent of paved roads and automobiles that revolutionized transportation. When farmers moved by horse and buggy, and later in Model A's and T's, they needed towns within a few miles of where they lived to supply their needs—small "market towns" such as most of those profiled in this book. When farmers began driving their postwar Ford pickups and Chevy sedans over improving roads, they could reach small cities 30 or 50 miles away in the same time it once had taken them to reach those small market towns or county seats. Likewise, wood-burning trains that needed water stops every few miles gave way to modern trains and trucks that could go hundreds of miles without stopping.

The result has been that many towns that were created to serve specific needs, such as railroads, have suffered the unintended consequences of advances in transportation. In some cases, the results have been beneficial, at least in terms of a well-sited town's growth. When, thanks to the automobile and highway construction, people living in small towns within a 50-mile radius of Hays, Kansas, could get to Hays in less than thirty minutes, things changed dramatically, and for the better, at least for Hays. It became a hub city for its region, and it is growing. Hays hosts the Wal-Marts and Marriotts and the car dealerships of the world— while the towns that were bypassed by the interstates are left with the Duckwalls, True Values, aging mom-and-pop motels, and small groceries. If they're lucky. If they're not lucky, they lose their hardware store, their variety store, their grocery, and their motel, along with their gas station and school and post office.

The seeds of what was to happen to transportation and agriculture were present during the 1930s but were put on hold by World War II. The postwar boom period saw enormous growth in highway building, automobile production, and mechanization of farming. About the same time that rural communities began to be affected by better highways and more automobiles in the 1950s, farm productivity began improving dramatically. Today, we grow about three times as much food on one-third of the land, using just two-thirds of the manpower, as we did before World War II.[1]

The 1950s was the last decade in which the small farm still dominated much of rural America and when it seemed like "every quarter section [160 acres] in the area had a different family living on it and off it."[2] It was

a time when the towns grew and prospered, when the opera houses actually had operas and the dance halls were packed on Saturday nights, when the schools were full of children and every town had an amateur baseball league and when a lot of them had movie houses and newspapers and doctors and dentists, and when bigger ones . . . had several groceries and mercantile stores, several car dealerships and farm-implement dealerships and banks.[3]

But it was not to last. In 1956, Missouri author and farmer Leonard Hall wrote prophetically about what he sensed was happening in agriculture and its effect on rural communities: "If family farming is eventually supplanted by factory farming, countless thousands of small businesses—and, indeed, small communities—are equally doomed. In such a system there would be no place for the country bank, the feed merchant, the equipment dealer, or any of the others who now supply the needs of farmers with at least fair efficiency and at a profit."[4] Hall lived long enough to see the changes he dreaded. In 1980 he wrote that "single crops on huge acreages year after year become the order of the day. Yields are boosted by applying chemical fertilizers. Crops are cultivated with chemical herbicides and sprayed with chemical pesticides. Farm-made manure and crop rotation became almost a thing of the past. Cattle, hogs, and poultry are raised in confinement. Steers in hundreds of thousands are fattened in giant feed lots; sows farrow on metal-slatted floors in high farrowing houses; broilers and laying hens by millions spend their short lives crowded into wire-floored poultry tenements."[5]

The history of family farming in Kansas is typical of the nation. As late as 1970 there were 87,000 family farms in Kansas. By 2005 a third of those farms had ceased to exist or had been combined with other farms, and the average size of a Kansas farm had increased by about a third from 550 acres to 750 acres. The decline in small livestock operations has been even more drastic. Over the same thirty-five-year period, poultry farms in the state decreased from 9,430 to 2,436, hog farms from 21,000 to 1,500, and dairies from 13,500 to 950. In addition, by 2005 the average age of farmers, as measured by membership in the Kansas Farm Bureau, was 58, and nationally about one-fourth of farm owners were over 65.[6]

After the decline of the family farm began to take its toll, roughly from the 1960s to the 1980s, there was a theory—perhaps more a hope— that the depopulation rural communities were experiencing was a temporary phenomenon. It was argued that the population losses were just a "correction" or "adjustment" to the artificial overpopulation that had been induced by government stimulation through programs like the 1862 Homestead Act. This theory maintained that rural towns would lose population until they reached a sustainable level. Everyone would concede that the 14,442 people who lived in Phillips County, Kansas, in 1900 were too many for the land to sustain. Therefore, as that number declined . . . to 9,273 in 1950, the consensus view held that a necessary accommodation was being made. Farms were larger, and a few ill-conceived hamlets had disappeared, but people thought that the county as a whole was poised to begin a period of lasting prosperity.[7]

But the hoped-for population stabilization—much less the recovery—that some believed was coming proved to be an illusion, and by the year 2000 it was clear that depopulation was not a passing phase and that in fact there was nothing to prevent small towns from unincorporating or disappearing entirely, as happened to Hanks, North Dakota (whose story is told in Chapter 6).[8] In the case of Phillips County, Kansas, by the year 2000 its population had decreased by another 35 percent from the 1950 level that some thought would represent a stable, sustainable population, and by 2005 it had dropped another 8 percent.[9] Throughout rural America, school consolidations and closings loomed, and the handwriting was on the wall. As it became clear that the population losses were not just a matter of adjustments but were continuing, the optimism that had once characterized the rural American began to give way to depression and pessimism. As a *New York Times* reporter noted in 2003, "From the Dakotas to the Texas Panhandle . . . a broad swath of the nation's midsection seems to have lost . . . its optimism. Polls show a quiet crisis in confidence, the one thing that had seemed a part of rural American DNA."[10]

Again, Kansas is fairly typical of what was happening. While between 1900 and 2000 the state grew from 1.47 million to 2.69 million people, a respectable gain of about 83 percent (and mostly in the urban areas around Kansas City, Topeka, Wichita, and a few university towns), many rural counties were shedding population at a prodigious—and unsustainable—rate of 2–3 percent a year— or over 15 percent each decade.[11]

Between 1900 and 2000, Ellsworth County in central Kansas went from a population of 9,626 to 6,525, a loss of 32 percent, and Mitchell and Ottawa Counties lost approximately 50 percent, although Ottawa County actually gained a few hundred people between 1990 and 2000, reflecting its proximity to Salina. Russell and Rooks Counties were on a roller coaster, with their populations increasing 57 percent and 14 percent between 1900 and 1950, thanks largely to the discovery of oil and natural gas, only to see their populations decrease by 45 percent and 37 percent by the year 2000.

Counties such as these contain a lot of small farm towns. The focus of this book is on such towns: communities that are the epitome of what rural America means. They generally contain fewer than 2,500 people and are not adjacent to major metropolitan areas. There is, for example, a world of difference between a small town on the outskirts of Indianapolis and a similarly sized town in truly rural Indiana, 100 or more miles from a major population center and more than 30 miles from even a small city. Small towns near metropolitan areas have a bright future economically, and their population growth and property values show it. From the point of view of demographics and growth, the issues facing such communities could not be more different from the issues facing rural farm towns. The university city of Lawrence, Kansas, and its neighboring towns—whose populations doubled from 1950 to 2000—are struggling to control growth, not attract it. At the same time, most small farm towns in rural areas are becoming an endangered species, unable to retain, let alone attract, population, and they are facing losses of even rudimentary services. There are important distinctions between towns that have a major asset, such as a college, and those that do not. Most of the towns that are the focus of this book do not have such inherent assets and are not within the benevolent shadow of a major metropolitan area.

If there is one key to a town's prospects for survival, or perhaps even growth, it is its schools. In community after community the economics of school finances have required school districts to consolidate. Typical examples are in Rooks and Ottawa Counties, in Kansas, where school consolidation, necessitated by the declining number of students, is in the process of creating ghost towns. In Rooks County, one of the losing towns is Zurich, situated between Plainville and Palco and about 7 miles from each. Both Plainville and Palco have public schools, while the school building in Zurich, a town which no longer has any significant commercial activity, stands empty. In Ottawa County, the decision was made in 2003 to close the middle school in Delphos and move it 15 miles to the county seat of Minneapolis. Delphos, which is still an attractive community, retains a bare minimum of basic community services, but residents fear families with small children will not want to move there and instead will move to Minneapolis. The result could be that their community will go the way of their neighbor Ada, another little Ottawa County town which lost its grade school in 1972 and now has no basic commercial services; Ada is well on its way to becoming a twenty-first-century ghost town.

The consolidation process has caused a lot of pain in rural America, and the fact that consolidation may be necessary doesn't make it any easier for the communities whose schools are closed. Unfortunately, there appears to be no end in sight. "Only 22 out of 105 counties have grown since 2000," said Jim Hays, a demographer with the Kansas Association of School Boards, adding that almost 60 percent of the state's school districts lost enrollment during the past year. "If that keeps going," he added, "it'll have a huge effect on schools."[12] Indeed, in 2006 alone four more school districts were consolidated with neighboring districts. The areas being consolidated all had something in common, in addition to depopulation: more than two-thirds of their residents were sixty-five or older. Typical was District 455 in Republic County, Kansas, a district whose area is larger than Boston and Philadelphia combined but has fewer than 100 school-age children. Consolidation addresses the economics of rural schools, but it can lead to a lot of time on the bus. In places such as Trego County in western Kansas, consolidation has probably reached its practical limits. Trego is twice the size of all five boroughs of New York City, four times the size of Denver, yet it has a single school district with both of its schools at the county seat of WaKeeney.[13]

School consolidation has also had other ramifications, reflecting the extent to which people in small towns identify with their schools. High school sports, particularly football, have strong traditions. On many Friday nights, virtually the entire town is at the game, and talk of football and rivalries with other towns dominates conversation. In rural Colorado these small town football traditions go back nearly 100 years. "Sports are part of us, and they've helped build our community," says Lisa Ault of Sedgwick County, Colorado.[14] But Sedgwick County has been losing population, including an 8-percent drop between 2000 and 2006, and the resulting school consolidation in the county means that yesterday's rival high schools, Julesburg and Revere, are now combined into a single team with a new identity: the Sedgwick County Cougars. It was a bitter pill for some to swallow, but enrollment at the two schools is half what it was just a decade ago. It has been worse in other rural Colorado communities, including the towns of Kit Carson and Aguilar, which have had to cut back to eight-man or six-man teams, and several rural Colorado schools have dropped football altogether. "It's just a sad reality of an agriculture-based economy," commented Bert Borgmann of the Colorado High School Activities Association.[15]

It may be a "sad reality," but that doesn't mean it is a good idea or that it results in better educations. There are many opponents of school consolidation who argue that small schools are better. The National Education Association (NEA) recently addressed the school size debate in a cover story in *NEA Today*. The article described the growing "small schools movement," a loose organization of educators and organizations such as the Bill and Melinda Gates Foundation, whose focus is on the benefits of smaller high schools in metropolitan areas, particularly in large inner-city schools in places such as New York, Chicago, and Los Angeles. Essentially, according to the NEA story, small schools offer better discipline, more opportunity for interdisciplinary teaching, and closer relationships. "We know by lunchtime which students are having a bad day," one teacher said. In contrast, larger schools may be more cost-effective, they can offer a greater variety of courses, and teachers don't have to wear too many hats. "At my previous school, you were just responsible for teaching," a teacher in a small school said, "here, I'm also the librarian and I'm in charge of writing grants, keeping the computer lab running, and 'Are we going to have uniforms next year?'"[16] Many of the school-size arguments pro and con are equally relevant to rural America, although even small school proponents are likely to agree that there is such a thing as being *too small*. Once schools reach the point that classes have just a handful of students—or two students in the entire school, as in the case of Bill, Wyoming—consolidation becomes a practical alternative (see chapter 8). "No Child Left Behind" federal legislation and the increasing emphasis on standardized test scores may also favor smaller schools. A study for the Rural School and Community Trust, a national nonprofit organization, found considerable evidence that smaller schools produced higher test scores, even for lower-income students, and also raised questions about the cost-effectiveness of larger schools.[17] A similar study was conducted for the Pennsylvania General

Assembly, focusing solely on rural schools; it concluded that there was no clear evidence that larger schools did any better—or worse—than smaller schools in providing a good education and that even the argument in favor of merging small rural school districts on the basis of cost-efficiency "is not supported by this study."[18] Absent from most discussions of rural school consolidation is any consideration of the long-term, and often devastating, economic and social effects of school consolidations and closings on the communities themselves. Studying rural schools in New York, Thomas Lyson, professor of rural sociology at Cornell University, found that "schools are especially critical to the social and economic well-being" of small communities and "vital to rural communities" where they are usually the recreational and cultural center for sports, theater, music, and other civic activities. He noted that "the money that might be saved through consolidation could be forfeited in lost taxes, declining property values, and lost businesses."[19] Unfortunately, at least for those small rural towns whose schools have been lost, the arguments in favor of consolidation have proven to be irresistible.

The *minimum* requirements traditionally thought necessary for a town to remain viable typically include a gas station, grocery, bank, doctor (part time), post office, restaurant, and school. Yet it is schools that are the key. As anyone with children can attest, schools are the glue that holds communities together. Virtually everyone I talked to understood that once schools leave town, it is just a matter of time before the other core services begin to disappear.

If schools are the key to survival, for most communities—and particularly for those that lack an inherent advantage such as a college, a county seat, or "bedroom" status to a nearby urban center—the key to growth is likely to be a strong and growing local business or a "purple cow"—something unusual or remarkable. "Purple cow" is a term associated with Seth Godin, author of the popular 2003 book *Purple Cow,* in which he argues, in essence, that in a herd of brown cows no one pays any attention to another brown cow but instead looks for something different, remarkable, unexpected: like a purple cow.[20] Although there is a community in Kansas that may have an actual purple cow somewhere (the grassroots art center of Lucas, for example, definitely has a large blue buffalo sculpture), the idea behind purple cows is that small communities that expect to grow need something special, which can take many forms. One of the most interesting examples is the small town of Fairfield, Iowa, where Transcendental Meditation (TM) is the attraction. Fairfield is the unlikely home to the Maharishi University of Management, with about 850 students, and twice a day much of the activity in Fairfield comes to a halt as the town's TM practitioners, estimated to be about a quarter of the population, pause to meditate. Having a TM center has attracted a wide variety of people to that part of southeastern Iowa, and one result is that Fairfield has a rich assortment of restaurants, art galleries, organic farmers, and eclectic small businesses. It also has a stable population. Jefferson County, of which Fairfield is the county seat, lost less than 1 percent of its population between 1990 and 2000, which, for rural America, is the equivalent of a population explosion. Asked about Fairfield's success, Mayor Ed Malloy, himself a TM practitioner, commended the town's tolerance for diversity and added, "If small-town America has a future, it's going to look something like this."[21]

Purple-cow examples in Kansas might include the Rolling Hills Wildlife Adventure just west of Salina, or a strong ethnic community like the one that exists in Lindsborg, or even a classic old hotel such as the Midland in Wilson. The equivalent of a purple cow, at least in terms of economic impact, may be a lake, or a business—such as Landoll Corporation in Marysville, the state prison in Ellsworth, or one of the many ethanol plants now springing up throughout rural America. It may also be a far-sighted and dedicated group of local leaders who are willing to work together unselfishly and reinvest in their community, as in Palco and Atwood. Or it may be a wealthy benefactor, such as Bill Haw and his efforts in Cottonwood Falls, or Bill Kurtis in Sedan. While purple cows and strong businesses by no means guarantee a community's success, they are valuable contributors.

Given the dominant population trends since at least the mid-twentieth century and the fact that most of the hoped-for "rural revival" has taken place in areas that are near urban centers or natural attractions, the communities that are most at risk in rural America are the small towns that are not adjacent to urban areas or amenities. More specifically, they are the communities with less than 2,500 people that the U.S. Census Bureau considers the core of rural America. These communities are where depopulation has been most severe and where it has been most difficult to attract in-migration.[22] Many are also places that have turned to giving away "free land" in an effort to attract residents.

Although the twentieth century seemed to end in a fog of gloom for rural America, there are signs in the early years of the twenty-first century that at least some people and towns are not going quietly into the night. The "free land" movement has called attention to communities' efforts to survive, if not grow, and throughout rural America there is evidence of towns trying to revitalize themselves. There are also examples of the growth of promising businesses, new and old, from specialized niche agriculture, ranching, manufacturing, and services to tourism, ethanol production, and entrepreneurial incubators. There may even be the prospect of some relief from the hardships caused by rural America's remoteness. The National Aeronautics and Space Administration (NASA) has launched a Small Aircraft Transportation System project that, if successful, may bring "air-taxi" jet service to hundreds of rural communities. NASA envisions the potential for an air-taxi system so cost-effective and ubiquitous that it would lead to what it sees as a new wave of migration from metropolitan to rural areas thanks to improvements in telecommunications as well as the development of the air taxi system.[23]

Although there are exceptions, there appears to be a pattern to the kinds of businesses that are successful in rural communities. Most of them are led by people originally from rural towns. These are expatriates who are returning to their roots—such as Chuck Comeau in Plainville, Kansas—or local entrepreneurs like J. W. Jung in Randolph, Wisconsin, who have been able to expand by relying on a stable, skilled local workforce that grew along with the business. Few success stories are the result of "elephant hunting," a term often used by economic development people to describe the strategy of attracting existing, sizable businesses with the lure of tax concessions, industrial parks, and airports.

This book tells the stories of some of the towns and businesses—the people really—that are trying to defy the odds and are fighting back after losing their school or being bypassed by a highway. It also tells about some of the places that are slipping away and that may be tomorrow's ghost towns.

What kinds of people look at the numbers—the depopulation, the poverty, the aging of a community—and take it as a challenge and an opportunity? Are they fighting an inevitable force that will one day overwhelm their efforts, or are they in the vanguard of a kind of broad-based and long-lasting revival that may save rural America?

Part 2

STRATEGIES IN THE
RURAL FIGHT FOR SURVIVAL

5
"Welcome Home" and the "Free Land" Movement

By the closing years of the twentieth century, many rural communities had begun to attract national attention by promoting "free land" in an effort to attract in-migration.[1] It was all strikingly similar to promotions from a century and a half earlier, the 1860s, when posters and newspaper ads lured people to the plains with slogans such as "Free Homes in Kansas," and "30,000 Free Homes in one of the Richest Valleys in AMERICA are WAITING for OCCUPANTS."[2]

The original "free homes" movement (by which was meant, in fact, "free land") was a response to what was taking place in the American West in the 1850s. Areas such as Kansas were occupied primarily by Native Americans. But with statehood arriving in Iowa in 1846, California in 1850, and Kansas in 1861, the federal government was anxious to encourage the migration of people from the east to fill up the new states and territories.

The Homestead Act of 1862, signed by President Lincoln in the midst of the Civil War, largely accomplished this. Almost 2 million people in 31 states claimed more than 270 million acres, an area greater than Kansas, Nebraska, and Texas combined. Much of the land homesteaded was in the plains states. Settlers received their land in quarter-section parcels of 160 acres for $18 (later enlarged to 640-acre full-section parcels) and were required to stay on the land for at least five years to obtain clear title. In addition, the Pacific Railroad Act of 1862, and later similar legislation, awarded vast amounts of land to the railroads for bringing rail service to regions that were as yet unpopulated, and much of this land was also offered to the public at very low cost.[3] It has been estimated that 25 percent of Kansas (and almost half of Nebraska) was settled by people using homestead claims, while another 10–15 percent of the state was settled by people who bought land from the railroads, typically at prices of $2–$10 an acre.[4]

Although many settlers abandoned their claims, many more stayed, and the Homestead Act and Pacific Railroad Act fulfilled their purpose of populating the United States west of the Appalachians. Of course, a century and a half later, things look different, as many of those places that filled up have begun to empty out, prompting the *New York Times* columnist Nicholas Kristof to label the Homestead era "one of the longest-running and most costly errors in American history."[5]

The homesteading idea was reborn in the late twentieth century. By the 1980s people began to realize that the strategy being followed by most small rural towns to try to stimulate population growth was not working very well. It was based on attracting large businesses, or "elephant hunting," as it is called in economic development circles. Communities vied with each other to attract a manufacturing plant or a distribution center—offering incentives in the form of land and tax breaks. Town after town across rural America taxed or borrowed to create "business parks" and airports. In Superior, Nebraska, community members

> taxed themselves to create an economic development fund. They put in a fiber-optic network for telecommunications. They shored up their high school. They zoned 30 acres at the edge of town for industrial use, graded it and put in utilities. At the center of the proposed industrial park sits the empty shell of a brand new building, built with the help of $145,000 in state money, on spec. Just outside town is a paved and well-lighted runway, although only a lone crop duster, flipped in a storm, rests upside-down on the tarmac.[6]

In most cases, such efforts produced nothing of value. Desperate rural towns competed against one another, a fact that businesses were not above exploiting. Elephant hunting proved to be a costly and uncertain path to growth, at best. At worst, companies came for awhile, took advantage of the economic incentives, and eventually departed for greener pastures or simply went out of business. In 2005 the High Plains towns of Lamar and La Junta, Colorado, already suffering from a persistent drought, got a dose of the downside of elephant hunting. Two of their largest employers, a pickle factory in La Junta and a bus manufacturer in Lamar, announced plans to close, resulting in the loss of 453 jobs—more than 10 percent of the area workforce.[7]

Economic developers decided to try another plan: instead of the "top-down" approach of attracting businesses, they decided to try the "bottom-up" approach of attracting and encouraging small entrepreneurs and families with school-age children. The bait included offers of "free land," supplemented with good schools and a safe, family-oriented lifestyle—a potentially attractive package when contrasted with urban areas saddled with sky-high housing prices, high crime rates, and poor schools.

This new version of homesteading appears to have had its roots in North Dakota or Minnesota in the 1980s, but the idea quickly spread to other states, including Kansas, Nebraska, South Dakota, and Wyoming.[8] The governor of Iowa started a similar kind of program that targets former Iowans, inviting them to receptions in places such as Phoenix and New York to try to sell them on the idea of returning home and extolling the attractions of the state, including one of the country's best public school systems. Some local Iowa communities also offer low-interest home loans to returning natives.[9]

The idea of giving away land has its critics, including John Cyr of the North Central Kansas Economic Development Commission, who believes it devalues the communities and makes them appear to be too desperate.[10] Another critic is geography professor and author James Shortridge, who concludes that "it is obvious that offers of free land in remote communities have little chance of reversing decades of economic decline," adding that indeed it is questionable "whether any program—local or national, private or public—can save the small plains town."[11] Yet even the critics acknowledge that the "free land" plan accomplished at least one thing—it attracted a tremendous amount of free publicity in the national media,[12] although that publicity was occasionally tainted by scornful remarks such as *Time* magazine's comment that "the only catch [is that] you have to live there."[13]

The plans have attracted attention despite the fact that the "free land" being offered is not in itself such a large economic benefit in a place where there is a lot of unused land; the lots offered are typically valued at

$20,000 or less. But to people in urban areas—particularly coastal areas where lots easily can cost over $500,000—just the notion of a place where the land is free can be an attention getter. Suddenly, people who had given up hope of ever building any equity in a home have an option to consider. And there are usually other benefits, particularly for those with school-age children, including help getting a loan and a job, credit toward a down payment, local tax rebates, and perhaps membership in a local golf club. Finally, there are the intangible benefits of being valued and being wanted and of having an opportunity to start a new life and perhaps get out from under a burden of debt.

In return for the land and other benefits, modern-day homesteaders typically must commit to build a house to certain minimum specifications and to occupy it for a certain period of time. Average housing construction costs are in the range of about $85,000–$150,000. Some communities require a preapproved loan before signing over title to the property.[14]

While the free land plans have not yet attracted as many people as some had hoped, most of the communities that have promoted it consider it to be a success in terms of the amount of free publicity it has generated. People have started to notice rural America, and not just prospective homeowners. "As a result of our free land campaign we've actually had lots of new business leads, in fact more within the past year—since we started the program—than ever before," said Roger Hrabe, Rooks County, Kansas, economic development director, and his comment was echoed by most other economic development people in "free land" communities. Whether as a result of the land promotion or other factors, Hrabe said Rooks County had attracted fifty or so small businesses by 2006, and although half of them have closed, many remain open, and several more are investigating opening in the county.

Two of the most ambitious "free land" plans are in Ellsworth County and the town of Marquette in McPherson County, Kansas. In Marquette, eighty lots have been given away, and the town's population, which had been 542 in 2000, had increased to 620 by 2007. Ellsworth County's "Welcome Home Plan" has offered building lots since 2003 in several towns, including the towns of Ellsworth and Wilson. The plan was the brainchild of the county's part-time economic development director, forty-nine-year-old Anita Hoffhines, who also owns marketing and real estate businesses and runs kansasfreeland.com, a web site for the twelve Kansas communities offering free land programs. "Trying to keep school enrollment up was the main reason for the program," she said, "but this is really a marketing tool to draw attention to the area, and it's done that."[15]

Hoffhines also mentioned a curious twist the program had taken, particularly in the town of Ellsworth—a community with a better-than-average existing housing base. "We can identify about 35 families coming here as a result of the program, and they've already added 50 full-time equivalent students to our school system, but not all the families bought our lots. Many people looked around and found good existing houses for sale, sometimes cheaper than they could have built, and they bought those, which is fine." What attracted people to the Ellsworth area? Hoffhines was asked. "They like the quiet, the fresh air, the friendliness and trustworthiness, the low crime rate—and really no serious crime—and the fact that their kids have smaller classes at the school and they can walk or bike anywhere without the parents having to worry about them. And a lot of people like the hunting and fishing, and like being close to Lake Wilson." Has there been anything people didn't like, or objected to? "Well, there *was* one family that objected to having to haul their trash to the town dump. That's about it."

Ellsworth is also one of many rural towns that have welcomed prisons as a reliable source of jobs. Perhaps the most famous such community is in Fremont County, Colorado. The town of Florence, population 3,653, is home to "Supermax," the highest-security federal prison, which housed Oklahoma City bomber Timothy McVeigh before his execution and now houses Theodore Kaczynski (the "Unabomber") and a host of organized crime and terrorist inmates. There are eight other state and federal prisons in the area that, taken together, form the largest employer in the county. Other towns have welcomed businesses such as feedlots. Sauget, Illinois, which, with a population of 250 is small, although not rural, has established a reputation for welcoming trash-transfer stations and other kinds of polluting business and industrial facilities that most communities try to avoid.[16] Sauget was formerly named Monsanto and was home to a chemical plant that was the largest producer of the controversial industrial chemical PCB, which has largely been banned from commercial use. "We were basically incorporated to be a sewer," said the Sauget mayor. The Environmental Protection Agency (EPA) operates a Superfund clean-up site in Sauget along Dead Creek, and the local EPA director calls the area "basically a soup of different chemicals."[17] Sauget also is home to several nightclubs and a minor league baseball team.

As previously mentioned, the other communities losing population have been central cities, and although there have as yet been no offers of free land in those places, most cities have invested heavily in urban redevelopment, including subsidizing small businesses willing to locate in certain neighborhoods. At least one city has actively tried to stimulate population growth. In 2006 and 2007 Buffalo, New York, which lost half its population from its 1950 peak of 580,000, sponsored "Buffalo Old Home Week" and invited back thousands of Buffalo expatriates for presentations about the attractions of their hometown, including a "Career Fair and Entrepreneurial Seminar" designed to appeal to people considering moving, or returning, to Buffalo.[18]

Although Buffalo and many other cities are hoping to reverse population losses, some cities have recognized the reality of their population losses—and the likelihood that the losses will continue—and have begun actively planning to become smaller, yet still vibrant, communities. One of the best-known such cities is Youngstown, Ohio, which has lost over half its population since the 1960s and recently began following an economic plan known as "controlled shrinkage."[19] Other Ohio cities are looking at the Youngstown plan, and the Cleveland Urban Design Collaborative at Kent State University has started a Shrinking Cities Institute to try to help Ohio cities become "smaller and smarter rather than bigger and better."[20] The "shrinking cities" movement is by no means limited to Ohio. The University of California at Berkeley held a symposium on the subject in 2007 that attracted people from five continents, including Europe where several Berlin-based "shrinking cities" projects are under way. Youngstown mayor Jay Williams, a former city planner, has embarked on a major campaign to close streets, clean out decaying neighborhoods, and replace them with parks and open space, actually reducing the city's population density. While Youngstown and similar cities have access to significant internal and external resources to help manage their depopulation, small rural towns for the most part do not. Their fate is in their own hands.

In the next five chapters I tell the stories of five counties or communities, several of which are part of the "free land" movement, that are battlegrounds in the rural American fight for survival. They are all small and remote—some very small and very remote—and all but one has been experiencing significant population losses. Together they provide a good showcase for what does work, and what doesn't work, in rural America. Several of the communities are examples of places that appear to be doing almost everything "right" in their efforts to combat depopulation, and they bear watching over the next decade as early indicators for determining if declining rural populations can be stabilized or if the twenty-first century will continue the emptying out of rural America.

6

Plainville and Rooks County: High Plains, High Style

Rooks County, Kansas, is home to approximately 5,386 people in the north-central part of the state, where the Smoky Hills begin to give way to the High Plains. Stockton is the county seat, population 1,465, and is about 41 miles north of the city of Hays in Ellis County, which has a population of 28,000. Stockton is also 15 miles north of Plainville, also in Rooks County, with a population of 2,029. Hays is growing. Plainville, Stockton, and Rooks County overall are not. Since 1910, Rooks County has lost half its population, and in just the first few years of the twenty-first century the county lost almost 5 percent of its population.[1]

Although Plainville is not the county seat, it is a larger town than Stockton and has more economic activity. Its success vis-à-vis Stockton may be due in part to its being closer to Hays, which is just 26 miles, or about a half hour away, but leadership also plays an essential role.

Assessing what's working well in Rooks County, Roger Hrabe, the county's economic development director, stresses the importance of leadership and the need for cooperation between businesspeople and local governments. Plainville and Palco have been good examples.

Plainville began its existence in 1870 when ranchers and farmers moved into the area, which was then known as "Paradise Flats." In 1888 the name was changed to Plainville, and the Union Pacific reached the town with a branch line. In the 1920s, oil and gas were discovered in the area.

Except for the Great Depression and the dust-bowl years of the 1930s, the seven decades from 1900 to 1970 were relatively good years for Rooks County, which reached a population of more than 11,000 in 1910 and hovered around the 9,000–10,000 range for the next sixty years.[2] Well into the 1950s and early 1960s Plainville was a prosperous town. Family farms still dominated rural America, and oil and gas activity was high. Candace Rachel, editor of the *Plainville Times,* remembers what it was like to grow up in Plainville in its heyday, and her memories could apply to most small rural towns in America:

> Plainville was a paradise for a kid in those days. A child could walk to the swimming pool and swim all day, then walk a couple more blocks to the baseball field and watch K-18 baseball in the evening, and walk home if necessary, without a fear.
>
> We went to the movie theater in groups, walking each other home afterward. There were at least two clothing stores here, with a few items available at the Duckwall's store as well. There was also a formal/bridal shop where people came from miles around.
>
> The streets of Plainville were full of smiling faces and chatting folks during the summer celebration and parade. There were games for the kids, huge sidewalk sales, a massive parade, and the rodeo for two nights. Everyone took part in the festivities, and the rodeo was packed—even when it rained, which it did most years.
>
> Christmastime was the same. Stores were full of people throughout the season, full of goodies to purchase and full of good cheer. It was pleasing to be downtown at night with all the Christmas lights along the streets and in the stores. I can still feel the wonderment of a child at Christmas, thanks to growing up here.
>
> In 1963 there were nine stores where a person could buy appliances. I couldn't tell you the names of the stores, but we did have both Sears and Montgomery Ward dealers besides Carmicheal's Coast to Coast (now Carmicheal's True Value) and Gary's Western Auto.
>
> The Rooks County Fair each August was also a highlight for just about anyone in the county. 4-H kids displayed their work, showed their livestock, and worked in the food stand during the week. The smells of livestock mingled with fried foods are something to behold and can grow to be very pleasant. You could see all your relatives and friends at the fair, and there, too, people smiled—a lot.
>
> Cap's Shoe Repair shop was always a Saturday morning stop for me as a kid, whether I had a reason to be there or not—the smell of leather always pulled me in for a chat. The bakery on Mill Street

added to those memories. We always had to have a fresh loaf of Harold's French bread for my dad. It was one of the first places I got to drive to alone in the car at age 14.

Duckwall's had fresh candy behind glass counters, and in the fall the front window was full of fresh caramel apples for sale . . . heaven. The store had bins of goods you could pick through in several tiers. It was a great store for a kid to ponder and make those important purchases. I still love a store with wooden floors. Carmicheal's is that way today.[3]

But much as she loved growing up in Plainville, Candace Rachel joined the many who began leaving the area in greater numbers in the 1960s, and when she returned in the late 1990s, the county's population had dropped by almost 40 percent. The rodeo and drive-in movie and new car dealership were gone, and most of the stores she had known as a child had closed. "The town looked a lot smaller," she said.[4]

Yet as she stayed in town and began working at the local weekly newspaper, which has a circulation of about 1,400, she detected some signs of renewal. "Since about 2000 the town seems to be getting more progressive," she said, adding, "I've seen former high school kids starting businesses and the city council beginning to spend some money on cleaning up the downtown, and coming up with a free land program to try to attract people. It also seems like more people are buying locally when they can instead of running to Hays for everything."[5]

There was concrete evidence of a willingness on the part of the people of Plainville to reinvest in their community when, in March 2006, voters approved a $3.46 million bond issue to renovate and expand the Plainville High School gym and upgrade many other facilities in the school district.

Plainville is close enough to Hays that it has developed into something of a bedroom community for its larger neighbor—and in turn there are those who live in Hays because of its amenities and commute to Plainville. As a result, Highway 183 between Hays and Plainville is a busy road—at least for rural Kansas—during morning and evening rush hours.

But it is likely that Plainville's greatest asset is its people. Plainville has been fortunate to have a number of successful business and community leaders, including, in addition to Hrabe, Rod Cellmer of Schult Homes, a maker of manufactured homes (a division of Clayton Homes, which is a Berkshire Hathaway company), Ben Quinton of the Plainville Health Center, Marvin Reif of Sticks and Stones, a yard-art company, and perhaps most notably Chuck Comeau of the DessinFournir Companies, one of the country's leading designers and manufacturers of high-end home furnishings.

The impact of DessinFournir on the community cannot be overestimated. The company was started by Comeau, who had grown up in Plainville, graduated from nearby Fort Hays State University with a degree in earth sciences, and worked in banking, ranching, and the oil industry—all major contributors to the economy of Rooks County. By 1993 Comeau, who was then 36, realized that while he enjoyed those businesses his greatest interest lay in architecture and interior design, interests and skills he had picked up on his own primarily as a hobby but that were consuming more and more of his time as he helped design and decorate homes for friends and family members.

While working on a home in California, Comeau met Len Larsen, who had a design background and, like Comeau, wanted to get into the furniture business. DessinFournir was born and was successful from the start when it was based in Los Angeles, although Comeau remained in Plainville with his wife and young children. The result was a tiring travel schedule and the challenge of managing a company from afar. Finally, in 1999, with DessinFournir becoming one of the top names in the industry, Comeau made the decision to move the company to Plainville. "People thought I was crazy," Comeau said, "but it turned out to be the best thing that could have happened."[6]

Although reducing his personal travel was important, there was much more behind Comeau's decision. Running the business in Los Angeles had presented many problems, including high labor costs, a business climate with difficult regulations, high taxes, very expensive rent and real estate prices, and a fickle workforce with high turnover.

By contrast, Comeau said, "People in Plainville have a great work ethic, an innate loyalty that's different from other places with more of a transient population."[7] The firm still has strong ties to Los Angeles, including a line of furniture designed by Kerry Joyce, a well-known Los Angeles interior designer whose clients include many people in the entertainment industry.

Not only was it unusual for a company such as DessinFournir to be in Plainville, but the way it was done was also unconventional—and very successful for the company and the town. Most manufacturing businesses in towns such as Plainville are located on the outskirts of town in large, nondescript, steel or concrete buildings. Sometimes this is for a good reason, as is the case for businesses that make farm equipment and manufactured housing and need a lot of storage and loading space and hangarlike working areas.

Yet in many cases there are other options, and there is no better example of this than the DessinFournir facilities. When Comeau moved the business to Kansas, the Plainville downtown area—as is common to most small Kansas towns—was characterized by a lot of empty storefronts and rundown buildings. Most businessmen would have taken a quick look downtown and then bought a few acres outside of town on which to place the customary kind of building. And most towns, anxious to attract economic activity, would have been delighted and perhaps even made the land available at below-market rates or with attractive tax advantages.

Comeau had different ideas. Where others saw blight and failure, he saw the potential for "style and atmosphere" and—just as important—for a unique and very appealing working environment, a kind of rural equivalent to the loft and warehouse revitalization efforts that have been so successful in the SoHos of New York and LoDos of Denver, as well as other major cities.

The first DessinFournir office, which is still the main office, occupies a renovated building—formerly an automobile dealership—at 308 West Mill Street, right across the street from the Plainville City Hall. As Comeau has expanded, other DessinFournir companies have taken over and renovated seven nearby downtown buildings, with three additional buildings yet to be completed. Each building has been renovated in a distinctive, but not inappropriate, style, and each is within short walking distance of the others—as well as of the banks, the library, the schools,

OPPOSITE: *Top: DessinFournir's headquarters is in this former car dealership in the heart of downtown Plainville. Center: DessinFournir's fabric businesses are headquartered in this renovated building in downtown Plainville. Bottom: The Pineapple Post gift shop shares the building with Classic Cloth.*

the hospital, the hardware store, "Tina's"—the lone downtown bar—and Comeau's own home.

As a result, Comeau has accomplished at least two things at once: he has created an attractive working environment for a creative group of businesses, and he has had a major impact on reinvigorating Plainville's downtown and making it a showplace, rather than an eyesore.

But it is not only the outward appearance of Plainville that has benefited from the decision to move DessinFournir to town. The company also brought almost eighty well-paying, interesting, and skilled jobs to a community hard hit by the collapse of the oil market in the 1980s and the continuing loss of population as young people move away.

The loss of its young people has been a chronic long-term problem for Plainville. The fate of towns that lose too many children, including Plainville's neighbor, Zurich, is a marginal existence at best—perhaps becoming a bedroom community for some nearby town or—at worst—becoming just an isolated cluster of a few houses with no services and a decaying infrastructure: a ghost town.

Rooks County Economic Development Director Hrabe described the problem. Plainville High School has 144 students, including approximately thirty in the twelfth grade. By all accounts Plainville is representative of Kansas schools in general, which tend to be better than average. The students receive a good education. The teacher-student ratio is about one to ten, and 97 percent of the students graduate. But following graduation, the students tend to fall into three groups. The first group doesn't attend college—deciding instead to get married or work at whatever jobs are available in the area or to join the military. The second group goes to college, which means leaving Plainville even if it is to go no farther than to Fort Hays State University in nearby Hays or to one of the other colleges and universities in the state, but they at least vaguely contemplate returning someday—most likely when they decide to raise a family. Some of these people actually do return, but at least half do not. The third group—the largest group—goes away to college and plans never to return to live permanently in Plainville. The arithmetic is clear: fewer than half, indeed probably less than one-third, of Plainville's children will remain in the area. And, of course, many of those who leave are among the better-achieving students. When this pattern is repeated year after year, the effects on a community such as Plainville are not difficult to discern, particularly when contrasted to what the community could become if most of the students decided to make their homes in Plainville.

But there are reasons why so many students leave such communities. Although jobs are often available, they have tended to be relatively low paying and often unchallenging. Farming appeals to many, but the declining need for farmers—and with it the decline of the family farm—is just one more long-term trend changing rural America. The other factor working against towns such as Plainville is simply the lure of the urban American lifestyle. Students who go off to college in Boston or Boulder quickly develop a fondness for the amenities and attractions available in an urban community.

In this context, it is easy to see why Comeau's vision is so promising. By doing business the way he has, he brought economic activity into the local community, he contributed to transforming downtown into an attractive—even trendy—area, and he made possible a lot of jobs that are unusual for such a community: well-paying jobs, creative jobs, fun jobs, career-path jobs. Suddenly, some of the students have options they never had before.

"I would probably be working late nights at a fast-food restaurant or mowing grass if it wasn't for this job," said Samantha Hixon, a junior at the Plainville high school whose after-school job is to produce catalogs for interior designers and the showrooms through which DessinFournir sells its products. "I know this usually doesn't happen in a small town like this," she added.[8]

Comeau has also introduced flexible hours in his workplace, so that people such as Hixon can balance their schedules, which in her case includes cheerleading and volleyball. While Hixon may well attend college after graduation, the existence of DessinFournir will provide her with options and opportunities she would not have had a decade before.

Regarding Comeau, and his effect on Plainville, *Plainville Times* editor Candace Rachel chooses one word: "Tremendous." "He encourages employees to become involved in community events and the city council, and projects such as the Saddle Club, and his people have a 'can do' attitude. I don't know how he does it, but people who work [at Dessin-Fournir] seem to become transformed into better citizens."

Of course the beneficial effects DessinFournir has had on Plainville are secondary to, and dependent on, the success of the business itself.

Comeau's decision to locate in Plainville and conduct business the way he does was based primarily on business and personal considerations, not the goal of downtown beautification or providing jobs. Comeau believed that one would follow the other, but he knew the business case had to come first. The benefits that Plainville enjoys as a result of Dessin-Fournir would not exist if it were not a good place to do business. But Comeau, along with other successful rural entrepreneurs, was able to "think outside the box." In this regard, he was lucky—because of his background he knew the hidden assets that rural communities such as Plainville could offer. More traditional entrepreneurs might simply locate a company such as DessinFournir in a crowded urban "fashion center" and never consider a rural option.

In a strange way, DessinFournir's location in Plainville instead of someplace like New York or Los Angeles has been something of a secret weapon in marketing. People in the luxury furniture business have no difficulty remembering DessinFournir, a company that in Comeau's words creates "products for basically one percent of the population who, subsequently, control 44 percent of the wealth"[9] It's that company in Plainville, Kansas, *wherever that is!* And Comeau enjoys a dream come true: living and working where he wants to live in a place that is good for him, his family, and his business. It is also a place where he can more easily, and more rewardingly, have a chance to make a lasting difference.

Ultimately, much of the success of any business comes down to its employees. Because of his background, Comeau knew the qualities of the potential workforce in Plainville: hardworking, well-educated, skilled, and loyal. "There are lots of good local people here," Comeau said, adding, "the quality of people in the rural communities I know about is second to none. And we've had no problem finding skilled workers—including people who used to work on oil equipment or farm equipment and now are creating products in our lighting business." Nor has it been difficult to get talent from elsewhere when necessary. "I've never had to solicit or use headhunters. The company's reputation tends to attract people."

But it has not been without challenges. One of the reasons for Dessin-Fournir's success, according to Ron Wilson, director of the Huck Boyd Institute, which fosters rural development, has been that Comeau "thinks big" and "looks beyond Kansas to the national and international markets."[10] That has meant travel, and the Hays Regional Airport offers just four commercial flights a day (to Kansas City and Denver). As a result, travel can often take a full day, with connections, and the option of driving four or five hours to Kansas City or Denver doesn't help much. Wichita offers a few more destinations, including Chicago, but it is three and a half hours away by car. Corporate and charter aircraft provide a solution, which Comeau has tried, but they are expensive, and he has concerns about safety. For the time being, inconvenient travel may just be a necessary evil for companies in places such as Plainville. Fortunately, the company actually operates through sixteen showrooms from New York to San Francisco.

Services such as telecommunications and shipping goods and materials, however, are another matter. Thanks to the ubiquity of overnight shipping, FedEx and UPS trucks service the DessinFournir businesses in Plainville at least as efficiently as if they were in a large urban market. Likewise, the area has good telecommunications services, including high-speed Internet access and cellular services, thanks largely to Nex-Tech and its parent, Rural Telephone Company. Rural Telephone is a cooperative that was formed by the people of Rooks and five other counties in 1951, a time when good telephone service in such rural areas was almost nonexistent. AT&T also nominally serves the region, but rural communities have never been a high priority for the major telephone companies. Fortunately for rural America, many small communities such as Monroe, Oregon (population 680) and Greybull, Wyoming (population 1,815) "have surpassed the cities . . . because of nimbler local telecom companies that have taken matters into their own hands. While behemoths such at AT&T Inc. and Verizon Communications are hamstrung by their large size and logistics of serving millions of consumers, many small companies have charged ahead by exploiting some weapons only available to firms of their size."[11] One such weapon is the Rural Utilities Service of the U.S. Department of Agriculture, which can pay for up to 80 percent of network modernization.

One problem often encountered in—but by no means limited to—rural communities is the narrow vision of some of those in town government and the local business community, sometimes tinged with jealousy and the remnants of old feuds. While entrepreneurs such as Comeau and others in Kansas may indeed "think big," a common complaint from businesspeople is that some members of town councils and zoning boards and some local bankers, are inclined to "think small" and to look for reasons why a project should not be done, rather than try to find ways to do it. Although Comeau's plans generally have been welcomed by the community, he occasionally has had to battle over such things as minor zoning variance requests. He has expressed frustration over such delays, and he believes that groups trying to promote rural business development, including the new Kansas Center for Entrepreneurship in Wichita, should perhaps help local governments better understand the needs of entrepreneurs and businesses. In his *New York Times Magazine* article about rural America, Richard Rubin relates the story of Shawn Oehlke who decided in 2004 to settle in Divide County, North Dakota. The county had lost almost two-thirds of its population since 1920, but Oehlke chose the location to start a high-technology company to make precision optics, including fast steering mirrors for the military. The local county and a business development group promised many benefits, but the reality was somewhat different, prompting Oehlke's wife Esther Oehlke, who is also the company's chief executive officer, to complain in a letter to the local paper, "We heard that North Dakota wanted small business [but we have encountered] . . . meetings put off, lack of vision in planning ahead, burdensome regulations that are used arbitrarily, counting cost instead of value—these are why businesses and people leave this town."[12]

Another problem mentioned by Comeau, and echoed by others throughout rural America, is the matter of low property values or, more specifically, the discrepancy between real estate appreciation rates in places such as Plainville and in cities such as Hays and urban areas such as Denver. (Interestingly, the retail price of DessinFournir's most expensive item is exactly the same as the median price of a home in Plainville!)

From 1995 to 2005 property values in many urban and suburban areas almost doubled, while in rural communities prices remained essentially flat. While this makes moving to a rural community attractive for someone coming from a city, it also has a negative aspect: if conditions don't change, it is unlikely the buyer of a home in a rural community will enjoy the kind of gain in value realized by his urban counterpart. There are, of course, two sides to this. Such gains are not assured, and, indeed, urban home prices began to weaken in 2006 and 2007 while demand in many rural areas for housing remained steady. Indeed, there have been some dramatic drops in housing prices in urban areas—Los Angeles in the early 1990s and Denver in the 1980s, for example—and also periods when appreciation has been modest (1950–1965).

Comeau obviously finds that a rural community works well for creative businesses such as the DessinFournir companies, and he also believes the rural environment is good for think-tank and research-oriented types of businesses because "life is simple here and good for people who need time to think and reflect." Yet he is not sure if there is a likelihood of any sustainable or significant rural revival based on attracting more people like him and companies like DessinFournir. Commenting on people who have left rural communities but are considering returning, he thinks that for a lot of them, "while the desire to return is there, particularly on the part of people from the traditional corporate world, the leap from corporate life to entrepreneurship in a rural community is a big one."

In assessing what rural plains towns can do to help themselves, Comeau brought up the purple-cow theory.[13] Referring to small plains towns, Comeau said, "These places need something special to attract some attention and give people a reason to take a look at them." As noted earlier, rural America is not without purple cows, including attractions such as Lake McConnaughy near Ogallala, Nebraska, and the Pawnee National Grassland in northeast Colorado. In Kansas, purple cows include the Lucas arts community and restaurants such as the Bunker Hill Cafe in tiny Bunker Hill and the Brookville Hotel in Abilene—which is actually a famous fried chicken restaurant. The Brookville Hotel drew people from near and far to the tiny town of Brookville, Kansas, population 259, before the restaurant moved to Abilene in 2000. A Hot Wheels festival in 2006 drew 10,000 people to Speed, Kansas (population 37) and to nearby Norton, where collector Jeff "Goof" Urban has a museum with some 8,000 Hot Wheels die-cast toy cars.[14] Cars are also the attraction at one of the most unusual purple cows in rural America, Carhenge near Alliance, Nebraska, a re-creation of prehistoric Stonehenge in England, but built entirely out of vehicles painted granite-like gray. In rural southwestern North Dakota the purple cow takes the form of huge roadside sculptures along a stretch of interstate called the "Enchanted Highway." Perhaps the ultimate rural American purple cow may emerge if

Carhenge is a remarkably accurate replica of the prehistoric Stonehenge monument. However, while Stonehenge had its beginnings some 3,000 years ago and was built of massive stone blocks in Wiltshire, England, Carhenge was created in 1987 by Jim Reinders and his family a few miles north of Alliance, Nebraska, and was built entirely of thirty-eight cars. The site is now maintained by a local group, Friends of Carhenge, and some additional automobile sculptures as well as a parking lot and picnic tables have been added to the site, which has attracted more than 80,000 visitors.

Amazon.com founder Jeff Bezos goes ahead with plans to build a giant spaceport near Van Horn, Texas, a town of about 2,100 people that lost 10 percent of its population between 2000 and 2005. According to a *Wall Street Journal* report, Bezos has bought almost 300,000 acres of land near Van Horn for a company called Blue Origin, which may start offering commercial space flights as early as 2010.[15] And there are towns, such as Tipton, Kansas, or Plainville's neighbor Palco, which may lack a real purple cow but survive because of the dedication of a few people who simply won't let the town disappear.

Despite continuing to lose population, Plainville can be considered a probable success story. There is—relatively—a lot going on in Plainville itself, and its proximity to Hays and an interstate highway would seem to bode well for the future. Indeed, if Plainville can't make it—that is, stabilize its population—it is difficult to see how other similar small towns will succeed. But, there *is* something tenuous about what is going on in Plainville and many other promising rural towns, as evidenced by the January 2007 closing of the Schulte manufactured homes plant in Plainville, a loss of 140 jobs. Progress is dependent on a handful of people and companies. Who would replace the people who went out on a limb

The Tin Family is just one of six enormous metal sculpture sets erected along a 32-mile stretch of Interstate 95 between Gladstone (population 248) and Regent (population 211) in North Dakota. Created by Regent native Gary Greff to try to attract visitors to the area, the Tin Family was built in 1993 largely out of scrap metal from local farms and junkyards. Welding took two months. The tin man is 45 feet tall, the tin woman 44 feet, and the tin boy 23 feet. Four more sculptures are planned for this section of the interstate, which is billed as the Enchanted Highway and claims to display the world's largest metal sculptures. (Courtesy of Richard Johnson)

to save the Midland Hotel in Wilson? Who would replace the Comeau family should they be unable or unwilling to continue their role in the Plainville community?[16] And who will replace Schulte homes? Who would replace the few people in each community who are creating purple cows and defying the odds? That question cannot be answered, and therein lies a significant vulnerability for many of these communities.

Palco, Zurich, Codell

Palco and Zurich are just west of Plainville. Palco is about 15 miles from Plainville, and Zurich is between the two, about 7 miles from each (see map, page 73). Physically, Palco is an unusually attractive community for western Kansas. Most of the homes are well maintained, the small "downtown" Main Street is active, the topography provides a few gentle hills and valleys, and the main highway is just outside of town, rather than through the middle, as is the case with most such towns. In many respects, Palco is a picture-postcard kind of small Kansas town.

The population of Palco is approximately 235, while Zurich is about 122. The area was settled in the 1870s and 1880s, largely by homesteaders. An early settlement in the area was Cresson, about a mile and a half northwest of present-day Palco, where a post office was established in 1879. By 1885 Cresson had a population of 200.[17]

Success or failure for a town in the late nineteenth century could be determined by where the railroads chose to lay their track, and so when the railroad reached Plainville in 1888 there was much speculation about which way it would go as it extended to the west. Enough Cresson citizens believed the path would go to their south that they moved most of the town to New Cresson at a spot southwest of present-day Palco and awaited the railroad. It never came; instead the railroad was built to the northeast toward Hill City—passing not far from where original Cresson had stood. Once again, most of the citizens decided to move, and in late 1888 they headed back north and located a town on some available land where the Union Pacific's branch line from Plainville and Zurich curved toward Hill City. And in a further effort to ingratiate themselves with the railroad gods, they agreed to name the new town after two Union Pacific managers, a Mr. Palmer and a Mr. Cole, hence "Palco." (The communities of Codell, Plainville, Zurich, and Palco received daily railroad service until into the mid-twentieth century. By the end, in 1958, service consisted only of Union Pacific "jitneys," seventy-four-passenger self-contained trains that were more like streetcars than passenger trains, and a slow freight train with some space for a few passengers in the caboose. Trains originated in Salina and ended in Oakley on a spur line from the main Union Pacific route that ran from Kansas City to Denver roughly along present-day I-70. The trip from Salina to Plainville took almost four hours by jitney and seven hours by freight, compared to less than two hours by car.)

In 1907 some cement sidewalks were installed along the town's main and virtually only street (named "Main Street"), but in 1913 other streets—and alleys—were laid out, although none of the streets were

Above: The Midwest Community Bank in Palco, with the town's grocery store in the background to the left. Below: Palco's survival depends on being able to support its school, pictured here in the foreground, with the Palco grain elevator in the background.

paved until the late 1920s. The mid-twentieth century was relatively uneventful for Palco, but the energy crisis and ensuing oil boom in the 1970s brought jobs, prosperity, and people. Palco's population reached almost 750 at the peak of the boom, and the high school had almost as many students as Plainville. But the energy market crashed in the early 1980s, reaching its bottom a few years later, and the late 1980s were difficult years for Palco, as they were for Zurich and most of Rooks County.

By 1990 Rooks County's valuation had declined 50 percent from a decade earlier, Palco's population had been reduced by almost 65 percent, and school enrollment was plummeting.[18] True, oil was cheap, and gas could be bought for well under a dollar a gallon at Palco's three gas stations and Zurich's one gas station, until all four closed their doors in the early 1990s. But Palco still had one critical asset: in 1955 it had won the battle with nearby Zurich for a high school, and in 1990 Palco still had the high school, plus the grade school, while the town of Damar to the north had the junior high school. Zurich had nothing. But the schools were losing students at such a rapid rate that further consolidation, or even a merger with another school district, threatened Palco's viability. Palco needed to stem the loss of people, or it might soon go the way of Zurich and so many other towns.

It turned out that in addition to its schools, Palco had another valuable asset: a small group of people, including Myron Keller, Monte Keller, and Charlie Allphin, who didn't want to see the town die and were willing to do what was necessary to save it. They formed Palco Community Economic Development (PCED) in 1990, a 501(c)(3) entity that could get loans and matching funds from government agencies. Fortunately for the group, Monte Keller was a banker and also had extensive experience in grant writing and in working with government agencies to obtain financing. Their first project was in 1994, raising $175,000 for Kysar Machine Products, a supplier of precision systems and pneumatic tools to companies such as Hallmark and Goodyear. Kysar had been one of the town's strongest local businesses since the 1970s but was threatened by the economic downturn of the 1980s. Kysar has survived and today employs seven people in Palco.

The development group's second project, in 1998, raised almost a half-million dollars, including $200,000 locally and a Small Business Administration (SBA) loan, for a combination gas station, body shop, and garage on Main Street on the site where an old grain elevator had been razed. The facility, which is run by Myron Keller, quickly became profitable, and in 2004 Keller received the SBA's national award as Young Entrepreneur of the Year. Underscoring the challenges of running a business in a remote, small town, Keller pointed out one of the keys to success: "You can't afford to displease any customer. Not one." Not only are there few customers to begin with, but word of mouth gets around quickly in such communities. The reputation of Keller's body shop is such that, in fact, he gets business from Hays and other locations far from Palco.

In 2001 Palco's only restaurant was put up for sale, and the town was faced with the loss of a business that was a local informal meeting place as well as a provider of breakfasts, lunches, and dinners. The members of PCED realized how important it was for a town to have such an amenity and raised $45,000 to buy the building, which they now lease to a restaurant operator who also pays the taxes and insurance on the business.

During the 1990s Palco still had a bank, the First National, but in 2003 the bank moved its headquarters to Hays, and in the following year Monte Keller led a successful effort by Midwest Community Bank to buy out the First National. Today Keller is the bank's president, and by 2006, the bank had more deposits as Midwest than it did when it was the First National.

By 1990 Palco's last doctor had left town, and the community was faced with doing without regular medical care, which would make it difficult to attract families with young children—or keep such families—and posed a hardship for Palco's retirees. Palco Community Economic Development spearheaded an effort to create a medical facility, helped secure a $90,000 grant, and renovated a Main Street building. In 2004 the Palco Medical Clinic opened its doors, staffed by two doctors from Plainville who operate the clinic two days a week. The development group also provided help to the community-owned grocery and was—along with the local Lions Club—a major contributor to the Little Roosters Day Care center,[19] which has twenty-three children enrolled and is a vital resource for a town trying to attract young families in which both spouses are working. The day-care center was a $102,000 project, with $40,000 raised locally and the balance obtained through grants and low-interest loans obtained from the U.S. Department of Agriculture's rural development program.

Having a local day-care center is important for small communities such as Palco, as Monte Keller explained:

> Some of our families are two-income families with small children
> and both parents working in Plainville or Hays, and if we didn't have
> day care in Palco they would take their children with them to day

care in Plainville or Hays, and they would begin to build all their community attachments to one of those places, not to Palco. Their children's friends and playmates would be from those communities, and in some cases when that happens the children end up going to school there as well. We just can't afford to let that happen.[20]

In 2001 the Palco city offices were renovated, with most of the funding coming from local residents, PCED buying the land, and Myron Keller as the unpaid project manager. In addition to space for the town council, the offices provide the town's ambulance and fire departments. Palco has also managed to keep its library, which is supported by the city through tax revenue.

Perhaps the biggest project Palco has faced was a major street-and-sewer overhaul for Main Street in 2003. The eighteen-month, $2.2-million-dollar project would have been beyond the resources of the town, but most of the money was provided by the Kansas Department of Transportation and the federal government. Getting the state and federal agencies to agree to put money into Palco, however, was not a foregone conclusion. According to Monte Keller, the main reason the money was allocated to Palco was because of the community's track record of involvement and reinvestment, which helped convince the government that money spent in Palco would not be wasted on a lost cause.

Even a brief history of what has taken place in Palco since 1990 is illustrative of the importance of the four necessary elements for a town's survival: leadership (in this case from the PCED), a town council that is generally supportive, local people who are willing to invest their own money in the community, and a school. There are many communities similar to Palco in Kansas where one or more of these four elements are missing, and most of those communities are either failing to live up to their potential or are beginning the downward spiral toward becoming a ghost town.

Yet despite the enormous efforts of the people of Palco and the leadership of PCED, the town is still in jeopardy. The key barometer of survival, school population, remains a persistent problem. In the 1970s—a time of rising oil prices that attracted workers to oil fields around Palco—the schools averaged as many as fifty-five children in a grade, but this dropped to twenty-eight in the 1980s. By 2004 the average high

Most rural towns with fewer than 300 people have had to close their libraries. Palco has managed to keep its small library open.

school class size was twelve, and the average elementary school class was ten. A high school with forty-six students and 7.5 teachers may well be an excellent place to get a good education—the Palco school district spends almost twice the amount of money per student as the Kansas average— but it remains a potential weak link in the Palco community. Thanks largely to higher oil prices beginning in 2005, Palco's schools have seen small increases in enrollment, but the numbers are still low, and gains in enrollment appear to be dependent on the vagaries of the oil market. A downturn in oil prices, which occurred in the 1980s, would again endanger the viability of the school, the school district itself, and, eventually, the town.

The second weak link in Palco, as elsewhere in rural America, is housing. "The economy around here has been strong lately, but we've pretty much run out of houses," said bank president Monte Keller in 2006. Basic economic theory would seem to suggest that the scarcity of housing stock should result in meaningful appreciation in home prices and the construction of new houses, but for the most part it hasn't happened in Palco, perhaps because the incomes of many in rural Kansas simply can't support higher prices. In addition, builders and lenders have been more interested in housing markets in metropolitan areas like Kansas City or even rural cities such as Hays and Salina, where the population is younger and incomes are higher.

Zurich

Less than 10 minutes east of Palco is Zurich, the town that lost its high school to Palco in 1955 and its K–8 school twenty years later. It has become essentially a bedroom community.

The demise of Zurich as an independent community is a story both of consolidation within the Palco-Damar-Zurich school district and of a community's unwillingness to accept change. After Zurich lost its high school to consolidation in 1955, it kept its K–8 school while its high school students attended school in Palco. In 1974 dwindling school enrollment again required consolidation, and the district proposed moving grades 6–8 from Zurich to Damar, leaving a K–5 school in Zurich. Under the plan, Damar would lose its K–5 school and small high school to Palco but would get the junior high school. Damar accepted the deal, but Zurich resisted and filed a lawsuit against the district demanding that it be allowed to keep all of grades K–8, not just K–5; it also sought to split off from the Palco-dominated district and join the Plainville district. Zurich lost the lawsuit and in the process lost all of its grades, with grades K–5 going to Palco and grades 6–8 going to Damar. Soon, Zurich's stores began to close.

The town still has about 120 residents, but no services. Because of its location, it is likely that Zurich will function only as a bedroom community to Plainville, Hays, and Palco. While bedroom communities can be successful as such, they run the risk of becoming increasingly characterized by dilapidated and abandoned buildings and vehicles. It is difficult to see why newcomers, and certainly families with children, would choose to settle in such towns, as opposed to Plainville or Palco. And housing prices can drop to the point where they attract a transient, undesirable element (including operators of methamphetamine labs), driving out the few remaining long-time locals.[21]

Zurich is somewhat similar to Ada, a town in Ottawa County that has become a ghost town, at least in terms of retail activity, alongside its more prosperous neighbors Delphos and Minneapolis. It does not appear that state or local officials or private groups have a solution for what to do with the Adas and Zurichs of the world. Once the downward spiral has reached a critical mass, communities lacking the essential elements that are present in towns such as Palco seem to have no options.

Abandoned buildings in what once was the small downtown area of Zurich.

If they are fortunate in terms of location—as Zurich may be, but Ada perhaps less so—they might endure as bedroom communities, but if not, they will suffer the fate of towns such as Hanks, North Dakota, which once existed to serve the cattle drives that went through the area. Hanks reached a population of 300 in the 1920s but was down to 150 by the 1940s as the cattle markets changed. By 1991 Hanks had 11 residents and voted to unincorporate. Today, Hanks has one resident, Debra Quarne. In the story of Hanks that was included in a *New York Times Magazine* article in 2006, she was asked what life was like in Hanks. "Quiet," she replied.[22]

Codell

Yet as bleak as Zurich's future may appear, it could have been worse. By 1916 the small town of Codell, just a few miles east of Plainville, had been in existence for almost fifty years and had a bank, a restaurant, a hotel, two churches, a school, and about 200 residents. In 1915 the town narrowly escaped a tornado, but on May 20, 1916, it was not so fortunate. A category F2 tornado (winds to 156 mph) ripped through the area just east of Codell, doing moderate damage. The community repaired and rebuilt, only to be hit by another tornado (an F3, with winds to 206

Codell's small park contains this memorial to the tornadoes that struck the town in three consecutive years and to its high school, which closed in 1965.

mph) on the same day the following year, May 20, 1917. The 2-mile-wide twister cut a path just west of Codell and destroyed the barns on six farms. A year passed. When the skies turned ominously dark on the afternoon of May 20, 1918, people could scarcely believe what was happening. Yet by nine o'clock that evening a category F4 tornado, bearing winds up to 260 miles per hour and capable, in tornado terminology, of doing "devastating damage," did just that. The tornado, accompanied by massive amounts of lightning and thunder, hail and rain, entered Codell from the south, where it already had killed five people in Ellis County. It went right through the center of Codell, destroying virtually everything. Yet—and not surprisingly—the people of Codell had been inclined to take tornadoes seriously given their recent history. They hid in their storm cellars ("'fraidy holes," some called them) and, miraculously, no one in Codell died. Not so fortunate were some farmers to the northeast, where the tornado went after leaving Codell. It killed four people who had not sought shelter underground. Only then did the tornado, having taken the lives of nine people and destroying scores of buildings in its 60-mile path, finally lose strength near Osborne.[23]

Cattle now graze in some places within the town of Codell, including on this lot where a house once stood before being leveled by a tornado.

That year, 1918, was the last straw for many of the people of Codell. The town, much of which was not rebuilt, never really recovered, although strangely enough the area has not experienced another tornado. Although it was predicted that Codell might become a ghost town, it actually achieved a measure of dubious fame in *Ripley's Believe It or Not*,[24] and to this day it exists as a small, friendly, well-maintained, unincorporated village, with a Baptist church, no retail activity—unless you count a couple of soft-drink vending machines—and no paved streets. The half-block of "downtown" Codell is empty now, save for a small oil company office, which also serves as the town's post office and notary public. The town, like Zurich, has no school. Its high school was closed in 1965 and its grade school in 1978, and for education and most shopping and services it is dependent on Plainville. Codell stands as a quiet monument to natural forces and a reminder that nature—in the form of tornadoes, insect invasions, dust storms, or limited water resources—is a force to be reckoned with in the High Plains.

7

Atwood and Rawlins County: Surviving in the Great American Desert

In general, the problems facing small rural towns increase in rough proportion to their remoteness from urban communities and major highways. This includes many towns in northwestern Kansas, including Atwood, the county seat of Rawlins County, a "frontier county" with fewer than three people per square mile. Atwood is 30 miles north of Kansas's major east-west highway (I-70) and the small city of Colby, 50 miles from the larger city of McCook, Nebraska, and 140 miles from Hays, the nearest sizable city in Kansas. Atwood is so far west that its metropolitan area orientation is centered more on Denver, Colorado (262 miles away), than on Wichita (317 miles) or Kansas City (400 miles).

Before the Interstate Highway System was built, beginning in the 1950s, Atwood was relatively well situated. At that time, Kansas had several east-west highways, including three linking the Kansas City–Topeka area with Denver and Colorado Springs. In northwest Kansas, Highway 36 went through Atwood, Highway 24 through Colby, and Highway 40, in the south, went through Oakley. To both east and west the situation was repeated, with three towns running north to south and three highways (see map, page 73). When it was decided to build one east-west interstate highway through the state, it was clear that two of the three towns in each area would be losers. The results would be of enormous importance to most of the towns, all of which were county seats. Just to the east of the tier of Atwood, Colby, and Oakley lay several other tiers of towns: Norton, Hill City, WaKeeney; Phillipsburg, Stockton, Hays; Smith Center, Osborne, Russell; Washington, Clay Center, Abilene.

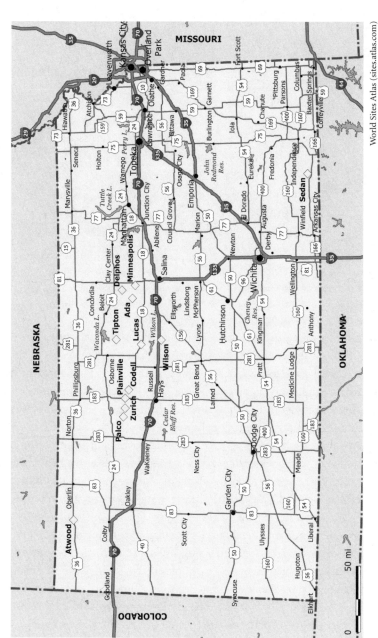

World Sites Atlas (sites.atlas.com)

Atwood's downtown is busy, even crowded at times, and has a good balance of small businesses, retail, and restaurants. In the background, and up a small hill, is the Atwood High School.

Although road maps that predate the interstate system often show U.S. Highway 24 as the principal east-west highway, the decision was made essentially to follow U.S. Highway 40 through most of Kansas until veering north to join Highway 24 in the far west. Some said the decision was influenced by the fact that Abilene, which was on Highway 40, was the home of then-President Eisenhower, yet for the most part the cities and towns along Highway 40 were already larger than their northern rivals. Norton was an exception. It was larger than WaKeeney before the interstate arrived, and—evidence that while location is important it isn't everything—it is *still* larger than WaKeeney and has in fact grown a little, while WaKeeney has shrunk by about 20 percent.

Atwood was among the losers. Its population has dropped by 20 percent since the interstate favored Colby, while Colby's has increased by 55 percent, and in 1964 Colby got a community college that might otherwise have gone to Atwood and that has an enrollment of over 2,000 students. Yet isolation also has its benefits. While towns close to larger cities have seen many of their businesses close because of the proximity of Wal-Marts, Home Depots, and large supermarkets, Atwood still resembles a reasonably complete and self-sufficient small town. It has an at-

In the mid-twentieth century most small rural towns had a new car dealership or two. Atwood still does. Beamgard Chrysler-Dodge-Jeep has been in the town for almost ninety years. Although the sign still lists Plymouth, Chrysler discontinued that brand in 2001. By 2007 Chrysler's own future was unclear, as it had been sold to a private investor group.

tractive and well-stocked supermarket, a health-care center, and even a car dealership that dates back to 1919 and is an increasingly rare thing to find in a small rural town. It also has a weekly newspaper, the *Rawlins County Square Deal*, with over 2,200 subscribers. Atwood's downtown area is not dominated by boarded-up and vacant buildings, and its residents tend to identify more with their own community than with a larger neighboring city.

Isolation also presents a danger. Being near urban areas may mean that towns lose businesses and services, but it also means that such communities are unlikely to disappear completely or lose so much population that they become quasi-ghost towns, lacking even the most basic services. If nothing else, they are likely to survive as satellite suburban communities of their larger neighbors. But because of its isolation, Atwood, and its neighboring towns of Herndon and McDonald, have no such crutch to fall back on.

In 1870 the Atwood area was open prairie, occupied by buffalo and other animals, and a few human nomads, including Indians, buffalo hunters, and cowboys driving cattle along the Texas-Ogallala Trail.

Looking west to downtown Atwood; the Rawlins County Courthouse is on the right.

Homesteaders, mostly from central Europe, Ireland, and Scandinavia, began arriving in the 1870s, and by 1880 there were several scattered family farms and perhaps 1,500 people. The last Indian raid in Kansas, in which seventeen settlers were killed, occurred about 20 miles east of Atwood in 1878. Atwood was laid out as a town site a year later and became the Rawlins county seat in 1881. Over the next few years—relatively wet years in which the rivers and creeks were often full—Rawlins County grew rapidly and eventually contained more than 7,000 people and eight towns: Atwood, Herndon, McDonald, Ludell, Achilles, Blakeman, Beardsley, and Chardon. The railroad reached Atwood in 1887. Today the county is home to fewer than 3,000 people, and several of the towns have disappeared. Herndon, with a population of just 150, has lost its schools. Atwood itself has seen a population decline from about 5,000 in the 1930s to about 1,250 today.[1]

Although Atwood, elevation 2,850 feet, is located on the generally flat and featureless High Plains, it was built on a picturesque site in the hilly Beaver Valley. Several parts of the town are built on hillsides, making it more similar in appearance to towns in eastern Kansas. Yet being a High Plains town, Atwood is relatively arid, averaging just 19 inches of rainfall a year. Its agriculture is heavily dependent on irrigation from deep wells for the equivalent of another 10 inches of rainfall needed for most crops. These sources are drying up and, in the case of water for Atwood itself, sometimes are failing to meet federal water-quality standards.[2] Aggra-

The nine-hole Atwood Country Club golf course has irrigated fairways and grass greens and is part of the Lake Atwood recreation area.

vating the situation is the drought that western Kansas and eastern Colorado have been in the grip of for much of the 1990s and early twenty-first century.

For many years the pride and joy of Atwood—indeed, the town's recreational center—has been Lake Atwood. The manmade lake is the focal point of a park in the north part of Atwood, which includes the local golf course. A sudden intense storm in 2001 led to a flash flood that did a lot of damage without helping crops very much. It also washed away much of the lakebed, creating a porous subsurface that drains quickly, leaving a lake that rapidly empties anytime water accumulates. A public/private project is under way to reopen at least the 28 acres of the lake near the golf course, an effort that involves mixing soda ash with the lake's bed to seal the lake floor.

The dry lakebed serves as an ominous symbol of the lack of water in the area, which may be an even greater threat to Atwood than its isolation. Atwood sits atop the Ogallala Aquifer, an underground reservoir of water made of layers of permeable rock and sand, bigger than the state of California and as much as 400 feet deep, which lies beneath parts of eight

For many years the center of recreation in Atwood was Lake Atwood. Two decades of drought and a porous lakebed have emptied the lake, although the community hopes to refill at least a portion of it.

western states. It supplies much of the water that has enabled crops to be grown and communities to survive. It is a resource that is running out. Estimates vary, but most people agree that, within the next fifteen to twenty years, some communities that depend on the aquifer may see their water supplies depleted and, within fifty to one hundred years, some areas will have exhausted their water supplies.[3]

Unfortunately, Atwood is looking to the falling Ogallala Aquifer as a continuing source for water for the town and for agricultural irrigation. But what might once have represented a long-term solution to the area's water problems can no longer be counted on, as the demand for the aquifer's water has increased just as the availability of that water has decreased.

Other water sources have been considered, including runoff from the Rocky Mountains just 300 miles to the west, but competition for those water supplies has become intense as well, with the growth of population centers along the front range of the Colorado mountains from Pueblo to Ft. Collins. As Chris Sramek, the Rawlins County economic development director, points out, farmers and small communities such as Atwood cannot afford to buy water in competition with wealthy metropolitan areas such as Ft. Collins and Denver.[4]

As with other rural Kansas towns, including those near larger cities, Atwood does a good job of educating its children and then losing them at an alarming rate. Most of them—roughly 80 percent—leave. Sramek believes jobs, rather than lifestyle, are the main problem in retaining Atwood's youth. It's the same story: farms require fewer workers per acre, and high-paying and professional jobs are few and far between. Although Atwood's largest employer is the county government, its most successful businesses are Beaver Valley Supply and J. D. Skiles, both of which manufacture farm and ranch equipment.

In its quest for a solution to declining population, Atwood has been more aggressive than many other towns. It instituted a "free land" program offering five lots, and although the program has attracted some publicity and lookers, Sramek believes it would be more effective if local builders were able to offer the kinds of upscale housing that some newcomers, including many retirees, prefer. Unfortunately, the homebuilding market in Atwood has been anything but robust, and what newcomers there are have generally bought existing houses. The relatively low housing values in the county have not attracted much interest on the part of homebuilders who do high-end work. Although Atwood has a 20-acre industrial park and an airport with a 5,000-foot runway and offers essentially free land to prospective businesses, like most small towns it has had little success attracting them. Instead, it has begun to focus its energies on attracting small entrepreneurs and independent business owners, as well as people looking for a second home—perhaps a hunting retreat. Rawlins County is a popular area for hunting deer, turkey, and pheasant.

Rawlins County's efforts at economic development have been substantial but ultimately disappointing. The town experienced a degree of success in the late 1970s under the leadership of a group of businessmen—the Atwood Ambassadors—which included Mike Hayden, who later became governor of Kansas and who now heads the state's Department of Wildlife and Parks. This group helped start several projects, including building the airport, a lumberyard, and a meat locker plant, and initiated the Early Rod Run, a classic-car racing and enthusiast rally that remains a major Atwood event to this day. Between 1970 and 1980 Rawlins County's population held up fairly well, which is to say that its decline was less than 7 percent. But in the 1980s and 1990s things deteriorated rapidly, and the county lost almost 30 percent of its population from 1980 to 2000.[5]

The 2000 U.S. Census confirmed that the depopulation of Rawlins County had continued and worsened despite the efforts of Hayden's group and a later initiative to try to sell the area as a center for hunting and second homes. Another local development group, made up primarily of people who had been small children when Hayden's efforts occurred, has begun to take shape.

In 2001 Chris Sramek, then thirty years old, returned to Atwood from Kansas City. Sramek was born on a farm 18 miles north of Atwood and had attended Atwood High School before going to the University of Nebraska, where he studied meteorology and climatology. After graduation he moved to Kansas City, working for a private weather consulting firm and doing weather reports for a local radio station. He liked the business, but wanted to live in Atwood. By 2001 he found that thanks to the Internet he was able to operate his meteorological consulting business, Decision Weather, from Atwood. The town has two high-speed Internet providers, as do many other plains towns, largely owing to the efforts of aggressive rural telephone companies such as Wilson Telephone and Nex-Tech. Sramek specializes in High Plains severe weather patterns, agricultural meteorology, and drought preparedness. He continues to work for private clients and do radio broadcasting. He also agreed to take on the part-time job of promoting economic development for Atwood and Rawlins County.

The new Atwood group differs from Hayden's group in several ways. By 2002 Atwood, like most small towns, had recognized the futility of trying to attract major businesses. Although Hayden's group had succeeded in attracting a few companies and invested in infrastructure, the business park remained mostly vacant, and the airport was underutilized and in need of maintenance. The new group decided to concentrate its efforts on convincing local businesspeople, farmers, and ranchers to reinvest in the community and on trying to recruit small entrepreneurs—people like Dawn and James Hampton, who run the town's drug

A common scene in small rural towns such as Atwood: children walking home from school. A sense of safety, security, and community are one of small-town rural America's strongest assets.

store but who also have branched out to create a custom pharmaceutical compounding business.[6]

The new economic development group also contains more women, and indeed it is Sramek's belief that women may hold the key to development in towns such as Atwood. Eleven of the twelve finalists at a 2006 Atwood entrepreneurial fair for students in western Kansas were young women, and he considers places like Atwood to be ideal communities for women, and particularly single mothers, thanks to low housing costs, good schools, safety and security, and a close sense of community. Rural communities are increasingly considered fertile ground for women wanting to become entrepreneurs. In Great Britain, an organization called Women in Rural Enterprise (WIRE) started in 1996 at a regional university and is now a nationwide institution. The founder, who was awarded an Order of the British Empire for her work, started WIRE when she discovered that although many of the people creating rural businesses in Great Britain were women, there was little or no educational or business development support tailored to their needs.[7] In rural

Maine, fourteen women entrepreneurs were featured in an article called "Telling Their Stories: Women Business Owners in Western Maine."[8]

Atwood began following a model for development called Home Town Competitiveness (HTC), which had its origins in Nebraska, where it is described as "a come-back/give-back approach to rural community building."[9] The model follows four basic tenets: developing leadership, energizing entrepreneurs, attracting and engaging youth, and stimulating charitable giving and using charitable assets as a development tool. The HTC idea is also reflected in Kansas's eight Small Business Development Centers, which target rural entrepreneurs and whose four-part program is very similar to HTC's.[10]

As a roadmap for development, and with an ambitious goal of doubling the county's population by 2020, the group—which is largely funded through private resources—produced a document titled "Rawlins County 2020," to identify and prioritize the needs of the county, which includes jobs and economic opportunities, growth and support of existing businesses, schools, healthcare, and water.[11] Four task forces were created, one addressing each of the HTC priorities.

Another difference between the efforts of the economic development groups of the late 1970s and the early twentieth century is that the Rawlins County project is part of a loose consortium of more than twenty communities from Nebraska to Texas called the Ogallala Commons. This effort to work together, and across state lines, represents a departure from some of the previous efforts at economic development, which too often ended up pitting community against community in the quest to attract large businesses.

The Ogallala Commons members hope that through their association and cooperation the participating communities can achieve more than they could alone, and that they can better address what in some cases are regional subjects, such as water resources and Great Plains culture and history. The Commons also targets developing what it terms "sustainable wealth . . . rather than [growing] by continued depletion of resources."[12]

The effort to increase charitable giving to the community has combined Atwood's HTC charitable assets task force with the existing Area Community Enrichment Foundation, a charitable organization that, mirroring the Commons effort, is working with likeminded communities from Colorado to the Texas panhandle on water issues. It has also

The community has restored Atwood's Jayhawk Theater, which shows movies and also provides a venue for plays and concerts.

been involved in community projects to raise money for the Rawlins County Health Center and to renovate both the Masonic Lodge building and the Jayhawk Theater, which are used for many community events. The goal of the charitable efforts is to try to make sure that at least 5 percent of the profits from sales of farms, ranches, and businesses in the area—which does have a significant amount of such wealth—remains in the community rather than all going to heirs and beneficiaries of the sellers, or to the government in taxes. And just as the other Rawlins County HTC teams are cooperating with their counterparts in other towns and states, so, too, the people working on stimulating charitable asset development are seeking to work regionally through a new High Plains Community Foundation.

Atwood's HTC efforts are too new for there to be any assessment of their success. Clearly they face major challenges, including securing sources of water. At the retail level, Atwood community leaders would like to see the area attract businesses such as a clothing store and a fast-food restaurant, which would appeal to youth. Other opportunities that have been identified include developing value-added agricultural businesses, including greenhouses, and raising natural beef and poultry, which would reduce the community's reliance on wheat crops. And although Kansas's new Economic Growth Act promises to put several million dollars annually into grants and tax credits for Kansas's entrepreneurs, there are fears that most of it will follow the path of earlier capital and end up in areas closer to the state's population centers and in larger businesses than the two- and three-person operations that are being sought by places such as Atwood.

8

Tipton: The Town
That Refused to Die

By most criteria, Tipton, Kansas, should be well on the way to becoming a ghost town. It's a town of just 243 people, located amid wheat and cornfields on the western edge of Mitchell County in north central Kansas, about 45 miles north of Interstate Highway 70 and 27 miles west of Beloit, the county seat. In 2003 its public school was closed.

Typical of many rural counties in the United States, Mitchell County reached its peak of population in 1900 when it was home to more than 14,647 people. It has been depopulating ever since and today stands at just under half the 1900 number.[1] Of those remaining 7,000 people, 4,015 live in the county seat of Beloit, which leaves just 3,000 people to populate the remaining 713 square miles of the county, an average of about 4.1 people per square mile.[2]

The Tipton area was settled by a variety of people, but predominantly German Catholics and Lutherans, who began emigrating to the region in 1871. At the time, the region was grassland, and buffalo were a common sight. Indeed, in 1871, the poem on which the song "Home on the Range" was based was written in Smith County, Kansas, about 30 miles from Tipton, describing a place where the buffalo roamed and the deer and the antelope played. But the newcomers were homesteading farmers, "sodbusters," who began planting the kinds of crops that continue to be grown to this day: red winter wheat, milo, corn, and sunflowers. Tipton became a town in 1877, the same year the first Catholic church was built, and in the next hundred years grew to perhaps as many as 450 people as a service center for the nearby farming communities. A Lutheran church was added in 1886, and in 1921 the Catholic schoolhouse, which is still in use today, was built. Although Tipton's streets weren't paved until 1969, and street signs weren't considered a necessity until the 1980s, Tipton

The Tipton Grocery on Main Street is one of the few retail establishments still operating in town. Since there are no restaurants in Tipton, the grocery does a good lunch-counter business.

was able to support a number of businesses, including various car dealers, groceries, restaurants, and gas stations. Tipton never had a movie theater. Movies were shown outdoors late on summer evenings, projected against the north sides of buildings. With virtually no crime, Tipton got by for many years with an unarmed town constable and a one-cell jailhouse until in the 1980s it was decided to hire a real policeman and buy a police car. Tipton's experiment with modern law enforcement was abandoned shortly thereafter, following the request by the officer to purchase a stun gun "to help maintain order." The town council decided their policeman was taking his job a little too seriously and closed the Tipton police operation in favor of a cooperative agreement with a neighboring town.[3]

Over the years Tipton became a very close-knit community, including many families whose ancestors went back several generations in the area, and also a very religious community. Although farming and ranching were what put Tipton on the map to begin with, the town's largest employers are building manufacturer Treb Construction and a farm equipment factory that is now the Kent division of Great Plains Manufacturing of Salina. Both were started by Tipton native Ken Hake, who also has a business restoring World War II jeeps and aircraft.

In 2003 Tipton received bad news from the Waconda public school district, which comprises Tipton and the nearby towns of Downs, Cawker City, and Glen Elder. Because of continued population loss, the Tipton elementary school (K–8), which had about 70 students, was going to be cut back to grades K–3, and Tipton's students in grades 4–8 would be bused to Cawker City, 15 miles away. The people in Tipton were convinced that the decision meant it was just a matter of time before even their K–3 school would be consolidated with a larger one in Downs. They opted out of the proposed realignment and their public school was closed. Tipton, it appeared, was fated to go the way of towns like Zurich.[4]

But it didn't happen. The descendants of the sodbusters, whose families had made the long nineteenth-century journey from Europe to Kansas by ship, train, buggy, horseback, and on foot and who had endured droughts, bitterly cold winters, stiflingly hot summers, plagues of locusts, tornadoes, dust storms, and an occasional confrontation with the native Indian population, were not about to see Tipton become a ghost town. At a town meeting in June 2003, Tipton voted to build and maintain its own private school—the Tipton Christian School—for grades K–6 (the Catholic high school next door to the site of the new school already had agreed to incorporate grades 7 and 8). Tipton had a formidable challenge: raise money, hire teachers, and construct a schoolhouse before the start of the 2003 school year just two months away. Beginning on June 22, and working long hours, the community came together. Much of the materials, including all of the windows, and most of the labor, was donated, as was the land. Those with skills built the structure, while everyone else pitched in by cleaning up, carrying materials, and bringing food and refreshments. While the fund-raising effort was getting under way to raise $250,000 for the building and first year operating expenses, a local woman offered an interest-free loan to allow the project to begin. Although the budget for the school included a requirement for annual tuition of $500 a child, the tuition covered only about 10 percent of the school's annual budget. Three full-time teachers and one part-time teacher were hired, and the man who had been principal of the public school in Tipton agreed to volunteer as principal. It was arranged for meals, and a few classes, to be provided by the high school.

Tipton volunteers built the town's elementary school in just six weeks during the summer of 2003. In the background is the town's high school.

Despite average high temperatures well in the upper nineties, and with the deadline of an August 25 opening day looming over the activity, the school was actually completed by the second week of August, almost two weeks ahead of schedule. On Monday morning, August 25, thirty-four students entered Tipton Christian School.

By all accounts, building the school not only helped ensure that Tipton would not lose one of its most important assets, but it also served to bring the community even closer together and to stimulate many of those who had left Tipton over the years to participate and help save the town. As is the case with many rural towns, Tipton has done a good job of educating its children. In 2006 both the high school and the grade school received the Governor's Achievement Award for proficiency in reading and math, which goes to the top 5 percent of Kansas schools and also takes into consideration attendance and graduation rates. In most years, every Tipton High School senior has gone on to college or, a few, to the military. In the 2006 graduating class of eight, for example, seven went to four-year colleges, one to a junior college. But the teachers and staff don't expect many to return. "Only farm kids come back," said the elementary school's Sandy Hake, "there are no jobs or businesses for the others." Yet even those who choose to live elsewhere tend to remain in touch with, and interested in, the Tipton community. Although Tipton no longer has a local paper, the community publishes an eight-page

The Tipton K–6 classes are small, but a new agreement with the school district in 2007 has improved the chances for the town to keep its local school.

quarterly titled the *Tipton Times and Alumni News,* which helps connect those who have left with those who remain. So much of the money raised for the Tipton Christian School came from Tipton alumni that in Hake's opinion, "it would not have been possible without them."

As remarkable as the Tipton story is, there's more to it. First, the closing of the Tipton public school, a modern and well-maintained facility with a large gymnasium, led to the sale of the building to the Tipton Academy, an accredited private boarding school for teenage boys at risk. The academy utilizes a variety of educational and behavior modification techniques to help students cope with their problems and, usually within a year, return to their own communities.[5] Places like Tipton are proving to be ideal for such schools, providing a secure, remote environment in which the students' needs can be addressed with a minimum of distractions. The school employs approximately twenty teachers and staff, several of whom have bought homes in Tipton and are expected to begin sending their children to Tipton schools. Tipton Academy represents one of the few opportunities for in-migration that has occurred in town for many years, and Tipton residents generally have been pleased with their interactions with both staff and students. The academy has encouraged students to get out into the community, and they can sometimes be seen raking leaves or shoveling snow for Tipton residents. In addition, the academy has started serving coffee and rolls in the morning to people in Tipton, whose last restaurant closed several years ago. Interestingly, in the fall of 2006 the owners of Tipton Academy opened Meadowlark Academy, a similar school for girls, located in the former middle school building in Delphos, Kansas, which was closed when the school was consolidated with the middle school in Minneapolis in 2003.

The latest chapter in the unusual transformation of education in Tipton occurred in 2006 when Tipton Christian School negotiated successfully with the Waconda School District and the Smoky Hill Educational Service Center in Salina, a consortium of public school districts, to begin receiving public funding beginning in 2007. The funding covers most of the school's salaries and supplies, leaving the local community with responsibility for the building and maintenance.

The Tipton school's partial return to the public funding school system was helped by the passage of time, allowing tempers to cool, and by some changes in personnel at the district level. In addition, getting Tipton back in the public system benefited the district financially. Operating as a completely private school had prevented the still-shrinking Waconda school district from receiving any state funds, but under the new agreement the district gets credit for the Tipton school's students. For the people of Tipton, partial public funding will mean easing the ongoing burden of almost continuous fund-raising to keep the school running and will introduce some benefits and efficiencies that include making it easier to maintain accreditation and making available more of the specialists and curriculum-enriching educational programs from Smoky Hill. The agreement with the school district probably will enable Tipton to retain its elementary school for the foreseeable future. Tipton may be unique: an isolated town of 243 people that still has its own school system for grades K–12. Yet even with this accomplishment, the people in Tipton are aware of the precariousness of their situation. The continuing exodus of high school seniors to college and then to urban America, coupled with a trend toward smaller families, creates a situation that is less than ideal. Grades 7–12 have fifty students, an average of just over eight per class. While the small class sizes help to provide a very good education, and an opportunity for students to participate in many activities, they also produce some unfortunate results. The school can no longer field a football team by itself and instead participates in a joint football program with St. John's School in Beloit, a school that itself averages only fourteen students per class. Tipton football players have to travel more than 50 miles each day for practice in Beloit. And it can be difficult to find the right combinations of students to participate in music and drama. Despite the difficulties of running a school with classes of eight people, the day may come when high school principal Gary Hake will be happy with such class sizes. Although three new families moved into Tipton in 2007, the elementary school is still very small: there are just thirty-one students, an average of fewer than five students per class. Third grade has only four students. Barring an infusion of students, once the elementary grades reach high school level the situation may become impractical. Yet it could be worse. Tipton elementary must look like Times Square to the student body at places such as Dry Creek Elementary (K–8) in Bill, Wyoming. Dry Creek's entire student body consists of two six-year-old first-grade girls. The staff and faculty consists of Sherrill Kilpatrick. Dry Creek is a designated "rural" school, one of four in Converse County. Normally, economics would have long since closed such schools, but many remain open in Wyoming, benefiting from the state's large budget surpluses as a result of oil, coal, and gas production.[6]

Perhaps technology will help small schools. The Tipton Academy relies heavily on computer and Internet-based instruction, and the high school takes advantage of instructional and distance-learning television, which make available many courses that small schools cannot provide, including physics, psychology, and foreign languages, as well as some advanced placement and college-level courses. More difficult to solve are the inherent social and financial challenges of running such small schools and maintaining a critical mass in which education and socialization can occur.

Thanks largely to its own efforts, Tipton has been granted an unusual "second chance" to maintain its community schools and, perhaps, its community. But there is little margin for error. If the depopulation of the Tipton area continues, the community may yet face its greatest challenge.

9
Ottawa County:
The Challenges of Becoming a
Rural Bedroom Community

The Ottawa County seat of Minneapolis represents yet another facet of rural America: a small town that is likely to survive and perhaps prosper as it is transformed by geography from a typical farming town into a new kind of community, one that is not a suburb but benefits from its proximity to a growing city. The county is also home to two smaller communities, Ada and Delphos, which are being left behind as Minneapolis grows.

The history of migration to—and from—Ottawa County, Kansas, is almost identical to that of the other counties in this chapter. The peak of settlement occurred in 1920 with almost 12,441 people, and the population fell continuously from that date until the 1990s, when it reached just 5,634. And then a strange thing happened. Instead of continuing to drop, the population in the year 2000 jumped to 6,123, an increase of about eight percent.[1]

The reason for Ottawa County's growth has much to do with its location, just 24 miles north of Salina. Salina is a city of 46,000 people, the largest city in north-central Kansas and the ninth largest in the state. A four-lane controlled-access interstate highway (I-135) connects Wichita with Salina and I-70, and although the interstate itself officially ends at Salina, the same kind of four-lane controlled-access *interstate-type* highway continues on north to Minneapolis as Highway 81 before reverting to a more typical two-lane rural road as it heads toward Nebraska.

One result has been that Minneapolis has emerged as something of a bedroom community of Salina. The attractions of Minneapolis to those

Above: The main street of downtown Minneapolis, Kansas, is generally well maintained and busy and contains several attractive older buildings. There are, however, few restaurants and retail businesses, reflecting the town's proximity to Salina. Below: In addition to a swimming pool and tennis courts, Minneapolis has a nine-hole municipal golf course.

working in Salina include housing prices that are at least 15 percent lower, coupled with a smaller, and perhaps better, school system, a more relaxed lifestyle, a small hospital, and some recreational facilities, including a pool, a city park near the Solomon River, a lake, and an attractive golf course.[2]

The other result has been that, while both the town and the county have maintained their populations, downtown Minneapolis has suffered. Few restaurants remain, the types of retail stores are very limited, and its two banks, grocery, car dealership, and two major manufacturers are headquartered elsewhere. The town still has a weekly newspaper, the *Minneapolis Messenger,* with a circulation of 2,100. But increasingly, people in the area shop in Salina, and about half of them work there, too, according to Economic Development Director Mark Freel. Freel himself was born in Salina, but grew up in Minneapolis, went to college at Kansas State University in Manhattan, where he worked following graduation, and then returned to Minneapolis when he and his wife decided to start a family.[3]

Despite the relatively strong population numbers for Minneapolis, the city has become one of the most aggressive promoters of "free land" in rural America. The reason, according to Freel, is that, in order to survive, "small towns need an attitude. They need people to believe their community represents the wave of the future, not the dying past." According to Freel, this attitude shift is occurring in Minneapolis, and he believes the success of the "Welcome Home" land program has helped.

Minneapolis is a place where the land promotion has been successful in real terms, as well as being a publicity generator, and twenty-six new homes have been constructed on "free land" lots, with an average home price of $135,000, more than twice the average price of a house in Minneapolis. The city made available twenty-four lots in its first addition, Sunrise II, and all those lots have been taken. Fifteen additional lots were made available in Sunrise III, and nine have been taken. Each lot is approximately 12,000 square feet. The city requires owners to have a contract with a builder within six months and construction to begin within twelve months. A $1,500 deposit is also required, which is returned if construction is completed within eighteen months. Although the lots themselves are "free," they come with a special assessment for infrastructure and utilities of approximately $12,000 payable over ten years, about half of which can be offset by a state tax rebate program for communities that have qualified neighborhood development plans.

Most of the people taking advantage of the land program did so, according to Freel, because they were interested in a good community to

Above: These new houses were built as part of the Minneapolis "free land" program.
Below: Minneapolis also has a number of substantial older homes, including this one just east of downtown.

raise their families: "a safe place for kids to walk, ride, and play. No stop lights. They can change their lives and build some equity." In return, they were willing to give up some things, including easy access to shopping, entertainment, and good restaurants.

In addition to its favorable location, Minneapolis has two other significant assets. It is the county seat of Ottawa County, and it has been home to all the schools in the North Ottawa County District since 2003, when the middle school in nearby Delphos was closed and consolidated with Minneapolis. It also has a strong manufacturing sector for a small town, and according to Freel, all of the town's industrial buildings are occupied.

Yet if Minneapolis is in relatively good shape for a small rural town, its future as an independent town is unclear. The location actually is a mixed blessing, according to Freel. "There's a sense that there is no crisis in Minneapolis because we're so close to Salina," he says. While its location and county-seat status assure that it will never become a ghost town, it faces significant challenges. First, of course, is the transition from an independent community to a bedroom community. As other towns near larger cities have found, the transition can be difficult as the character of the population, and the quality of life, undergo changes. Many of the people working in Salina tend to consider themselves more a part of a "greater Salina" community than of Minneapolis.

Bedroom community or not, Minneapolis also has some of the same chronic problems of other small rural towns; including an aging population and an exodus of young people to the cities. In addition, and in contrast to places such as Plainville, Palco, Atwood, and Tipton, the evidence of a community-wide commitment to economic development and reinvestment is mixed. While the community has supported the free land program, it decisively rejected a $9.4 million school bond issue in March of 2006, then rejected two of three school bond issues in November 2006, although the one that was approved was the largest, $5.47 million for expansion and remodeling projects at the Minneapolis schools.

The controversy over the bond issues, Freel believes, is in part due to complacency caused by the perceived benefits of the town's proximity to Salina. "Unlike many small towns in Kansas," Freel says, "some people here don't think we have anything to worry about." It is a frustrating situation for Freel, with his belief that small towns need an "attitude" and need to be continuously reinventing and improving themselves. Or, as a 1970 presidential task force on rural development warned, if "a community lacks leadership, if it lacks local concern, if it isn't convinced that it should become a better place to live—then perhaps it shouldn't."[4] Yet the problems facing Minneapolis pale in comparison to those facing its neighbors to the north and west, Delphos and Ada.

Ada and Delphos

As late as the 1960s, the small Ottawa County town of Ada was relatively prosperous, and Delphos was sufficiently robust that it enjoyed something of a rivalry with Minneapolis. While the towns weren't growing, they were at least doing no worse than most other small towns and were successfully serving their surrounding farming communities. Each town's focal point was its large grain elevator, but they also had a school, a few retail stores, and services. Most people living in Ada and Delphos had little need to travel the twelve miles or so to Minneapolis, let alone to Salina.

Then, in 1965, the diminishing population began to take its toll. Ada's high school was closed and consolidated with the high school in Minneapolis. Seven years later, Ada's grade school closed and consolidated with the middle school in Delphos. One by one the town's stores closed, as did one of its churches. Today Ada, which still has an attractive location, with many mature trees, has only the seasonal activity of the grain elevator to remind it of better times. With no school, parents moving to the area opted for Delphos or Minneapolis. Families and young people deserted Ada. Homes became difficult or impossible to sell.

Today, driving through Ada on a late afternoon during harvest time, the only sign of life "downtown" is at the elevator. There is no post office. No gas station. No grocery. No library. No town offices. The few remaining attractive and well-maintained houses are outnumbered by houses in disrepair, some with yards that are cluttered with cars, trucks, and trash. On such afternoons in more fortunate towns in rural America one would see children walking home from school, talking and playing, and one would pass by people mowing their lawns or tending their gardens. The people would—most likely—wave. But in Ada the streets are eerily empty, almost as empty as the area must have been in 1872, the year Ada was founded: few children, few people at all, few cars, other than those rusting on the lawns. It is close to being a twenty-first-century ghost town.

It is the ghost of Ada that is haunting Delphos. The school in Delphos lasted thirty-eight years longer than the school in Ada, but in 2003 it was closed by the North Ottawa school district following a long and bitter battle.

Downtown Ada, empty at noon on a day in early fall.

Delphos was founded in 1867, about the same time as Minneapolis. The 1860s in Ottawa County were marked by Indian raids, including one in Delphos in 1868 that had tragic consequences for Anna Morgan, a young newlywed, who was taken captive by the Sioux and traded to the Cheyenne who held her for six months in Oklahoma until she was rescued by General George Custer. The harrowing experience forever changed Morgan's life. According to a history of Delphos written by Clayton Hogg, after returning to Delphos Morgan gave birth to a half-Indian child, who died two years later, then had three more children before she was divorced. She lived alone for many years, plagued by mental illness, and died in a mental hospital in Topeka in 1902. She is buried in Delphos along with her Indian son.[5]

For much of the twentieth century Delphos prospered, and at one time it had a hotel and an opera house, along with other retail and service facilities, all laid out around a central town square. In 1971 the quiet town made national news when a sixteen-year-old boy reported seeing a "flying saucer" on his farm. His family corroborated the story, and the evidence included a white circle on the ground where, it was said, the saucer had landed. Subsequent investigation and testing cast doubt on the source of the white circle, but the event was considered sufficiently momentous that the *National Enquirer* paid the family $5,000 for their

A vacant lot in Ada.

story, and the sighting was ranked the best UFO sighting of the year by "a panel of UFO experts."[6]

With a population of approximately 450, down from a high of 750 in the 1940s, Delphos is the third largest town in Ottawa County. The closing of the school in 2003 was "a real blow" to the town, said Tom McGavran, president of the Ottawa County Bank in Minneapolis and the State Bank of Delphos, who was born in Ada and lives in Delphos. "There is not much left," McGavran said in late 2005, adding that "the Delphos community grocery store is a small nonprofit."[7] But within a year that grocery store became another victim of school consolidation, and closed its doors.

Delphos joined the ranks of towns with empty school buildings. In some cases such buildings have been used as community centers, but increasingly such buildings have been marketed to businesses for conversion to other uses.[8] Delphos decided to try to attract a buyer, and in early 2006 succeeded. The building was leased—with an option to buy—to the same company that runs the Tipton Academy boarding school for boys, and it opened in the fall of 2006 as the Meadowlark Academy for girls. As was the case with Tipton, staffing the school brought new residents to Delphos, at least partially compensating for the jobs lost when the public school closed. In addition, the school may try to help make up

Downtown Delphos has few remaining businesses, and there is little traffic on this fall afternoon.

for the closing of the community grocery store and is considering operating a small food market run by the staff and students at the school.

Notwithstanding the Meadowlark Academy, it may be difficult for Delphos to attract significant new businesses and, without a public school, the probability is that the town will continue to lose population. The average age of the population of Delphos (currently forty-two years old) will continue to be considerably older than the average for Kansas (thirty-five). Indeed, almost one-fourth of the people in Delphos are over the age of sixty-five, while for Kansas as a whole the number is closer to one-tenth.

While there are considerable public and private resources for the needs of declining metropolitan communities such as Youngstown, Ohio,—and even a few for small cities such as Minneapolis and Plainville—towns such as Delphos, Tipton, and Palco have far fewer options and few places to turn to for help. And it is difficult to escape the conclusion that the outside world has long since written off places such as Ada and Zurich. At some point, towns pass the "point of no return" in terms of the prospect for any kind of economic revival, and local reinvestment dries up as people conclude that it would just be throwing good money after bad.

There is not a lot for Delphos teenagers to do in town. Here, during harvest time, a few wait by the side of the road, hoping to sell soft drinks to farmers driving their trucks to the Delphos grain elevator.

To the extent towns such as Palco and Tipton succeed in maintaining their viability, their success derives from their still having a school and from their own initiative, particularly from their willingness to invest in their future—an investment that can open up state and federal funding sources. "Before people go looking for outside help, they need to invest locally themselves—time, money, or both," says John Cyr of the North Central Kansas Economic Development Commission, adding "a positive local attitude encourages people to reinvest in their towns. The original settlers were promised nothing but an opportunity, but today it seems that most people want guarantees."[9]

If there is hope for towns such as Delphos, it may lie in what Cyr calls "a redefinition of what 'community' means." He pointed out that towns like Delphos and Minneapolis used to be very independent. They were rivals, and the people who lived there identified very strongly with their town. "They even tried to steal businesses from each other," Cyr said, "but in the future they need to be thinking in terms of interdependence, not independence, and to define their community more broadly and encompass neighboring towns. Everybody can't have everything anymore."

A good example of redefining community is in Oberlin, Kansas, the county seat of Decatur County, where people began redefining their community long ago. In the 1960s an effort began to treat the entire county as the "community," which meant, for example, distributing the proceeds from Oberlin's annual carnival to other towns, in the county and cooperating with each other on economic development. In 1970, the people in the county created a unified county chamber of commerce, replacing three independent town chambers of commerce, and today the Oberlin/Decatur County web site also features information about the other towns in the county.[10] Despite the county's efforts, and underscoring the strength of the rural depopulation trend, the county has suffered only slightly less population declines than neighboring counties. Decatur County's population fell from 5,778 in 1960 to 3,472 in 2000, a 39 percent decrease. Still, it was better than Rawlins County to the west, whose population dropped by 43 percent over the same period. In addition, Decatur County's income levels have increased modestly in recent years and, as I examine in some detail in the section about Dave Rose and eBay, the small Decatur County town of Jennings has attracted a new and promising business.[11]

What is true for small communities within a county or a school district holds true regionally as well. Counties were laid out when travel was by horse or foot, and people wanted to be able to reach their county seat or market town in less than half a day. Thanks to highways and cars, much of the "county seat–market town" function in rural areas has been transferred to larger cities, which are the de facto hubs of a new kind of unofficial, unplanned community: a multicounty service area in which people in the smaller towns are trying to adjust to the new order and to figure out what people such as Cyr mean by "redefining community."

Perhaps improvements in technology, transportation, and communication may help to create this new kind of "community." Cyr noted that people considering moving to—or staying in—a rural town have traditionally demanded certain core services, including a grocery, bank, gas station, hardware store, and post office. If they have children, they are likely to want at least an elementary school. He believes most people are comfortable with having medical services available at the county seat or other larger nearby town, or perhaps having a part-time local clinic. Yet economics make it uncertain whether towns that are the size of Delphos can continue to offer all the basic services. The population declines have already closed the local Delphos school and forced the closure of the small community-run grocery.

While technological innovations such as air taxis may someday help rural America, there already are technologies that can contribute to providing services and amenities for rural life. Since gas stations and banks are considered essential, it is likely that automated self-service pumps, ATMs, and Internet banking can address most of those needs. And since improvements in transportation work both ways, it would seem to be practical for county and regional hubs to provide smaller towns in their areas with access to mobile or part-time local storefront clinics or service centers for both specialized and routine government and medical services. The Rural Assistance Center was created in 2002 by the U.S. Department of Health and Human Services specifically to help rural communities access information about programs and funding that can help them provide health and human services to rural residents. The Rural Assistance Center has helped bring about hundreds of programs in forty-seven states, from the Northwest Kansas Rural Stroke Project, which conducts quarterly stroke prevention clinics and physical examinations at senior centers, to the Sierra Mobile Clinic which serves 1,500 patients in a rural California county.[12] Rural patients may also benefit from the increased use of remote monitoring devices, made by companies such as Boston Scientific and Medtronic, which can help patients with heart problems, diabetes, and other ailments.[13]

Finally, while the local school is not likely to return to a town such as Delphos, there is no reason why people can't get used to the idea of traveling fifteen minutes to see their children in a play or a game at a school in a neighboring town, and thanks to e-mail they may be able to keep up with their children's teachers and school activities almost as well as before. True, it is not quite the old community, but as Cyr noted, "everybody can't have everything."

10

"The Amazing 100 Miles": Tourism in Rural America

In an effort to attract tourism, states and localities often create regional promotional campaigns. In Nebraska alone, there are nine scenic and historical "byways"; eastern Colorado has the "Colorado's Central Plains," an association of ten small-town museums and attractions from Limon to the Kansas border;[1] and there are several organizations promoting interest in Route 66 and the towns and cities along what remains of its route from Chicago to Los Angeles. Kansas, too, has several such promotions, including "The Amazing 100 Miles," created by a group of central Kansas towns, counties, and businesses in 1998. The 100 miles in question (actually 98 miles) are from Salina in the east to Hays in the west, along Interstate Highway 70, and ranging north and south of the highway to include more than 4,000 square miles and twenty-seven cities and towns. Geologically, the area is within the mixed-prairie grasslands known as the Smoky Hills region.[2]

The coalition was formed in an attempt to attract the attention of people in some of the more than 12,000 vehicles a day that traverse central Kansas on the Interstate highway, people who—the coalition members suspected—were inclined to treat most of Kansas as a necessary inconvenience on their travels to and from Colorado and points west and Missouri and points east.[3]

The area includes two major, economically healthy Kansas cities, Hays and Salina. It also includes counties, cities, and towns that are fighting depopulation. The two counties that are in the middle of the 100 miles are Ellsworth and Russell. Ellsworth's population peaked in 1910 at 10,444, and by 2000 had dropped to 6,525, while Russell, where oil and gas were discovered in the 1930s, reached its highest population in 1940 at 13,464. By 2000 Russell County's population had fallen by 45 percent to 7,370.[4] Most of the other small towns in the Amazing 100 Miles also lost population. As a result, by 2000 communities such as Ellsworth, Wilson, Lincoln, Kanopolis, Marquette, and Holyrood were eager participants in the "free land" campaign.

The plight of the small towns within the Amazing 100 Miles territory is further evidence of the extent and pervasiveness of rural depopulation. For the 100 miles is not an unappealing area, nor is it particularly remote. Most communities are within a short drive of I-70 and a regional city, and most of the topography within the 100 Miles area is made up of gentle hills and prairie. The region also offers some notable purple-cow types of attractions, including two large lakes; the 41,000-acre Cheyenne Bottoms wildlife wetlands in Barton County, south of Russell; and the Rolling Hills Wildlife Adventure museum and zoological park near Salina. Other attractions include the twenty-eight-room Midland Hotel in Wilson, a well-restored classic railroad hotel of the type that once could be found in many rural towns served by passenger rail; the Swedish community of Lindsborg; the restored Chestnut Street District and the Sternberg Museum of Natural History in Hays; and the grassroots art community of Lucas. Two of these towns, Wilson in Ellsworth County and Lucas in Russell County, represent good examples of attempts on the part of people in small, rural communities to attract tourists from among the many people speeding by on I-70. The towns are at either end of the 18-mile Post Rock Scenic Byway, named for the distinctive limestone rock found in the area and used in fences, markers, and buildings.

Wilson: The Czech Capital of Kansas

In 1865 Wilson began life as a stagecoach stop, which was located just south of present-day Wilson and served travelers along the Smoky Hill Trail to Colorado. The community, which was officially named Wilson in 1873, attracted homesteading immigrants from central Europe, particularly from the present-day Czech Republic. Many of the newcomers helped build the Kansas Pacific (later Union Pacific) main line from Kansas City to Denver. The route ran right through the center of Wilson, which became a major service and station stop for the railroad.

Wilson was settled in the 1870s by many immigrants from what today is the Czech Republic, and it has tried to maintain its Czech identity and promote it as a tourist attraction.

In 1899, on the site where the Midland Hotel stands today, the Power Hotel opened to serve railroad passengers. The hotel burned in 1902 but was rebuilt as the Midland Hotel and prospered along with Wilson until the Great Depression, when, at one point, the third floor was used as a chicken coop. The hotel revived thereafter and was often busy during the 1950s and early 1960s but began to struggle again after passenger traffic on the Union Pacific came to an end in 1972. Although it surfaced briefly as a setting for scenes in the 1973 movie *Paper Moon,* with Ryan and Tatum O'Neal, in 1988 the hotel closed.[5]

Wilson itself had seen better days. From a population of as many as 1,400 in 1964, when nearby Wilson Dam was being built, Wilson had fallen to below 1,000 by 1990 and to less than 800 by 2000, when more than one-fourth of the population was over the age of sixty-five and the median age was forty-six. Despite its location just two miles off I-70, just fifteen minutes from 9,000-acre Wilson Lake, and its history as "the Czech capital of Kansas," Wilson seemed to be stagnating. The local newspaper, the *Wilson World,* had closed its doors, as had most other downtown businesses.

Although Wilson tried to promote its ethnic heritage, by 2007 many of the descendants of the original Czech settlers were themselves elderly,

Wilson's downtown has suffered from the closing of many of its retail and service businesses, including its newspaper, the Wilson World.

and the community had become more heterogeneous over the years. Wilson's ethnic festival in late July suffered in comparison to the Swedish festivals at Lindsborg, Kansas, a much larger city.[6] Perhaps Wilson's strongest assets as it entered the twenty-first century, other than its location and proximity to I-70 and Wilson Lake, were its schools—with over 200 students enrolled in the grade school and high school—and Eschbaugh Advertising, the largest employer. A potential asset, the still-impressive Midland Hotel, was—like so much of downtown Wilson—vacant and boarded up in 2000.

While Eschbaugh Advertising was unlikely to draw any tourists, it was, and is, a good example of the kind of homegrown businesses that can succeed in rural America. The company was founded in 1952 by George Eschbaugh, a Wilson native. Eschbaugh returned to Wilson following service in World War II and started an advertising agency but soon concentrated on graphic arts. The company, housed next to his home on a farm just west of Wilson that had been in his family since the 1870s, grew into a successful specialty advertising graphics business, with sales in over twenty states, all through agents and sales reps. Eschbaugh disdained the notion of direct sales, just as he disdained accumulating debt or advertising his own business. Even as of 2007, the company had no web site.

George Eschbaugh died in 2005 at the age of eighty-six, and the company was taken over by his son, Steve, who had joined the business in 1987. With forty employees, Eschbaugh advertising continues to operate almost exactly as it had under the senior Eschbaugh, with little debt, no advertising, no sales force, and with the company's buildings still hidden away on the farm, almost invisible to the casual eye.[7]

For a community such as Wilson, people such as George Eschbaugh are a dream come true. Eschbaugh was a talented artist and a good student who attended Wilson schools and went on to receive a degree in commercial arts in 1940 from the University of Kansas. Following graduation he went to work for an advertising agency in Kansas City, and when war broke out he joined the Army Air Corps where he served as a captain doing intelligence work and drawing maps. After the war, it might have been expected that Eschbaugh would return to Kansas City, if not go someplace such as New York or Chicago, to pursue a career in advertising. Instead, he chose to return to Wilson. Wilson in those days was quite different from Wilson in the twenty-first century. Thanks to a variety of economic booms in the area in the 1950s and 1960s, including the construction of Wilson Dam, the opening of a (now-abandoned) missile base nearby, and increased oil production, Wilson at midcentury was prosperous, as evidenced by its two drugstores, three grocery stores, four bars, nine gas stations, and a couple of new car dealerships.

Eschbaugh tried several pursuits when he returned, including farming and manufacturing a liquid silver cleaner that he called Kleen Sheen. It was while he began designing and producing labels for Kleen Sheen that the idea of doing graphic design for advertising occurred to him. He relegated farming to a hobby and opened an advertising agency that soon began specializing in design and screen printing of labels, decals, posters, and banners for advertising, promotion, and product identification, initially in the farm implement business.

Although Eschbaugh had opportunities to move and expand, he stayed rooted in Wilson, never far from where he had grown up, building his business and reinvesting in the community, serving on the board of directors of a local bank and hospital, and supporting a variety of community activities and initiatives. Except for his years at college and during the war, Eschbaugh's life centered around his rural beginnings. In

The renovated Midland Hotel is one of the best surviving examples of a traditional "railroad hotel" in rural America. It is just a few hundred feet from the Union Pacific tracks, where several freight trains still come through town. The last passenger train serving Wilson stopped service in the early 1970s.

short, Eschbaugh was an example of the kind of rural American who has become increasingly rare.

One of Eschbaugh's community interests was the nonprofit Wilson Community Foundation, a group of Wilson businesspeople, including former mayor, Larry Ptacek, who in 1997 turned its attention to downtown Wilson and the Midland Hotel. The group hoped to help revive the town by renovating and reopening the hotel, which it believed could become the kind of attraction that would draw visitors and help put Wilson back on the map.[8]

The group raised $2.45 million in a combination of state and federal loans, grants, tax credits, and local gifts. The money, together with much local volunteer effort, culminated in the 2003 reopening of the hotel, which—as a prime example of a classic railroad hotel—is on the National Register of Historic Places of the U.S. National Park Service. The Wilson Foundation also undertook to renovate the town's Sumner Hardware store, a renovation that has been stalled because of flooding caused by roof problems, and helped with the conversion of an old school building to assisted living apartments. The new Midland Hotel has twenty-eight rooms, a restaurant, a library, and a bar. The interior was furnished with Mission-style furniture, in keeping with the original woodwork.

But the Midland Foundation soon found that running a hotel was, if anything, even more difficult than raising money and renovating. As of 2007 the hotel had seen four managers come and go, and the dining room and tavern were open only on weekends. The hotel did a good business during the summers and was sometimes sold out on weekends. But on too many nights, particularly during the winter, few of the rooms were occupied. It had proved to be more difficult than anticipated to attract travelers on a regular basis from I-70 and from the bland familiarity of the chain motels in Salina and Hays. Those who did venture off the interstate found that, while the Midland Hotel was comfortable and even memorable, Wilson itself had little to offer. With the upscale Midland bar and restaurant closed four days a week, visitors had to try to get to one of the town's few other eateries before they closed.

It had been hoped that locals would take advantage of the restaurant and tavern, but not enough of them did. The fact that people in Wilson did not better support the hotel is significant because if there is a single most repeated—and very valid—complaint about life in rural America it is that there aren't enough good restaurant options. The inability of the Midland restaurant and bar to thrive and attract people from perhaps a four-county area may indicate something about the Wilson community, but it also underscores how difficult it can be to create and run a consistently high-quality restaurant in a small town.

In fact, the Midland Hotel project also revealed a problem within the Wilson community. As is the case with many small towns, there was some resentment and jealousy about the Wilson Foundation's efforts, and even the foundation members realized they had failed to get a true community-wide "buy-in" to the effort. There were concerns that the Midland tavern might hurt the other downtown bar and that the restaurant might take business away from the one or two other restaurants in town. Not unreasonable concerns, to be sure, but the kinds of worries that might have been allayed if the Wilson Foundation had been able to cultivate a broader base of support for the project. If the foundation had been able to convince more people that the hotel could attract thirty or forty visitors every day to Wilson, a town that draws few tourists, and thereby would increase traffic for all the other local businesses (the strategy of so many fast food restaurants), the concerns might have been eased.

The other weakness that the hotel project uncovered was that Wilson was a community in transition and had not been able to develop the kind of strong and unified leadership that is essential for towns to survive. Small towns don't have the luxury of being able to afford deep personal or policy-related splits within their communities. By 2006 many of the people like George Eschbaugh who had led Wilson during its more prosperous years were dead, and some of those still living were unable or unwilling to reinvest their time or money in the community. Somewhere along the way from the 1960s, when Wilson was lively, to the early 2000s when it often seemed to be almost deserted, the town had lost its way, or, as one resident put it, "It failed to transform itself into something that is needed."[9] An example of Wilson's predicament may be the Czech Opera House and Museum and, around the corner, the Wilson Recreation Center and bowling alley. The recreation center, one of few such options in Wilson, is closed, and the Opera House, which in Wilson's heyday showed movies and housed a variety of activities, is in need of repair and upgrading. By 2006 it was attracting few people, tourists or locals.

As a result of the difficulties surrounding the Midland Hotel, the Wilson Foundation struggled to meet the requirements of its grantors and lenders, and more than three years after opening its doors was still struggling just to break even.

Compared to most of the other towns profiled in this book, Wilson is—at least on paper—well-positioned for the future. It is not as remote as Atwood or as small as Tipton and Palco. It is not so close to larger cities that it risks being "suburbanized," yet it is close enough that people in Wilson have easy access to Ellsworth and, if necessary, to Hays and Salina. It has a good grocery, which added a hardware section in 2006, a bank, a local medical clinic that is open twice a week, and a modern hospital nearby, in Ellsworth. It has one of two "Kansas Originals Market and Gallery" stores in the state, which sells products, crafts, and art indigenous to Kansas. Its schools are not threatened with consolidation or closings. It has an identifiable ethnic heritage on which to build, is well located to be a service center for Wilson Lake, and is at the starting point for the Post Rock Scenic Byway. It also has a purple cow in the Midland Hotel.

While there are many communities in rural America that appear to be fighting losing battles because of factors which are beyond their control—location or a failing water supply or school district politics, for example—the challenges facing Wilson seem to involve primarily internal considerations, particularly the town's ability to generate the kind of leadership that can help create a unified community that can make the most of Wilson's assets, including its purple cow.

Lucas: "Expect the Unexpected"

Lucas, Kansas, is a town of 436 people in Russell County, located about 18 miles north of I-70 on Highway 232, the Post Rock Scenic Byway, and is six miles from Wilson Lake. It was founded in 1887 and settled primarily by German and Czech immigrants and also by Samuel P. Dinsmoor, a forty-five-year-old teacher, farmer, and Civil War veteran from Ohio. How and why Dinsmoor picked Lucas is unknown, but his choice proved to be a fateful event that would shape the town's future in ways unknowable to anyone at the time.

Dinsmoor actually left Lucas for awhile, farming in Nebraska and elsewhere in Russell County, but in 1905, at the age of sixty-two, he, his wife, and four children returned to Lucas. He bought a lot in town where, in 1907, he built an unusual eleven-room log cabin—unusual because in place of wooden logs he used logs carved out of local limestone. He had no sooner finished the cabin than he began work on an even more unusual project: a large reinforced-concrete sculpture called the Garden of Eden. For the next twenty-two years Dinsmoor, usually working alone, created a work of art around and over his house—to a height of 40 feet—that contained more than 113 tons of cement in the form of 150 statues supported by 29 concrete "trees." The sculpture expressed Dinsmoor's conception of the Bible and the story of civilization.

During the construction, Dinsmoor's wife died and, at the age of eighty-one he married his twenty-year-old housekeeper. They had two

Above: Visitors arriving in Lucas on Highway 18 quickly realize they are entering an unusual community when they are greeted by "The World's Largest Souvenir Travel Plate." Below: Lucas's most famous attraction is the limestone-and-concrete Garden of Eden, which surrounds S. P. Dinsmoor's "log cabin" house made of native limestone.

children. Dinsmoor died in 1932 at the age of eighty-nine and was entombed along with his first wife in a glass-and-concrete mausoleum he designed, built, and incorporated into the Garden of Eden.[10]

The art scene in Lucas was quiet for the next eighteen years until 1950, when Florence Deeble, a local schoolteacher who had watched Dinsmoor's Garden of Eden take shape as a child, began creating concrete sculptures of postcard scenes in the backyard of her house. The Deeble creations portrayed scenes such as Mount Rushmore, Estes Park, Colorado, and an Arizona landscape. She was soon joined by Ed Root, a local farmer who was injured in an automobile accident and turned to making sculptures out of concrete, glass, metal, and stone. The sculptures adorned his farm until the property was covered by Wilson Lake in 1965, when they were rescued by members of his family and eventually given to the Kansas Grassroots Art Association.[11]

Root died in 1960 and Deeble in 1999, but the Deeble house and the Root collection are now part of the Lucas Grassroots Art Center, headed by Rosslyn Schultz, who likes to tell visitors, "Stuff here is kind of weird." Schultz, sixty years old, is a native of Salina, but has lived in Lucas since marrying her husband, Steve, in 1965. Steve is a wheat farmer, and in the 1970s Rosslyn began creating a wheat-based folk art known as Wheat Weavings. She began to show her weavings at shows throughout the Midwest and also began teaching the craft. In the late 1980s she and five other local women formed the Lucas Arts and Humanities Commission to promote teaching art in the local schools.

There might never have been a Lucas Grassroots Art Center, however, had it not been for a letter the town council received in 1990 that contained an offer to sell the town the limestone sculpture collection of Inez Marshall, a well-known Kansas folk artist, for $70,000. Marshall had done most of her work—using the same native stone that Dinsmoor had used for his Garden of Eden—in tiny Portis, Kansas, about 40 miles north of Lucas. The Lucas town council expressed interest but turned the matter over to Schultz and her Arts and Humanities Commission, saying that if they could raise $35,000, the town would contribute the rest. To everyone's surprise, they raised the money, and the Marshall Collection came to Lucas. Of course, it needed a place to be exhibited, which led to much more fund-raising and, in 1995, the opening of the

Above: When Lucas acquired Inez Marshall's limestone sculptures in 1990, including this Model T Ford, it marked the beginning of the town's emergence as a center of grassroots art in America. Below: One of the more unusual exhibits at Lucas's Grassroots Art Center is that of Herman Divers. Using only pull-tabs from beverage cans, Divers constructed a variety of sculptures, including a room full of furniture, a full-size roadster, and this motorcycle.

A recent addition to the Lucas grassroots art scene is this display of "American Fork Art" by Lucas artist Mri Pilar.

Grassroots Art Center with Schultz as director and Doris Johnson, who lives in nearby Luray, as associate director.

The grassroots or folk art tradition—terms that generally refer to art created by people who have not been professionally trained as artists—has flourished in Kansas, which, for reasons no one has been able to explain, is considered one of the grassroots art centers of the country. According to Schultz, Kansas trails only California and Wisconsin in the vitality of its grassroots art. Since Dinsmoor and Deeble first picked up their trowels, grassroots art has taken hold in Lucas and given the town its identity, at least in terms of the outside world. Today, scores of grassroots artists' works are on display in Lucas at the downtown art center or at places such as Erika Nelson's house, the home of "The World's Largest Collection of the World's Smallest Versions of the World's Largest Things Traveling Roadside Attraction and Museum."[12] Another grassroots artist, Mri Pilar, transformed the interior of the Florence Deeble house into a bizarre display of Mylar, silver insulation, and hundreds of eclectic objets d'art, and in 2006 she opened an exhibit of "fork art" in downtown Lucas.

In the late 1990s the old Isis Theater was restored by Lucas community volunteers and reopened in 2000 as a modern 195-seat multipurpose theater.

Lucas's reputation has attracted formally trained artists, too, such as Eric Abraham, a ceramics sculptor whose home and studio occupy a former Chevrolet dealership not far from the Grassroots Art Center on Main Street. Thanks to grassroots art, and Lucas's adoption of it, the town has also hosted two Smithsonian Institution exhibits, "Yesterday's Tomorrows: Past Visions of the American Future," in 2002, and "Between Fences," a cultural history of fences and land use, in 2006. Lucas is one of the smallest towns to host such an event. Although not everyone in Lucas is pleased at their town's unusual prominence in the world of grassroots art, most seem to have embraced it, and some even display their own forms of grassroots art.

Art, however, is not Lucas's only asset. In 1998 a group of eleven people got together to try to save the old, boarded-up Isis movie theater. They formed a nonprofit group and set to work. Relying almost exclusively on volunteer labor (over 4,000 hours) and $128,000 in donations, including $40,000 from the city, the modern, 195-seat Lucas Area Community Theater opened in 2000. The project was successful from the start, drawing customers from the many neighboring communities to watch first-run movies every weekend as well as music performances and high school plays. In 2005 the theater received a grant from the

Kansas Small Towns Environment Program that enabled it to add a 1,700 square foot half-million-dollar addition providing dressing rooms, prop rooms, and bathrooms, which has enabled the building to be used for a much wider range of live theatrical performances.

While the theater is not as unusual as the grassroots art, it gives the town another solid attraction and a resource that is particularly popular with the area's young people. Throughout rural America, saving and renovating the local theater has become a focal point for efforts to maintain an entertainment and cultural center for the community. Lucas's efforts have been duplicated in places such as Julesburg, Colorado, where the eighty-seven-year-old Hippodrome Theater recently reopened as the Hippodrome Arts Centre.

Lucas shares its schools with Luray, a town of 200 people 10 miles to the west. Lucas and Luray originally each had K–12 schools, but in 1977 Luray's high school was consolidated into the school at Lucas, with Luray retaining the K–8 school. The schools have 139 students, representing an average class size of ten and a teacher-student ratio of about eight to one. Lucas has all the basic necessities a rural town needs, plus a Ford dealership, a golf course in Luray, a couple of restaurants, a bed and breakfast, a florist, a library, and a newspaper—the weekly *Lucas-Sylvan News*, which also serves the community of Sylvan Grove 10 miles to the east. It also has Brant's Meat Market, a town gathering place that has been in business since 1922 under family ownership and is known for its smoked meats, sausages, and the dry wit of the proprietor, Doug Brant. The city's largest employer is a division of Great Plains Manufacturing of Salina, which has five farm equipment manufacturing plants in rural Kansas—including the one in Tipton. Great Plains, like the city government, is a reliable supporter of community efforts such as the theater, art museum, and downtown beautification efforts. Lucas also averages about 25 inches of rain a year, enough to give the area an opportunity to grow corn and other nongrass crops. Yet Lucas continues to lose population and today is 40 percent below its 1950s population of about 750.

Lucas is a city that has exhibited a high level of community involvement and unity and has much to show for it. Still, Schultz, head of the Grassroots Art Center, has a wish list for the town: a "quirky" place to eat—in keeping with the art—more and better housing, better job opportunities for women, and a public restroom to help handle the crowds when tour buses pull into town. She also thinks the area could use more lodging, and, in fact, there are plans to reopen the old Lucas Hotel as a hotel and art gallery.

While Lucas may be one of the most unusual attractions in Kansas, there are enough others to keep the Kansas Explorers Club busy. Every month the club's several thousand members receive the *Explorer Newsletter,* published by Marci Penner of the Kansas Sampler Foundation, whose mission is to preserve and sustain rural culture.[13] The Kansas Explorers sponsor group tours to attractions in the state, and the newsletter highlights interesting events, people, and places—for example, a listing of some two dozen Christmas festivals and an article about unusual water towers, including one in Smolan that had been converted into a residence and a pair of water towers in Pratt labeled "Hot" and "Cold."

Lucas and Wilson lie at either end of the Wilson Lake area, two small towns fighting depopulation with a variety of weapons, including their purple cows. By all accounts, Lucas recently has been the more cohesive and progressive of the two communities, yet it remains to be seen if either town can stabilize its population, let alone reverse the downward trend.

11

Sedan: Community Building from the Top Down

Sedan, Kansas, is a community of 1,306 in the southeast part of the state, about 10 miles from the Oklahoma border. It is a relatively isolated town: 40 miles from the cities of Independence and Coffeyville in Kansas and Pawhuska and Bartlesville in Oklahoma. The nearest metropolitan cities are Wichita and Tulsa, both 95 miles away. The closest interstate highway, I-35, is 70 miles to the west, and I-70 is more than 190 miles to the north. It even is becoming a little more isolated as U.S. Highway 166 and Kansas Highway 99, which once went through downtown Sedan, are being rerouted a few miles to the west of town, but the change will reduce the truck traffic on Sedan's Main Street.

Sedan, which became the county seat of Chautauqua County in 1875, is in the Chautauqua Hills, similar and adjacent to the Flint Hills geological area, and is characterized by rocky, rolling hills covered with oaks and prairie grasslands, a combination that is sometimes referred to as "cross timbers." The valleys along the Caney River in the county contain some good farmland, and the area receives enough rainfall to farm without intensive irrigation. The area has always been prime pastureland, and the economy is heavily dependent on cattle ranching and, during the 1800s, on the commerce that developed along cattle trails from Texas and Oklahoma to railheads north of Sedan. Oil was discovered in the area in 1904 and in recent years hunting has contributed significantly to the area's economy. Yet despite good rainfall and attractive topography, the area's population has been declining. From a peak of about 12,000 in the early twentieth century, the population of Chautauqua County has fallen more than 65 percent to 4,109. Sedan's drop has been less severe, from just over 2,000 in the 1950s to 1,306 today.

For decades the preferred meeting place for Sedan's farmers and ranchers has been the tiny Green Door Café on Main Street, where a full breakfast can be obtained for about $3 and coffee refills are free.

Sedan was a relatively prosperous town well into the 1970s, with five groceries, three new-car dealerships, and several dry goods merchants. But in the mid-1980s, as the impact of falling oil and cattle prices was felt, Sedan's retail stores began to close. Today there is one small grocery, and the car dealerships are in larger cities like Independence and Bartlesville. There is no place in Sedan to buy clothing or linens and, for that matter, no coin laundry or dry cleaner to clean them. Where once there were eight oil company offices in Sedan, there remain but two today.[1]

Almost the only reminder of Sedan's days of commercial prosperity is Ackarman Hardware, which has been in business since 1879, although it is no longer operated by the Ackarman family.

In 1988 a small group of Sedan residents decided to try to do something to drum up business for the town. Nita Jones, a local businesswoman, recalls that in 1987 thirteen stores closed on the town's two-block Main Street. Shocked into action, but not demoralized, Jones's group of "Dreamers and Doers" formed the "Save Our Sedan" committee. For their first project they decided to capitalize on the strong and universal appeal of *The Wizard of Oz*. They were not dismayed by the fact that L. Frank Baum had never specified *where* the scenes in

Sedan's oldest continuing retailer is Ackarman Hardware. It began business when Rutherford B. Hayes was president and Kansas had been a state for just eighteen years.

Kansas took place or by the fact that he seemed to have had in mind a flatter, bleaker, and less verdant place than Chautauqua County. Baum had specified only "Kansas," and Sedan was certainly in Kansas.

Since the Kansas towns of Wamego and Liberal already had Oz Museums (Liberal's with a 1909 version of "Dorothy's Farmhouse"), the Save Our Sedan committee decided to create the world's *longest* Yellow Brick Road. The Sedan city council agreed, and over the next few years the sidewalks of downtown Sedan were torn up by volunteers and inlaid with yellow bricks, which the committee sold for $10 apiece. Today almost 11,000 bricks make up the "road" through downtown Sedan, each bearing the name of a donor, including celebrities such as Brooke Shields and Whoopi Goldberg and people from all fifty states and twenty-eight foreign countries. Today the Yellow Brick Road is beginning to look a little worn and in need of a fresh coat of paint, but it is estimated by Jones, now sixty-eight and Sedan's unofficial booster-in-chief, that it still attracts almost 50,000 visitors a year.

At about the same time the Yellow Brick Road project was getting under way, a retired building contractor by the name of Don Armstrong

Sedan's biggest tourist attraction, the "Yellow Brick Road," is actually a yellow brick sidewalk through downtown. It's made up of over 10,000 donated and inscribed bricks.

began tackling the renovation of a couple of downtown Sedan's deserted buildings and also led volunteers in the creation of the Hollow, a flower garden park in downtown Sedan on a lot that had been used as a junk-yard.

As was the case in Palco and Tipton, the efforts of a handful of people like Jones and Armstrong may have saved Sedan. "People have to learn to pull together instead of apart to make a community work," said Jones, "and that's what Sedan has learned to do, learn to work together, whether you like each other or not. Works for me!"

Volunteer efforts such as the Hollow and the Yellow Brick Road, along with longtime businesses such as Sedan Floral, one of the nation's largest suppliers of bedding plants, and Economy Manufacturing, which makes truck beds, helped to keep Sedan alive, if not growing, until 1995, when Bill Kurtis arrived. Kurtis, then a CBS news anchor and correspondent based in Chicago, was raised in nearby Independence, Kansas. On a visit to see his parents, Kurtis explored the countryside west of Independence and came to Sedan, where he was struck by the beauty of the area and the potential he saw in it for a tourist destination and arts center. He also

A former dumping ground in downtown Sedan has been turned into a sunken garden, the "Hollow," and also contains a small historic schoolhouse and museum.

reconnected with the land itself, including some pastureland just north of Sedan that had been owned by his grandfather. In 1996 Kurtis bought the 6,000-acre Red Buffalo ranch, later adding more land to bring his total acreage to 12,000. He also plunged into the work of renovating Sedan, and by the time he was finished he had bought and renovated eleven buildings, most of them along Main Street and many of which he leased to entrepreneurs and artists at far below market rates.

Kurtis's vision combined an appreciation for the natural prairie grasslands typical of the Flint Hills and parts of the Chautauqua Hills—a potential international tourist attraction in itself, he believed—with his conviction that towns such as Sedan could replace much of their previous commercial activity with a variety of tourist attractions, including arts, crafts, and hunting. The impact of Kurtis on Sedan was difficult to overestimate. "It was kind of like a tornado coming through town," one resident told me. Sleepy Sedan was suddenly being transformed. Main Street began to look alive again, and Kurtis, along with Chuck Dye and others in the community, even kicked off a community effort to renovate and reopen the town's impressive, but empty, thirty-two-room hotel.

Above: Bill Kurtis's Red Buffalo Ranch, just north of Sedan, where grass-fed cattle are raised.
Below: A block of downtown Sedan, including many buildings restored by Bill Kurtis. Three of
Kurtis's businesses are located on the block: Tallgrass Beef Company, the Red Buffalo Ranch,
and the Red Buffalo gift shop.

The Sedan community plans to restore the old Sedan Hotel and add an upscale restaurant.

Interestingly, a similar effort at "top-down" revitalization and historic preservation was taking place elsewhere in the Flint Hills and nearby areas. Kansas City businessman Bill Haw was renovating buildings and opening businesses in Cottonwood Falls, the county seat of Chase County, which like Chautauqua County lost almost two-thirds of its population during the twentieth century.

Both Kurtis and Haw had highly successful careers in metropolitan areas, but they also had strong rural roots and hoped that their efforts could help the small towns on which they had focused to avoid, or at least reduce, further depopulation.

Kurtis's "pump-priming" efforts in Sedan began to change in 2005. He realized that there were limits to what he could do—and how long he could do it—all by himself. He decided the time had come to begin to move the Kurtis development efforts into the hands of the people who would, ultimately, have to make it work. Rather than continuing to lease his buildings, he began selling them—retaining only the buildings that house the business and marketing side of his ranching business, the Red Buffalo gift shop, and an art gallery. Perhaps his decision to back away from such heavy involvement in building renovation and the revitalization of Sedan had something to do with changes taking place in his ranching business. As Kurtis was becoming more familiar with raising "grass-fed" cattle, consumers' tastes were changing.

The 1990s saw the emergence of a strong demand for natural and organic food, including the growth of retail companies such as Whole Foods, suppliers such as Earthbound Farms, Coleman Natural Meats, and Petaluma Poultry, and restaurants such as Goodtimes Burgers, which makes its hamburgers out of natural beef, and Chipotle, which uses many natural and organic ingredients. In 2007 Chipotle began running ads touting its natural meats and adding "Factory Farms Suck!"[2] The 1990s also saw broad acceptance of higher pricing than would have been thought possible just a few years before. Consumers who thought nothing of paying three or four dollars for a cup of flavored coffee or two dollars for twelve ounces of bottled water stood in line at natural foods markets to buy a few ounces of dolphin-safe tuna salad for five or six dollars or hamburgers made from naturally raised beef for twice what Safeway was charging for conventionally raised beef.

The marketing of grass-fed beef may be one of the last big opportunities in the natural foods movement. Virtually all other beef, even from "natural" beef companies such as Coleman or Niman Ranch, is corn fed or, at best, grass fed for a year or two and then sent to a feedlot for a little extra fattening on grain before going to the slaughterhouse. For reasons that are beyond the scope of this book, "corn-fed" beef became synonymous with high-quality beef in the years after World War II, despite the fact that cattle have a difficult time digesting corn and that corn-feeding often involves massive feedlot operations.[3]

Advocates of grass-fed beef argue that grass feeding is better for the cattle (more digestible), the consumer (less total dietary fat, more omega-3 fatty acids, or "good" fat), and the environment (more sustainable: the crop renews itself; the animals require fewer drugs and hormones).[4] Another advantage of grass-fed beef is that it may be less susceptible to bovine spongiform encephalopathy (mad cow disease), which was discovered for the first time in the United States in a domestic dairy cow in 2003 and has been a continuing concern ever since.[5] Interestingly, one of the most vocal proponents of corn-fed beef is Kurtis's historic preservation counterpart, Cottonwood Falls's Bill Haw. Haw is president of National Farms, which operates large traditional feedlots, and he disputes the claim that grass-fed beef is healthier for people, although he concedes that corn feeding can create health problems for cattle.

But most important—and potentially of most interest to Kurtis and the others who are trying to gain market acceptance for grass-fed beef—Haw believes "the American public has cast its vote resoundingly that it prefers corn-fed beef to grass-fed beef. It does tend to be more tender. It does tend to be more flavorful. The grass-fed beef does not have as much external fat. It does not have as much marbling. It does not have as much total fat. But the preference vote is in and it is clearly for corn-fed beef."[6]

Notwithstanding Haw's assessment, the grass-fed beef versus corn-fed beef battle is not over. In a 2006 *New York Times* beef taste test, several brands of grass-fed beef were praised, including Kurtis's Tallgrass Beef ("superb flavor, juicy, tender"), and food critic Marian Burros found some "rich, juicy, and tender" grass-fed beef being served at New York restaurants.[7]

In addition to debates about health and flavor, there are other issues facing people such as Kurtis who are trying to expand market awareness and acceptance of their product. By its nature, grass-fed beef tends to be raised by a small number of independent ranchers, and since it does not end up in large, centralized feedlots, shipping in volume can be a hurdle. The prospect of getting grass-fed beef to the marketplace on anything like a national scale is daunting, requiring the creation of production and distribution channels and quality-control methods that will stand up to the demands of retailers and their consumers. As a result, most grass-fed producers—companies such as Thousand Hills Cattle Company in Minnesota and Mesquite Organic Foods in Colorado—limit their distribution to within a few hundred miles of their processing facilities.

Although most grass-fed cattle ranchers are uncomfortable with trying to meet the demands of the national markets, Kurtis is not. In 2005 he created the Tallgrass Beef Company, based in Sedan and using his own Red Buffalo ranch as the initial supplier. Kurtis's hope is that Tallgrass can do for grass-fed beef what Coleman and Niman did for natural beef: create a national brand. If this is to occur, it will require creating a consortium of ranchers, a distribution and transportation network, high-quality processing plants, and a marketing organization. The opportunity that Tallgrass presents, and the amount of time, effort, and money needed to bring it about, may well have helped influence Kurtis's decision to scale back his renovation efforts in Sedan. But in any event, if Tallgrass is successful it will be a boon to the town, which is likely to remain the headquarters for the company.

The future of Sedan without the same level of investment by Kurtis will depend on the ability of the town to work cohesively on projects and to do more regional marketing with other southeast Kansas communities. It will also test the theory that a commitment to the arts can be the driving force behind restoring small towns, a theory that has proved successful in Lucas but may be more difficult to accomplish in Sedan, which is more remote and is focusing more on attracting professionally trained artists than on Lucas's quirky grassroots art niche.

Despite its isolation, Sedan has several things in its favor. Thanks to the efforts of people such as Bill Kurtis, Don Armstrong, and Nita Jones, it has a relatively lively and interesting downtown, including several artists' shops and studios, a well-stocked hunting store, and a good hardware store. It has seven restaurants, an attractive golf course and town park, some strong local businesses, government jobs that go with a county seat, a prosperous ranching economy, an improving energy economy, and community-wide wireless Internet access. It has Mel's General Store, run by Nita Jones's daughter, and a small theater, which while not as well-restored as the one in Lucas nevertheless still provides the same kind of amenity—inexpensive first-run movies, occasional plays, and low-priced popcorn and soft drinks. Perhaps most important, it still has a healthy school system, with more than 400 students enrolled in grades K–12. It is lacking a high-end restaurant and upscale lodging, although that gap may be filled if the downtown hotel, which has been closed since the 1960s, reopens on schedule.

But despite its advantages, and Kurtis's investments, Sedan has continued to lose population, particularly its young, and it has seen its welfare and retirement populations grow. One of the biggest businesses in Sedan is its nursing home, with eighty-two residents. This demographic pattern has resulted in a small labor pool, particularly of skilled younger workers, leading Kurtis to express concern that if places such as Sedan can't do something to stem their population losses, "they can get too small" to attract business and remain viable.

The next decade will tell whether the "top-down" redevelopment and historic preservation efforts of people such as Kurtis in Sedan and Haw in Cottonwood Falls will yield lasting benefits for the towns and whether they will prove to have marked the turning point in their communities' efforts to survive or will be viewed as interesting—but ultimately doomed—attempts to reverse an irreversible trend. It may well be that the greatest and most long-lasting impact Kurtis and Haw have on their communities will be tied more to the success of their business ventures—much as has been the case with Chuck Comeau's DessinFournir in Plainville—than on their high-profile downtown renovation efforts.

12

Selling Rural America: Dave Rose and eBay

It is said that the Chinese symbol for danger or crisis also connotes opportunity. If the depopulation of rural America qualifies as a crisis, perhaps no one has been better at finding an opportunity within that crisis than Dave Rose. His is an emerging and unusual "story behind the stories" of many small, declining rural towns.

In 2002 Rose, then a 52-year-old claims manager for Farm Bureau Insurance in Kansas, began experimenting with using the Internet to sell salvage vehicles his company had acquired. The experiment worked, and the company began getting more than the vehicles' nominal salvage value, thanks to Rose's clever Internet marketing, primarily through eBay.[1]

In 2003 Rose was offered early retirement from the insurance company and took it. But a friend, who was a city councilman in Gaylord in north-central Kansas, asked Rose if the Internet marketing techniques he had developed to sell salvage vehicles might be used to help sell real estate. The property in question was an unoccupied school building in Gaylord, a town of about 170 people in Smith County, that had been closed when the school was consolidated with a school in the county seat of Smith Center. The Gaylord town council was concerned that it might be unable to sell—or even give away—the building. Rose agreed to try, and he and a son who was skilled at operating computers and building web sites put the school building up for sale on eBay, accompanied by lots of photographs and extensive descriptive information about the building *and* the community. Rose realized early in the process that it was going to be necessary to sell the community as well as the property. The building soon sold for $25,000 to a couple from Seattle, Gwen and Oliver Archut, who ran TAB-Funkenwerk, a niche audio electronics business that manufactures, renovates, repairs, and sells a line of esoteric, high-end audio recording studio components, such as microphone pre-amplifiers, that appeals to audiophiles and musicians like Keith Richards.

Not only did the town get money for a building they had been worried might be worthless—or, worse, might have cost them tens of thousands of dollars to demolish and remove—but the new owners brought a successful business to the small and remote town of Gaylord. In addition to being pleased with the amount of space they were able to buy for a sum that would buy a nice tool shed in Seattle, the TAB-Funkenwerk owners also were delighted with the work ethic they encountered in their Kansas employees, enabling them, in Dave Rose's words, to get "twice the work at half the wages" they would have paid in Seattle. And although townspeople were unsure how the Archuts would adapt to rural life, they appear to love it: "There's a difference between living and existing," Oliver Archut told *Los Angeles Times* writer Stephanie Simon. "In Seattle we were just existing. Here we can live."[2] In addition to Gaylord, the *Times* article featured school sales in Upham, North Dakota, and the towns of Paradise, McCracken, and Morland, Kansas, as examples of the "dozens of communities [that] have turned to eBay to sell schools shuttered for lack of kids. They've attracted tremendous interest from entrepreneurs seeking a bargain and an escape."[3]

Rose was sufficiently impressed with the Gaylord transaction to start a company called Midwest eServices, Inc., to market similar properties on its own web site and through eBay, Loopnet (a commercial real estate listing service), and other Internet marketplaces. He contracted with a web server company in Denver for the large amounts of storage and bandwidth needed for his data-intensive sales packages and refined his skills of selling, not just the property in question, but the community, the region, and the benefits of rural life in general. He quickly began signing up other towns, school districts, and private sellers. Most of his properties are in rural Kansas, Oklahoma, and Colorado, but he has sold property from as far away as North Carolina and Washington State, and he has received an inquiry from a property owner in France who was impressed with the way Midwest eServices presents its properties.

As the business developed, Rose not only provided sellers with an effective and powerful marketing tool but also helped them evaluate potential buyers and their business plans. Indeed, from the beginning, Rose saw his job as having two components: selling unused or underused buildings to people who could use them productively, and also helping bring new blood into rural communities that desperately needed it. As a result, he now works closely with the Kansas Department of Commerce, tipping them off to small businesses that have expressed an interest in rural properties so that they can help local communities prepare an attractive package of benefits and support.

It was Rose who sold the former public school in Tipton to the Tipton Academy, which brought much-needed revenue *and* a new business to the town of Tipton. And in Delphos Rose himself jumped in and bought the former public school, then worked out a lease-purchase agreement with the Meadowlark Academy.

One of Rose's most successful efforts took place in Jennings, a town of only 135 people in northwest Kansas that is remote—even by rural Kansas standards. In 2006 Jennings lost its K–12 schools, which had only thirty students, and its Prairie Heights school district was dissolved and folded into the K–12 schools in Oberlin, 34 miles away. Rose was contacted to try to find a buyer for the Jennings school building, and after an extensive marketing effort, and with considerable help from people in city, county, and state government, the building was bought in 2006 by Bus Coach International (BCI), a seller and operator of tour buses. Bus Coach International set up its North and South America distribution center in the 38,000-square-foot Jennings school building, and plans to build another 20,000-square-foot facility. Planning has also begun for a 7,000-foot airport runway to serve the BCI operations. By early 2007 BCI had created twenty-five new jobs in Jennings and plans to increase the workforce to 135 by 2008 as it reduces its operations in California and Arizona. Because many of BCI's buses are customized and renovated, the Jennings facility also is likely to attract some supporting businesses, including providers of restoration and upholstery services. The BCI project in Jennings was accomplished without tax abatements or other financial incentives, although any new airport runway is likely to require government funding.

Another Rose success is in Atwood's neighbor, Herndon, Kansas (population 140), where the abandoned school building was sold to Cencast, an Oregon-based investment casting company that manufactures products for medical and other precision uses, including artificial joints. The company was so impressed with Herndon that initially it considered moving its entire operations there, Rose said, but some of its Oregon employees objected and as a result the Cencast operation in Herndon will be a support facility for the Oregon headquarters.

In 2004 Rose took on the job of selling an empty school building in the town of Buffalo, a community of about 1,100 people in northwestern Oklahoma. Within four months the building was sold to a company from Florida that provides support services and supplies for people who home-school their children. The business now has seventeen full-time employees and adds part-time help—primarily local high school students—during peak times. "I can't even begin to describe what a boon to our community this venture proved to be," said James Leonard, economic development director for Buffalo.[4]

Rose has sold properties to a diverse group of people, including artists looking for large and inexpensive work spaces, home buyers, people looking for vacation and hunting lodges, and investors, including one who bought and renovated a building in Hill City, Kansas, which now houses a cell phone company, a restaurant, an insurance agency, and an apartment. Rose's business is sufficiently novel that it has attracted the attention of newspapers such as the *Boston Globe* and of other real estate companies.

Rose believes demographics, technology, low costs—and a concern for security—are on the side of rural America. He sees the possibility that Internet-based businesses may help keep young people in their communities and believes that many of the millions of baby boomers who are reaching retirement want the kind of lifestyle that he thinks rural America can offer: safe, friendly, and inexpensive. Costs are also on the side of rural America, Rose believes. While a few of the properties he markets are in poor condition and have been empty for too long, most of the buildings are in good condition (some just recently updated), are well built, and cost from $1 to $4 a square foot. Wages are low, too, sometimes half what would be necessary in urban markets, unions are rare, and workers tend to be loyal. In addition, in many rural communities zoning and other regulations are far more relaxed than in cities, and small towns can be more welcoming to small businesses than bigger cities. Rose's enthusiasm for rural economies found support in a four-part 2006 *Wall Street Journal* series "Still Built on the Homefront," about U.S. manufacturing companies that have resisted the lure to move operations out of the country. Many not only have remained in America, but in rural America, including the Viking Range Corporation in Greenwood, Mississippi, Bobcat Manufacturing in Gwinner, North Dakota, and Arctic Cat Snowmobiles in Thief River Falls, Minnesota, settings that company executives believe provide a loyal workforce and "[breed] the kind of culture where problems are solved with the can-do, make-do ethos of the farm."[5]

Rose's business has grown rapidly from the first Gaylord school in 2003, and by 2006 it employed nine licensed real estate agents in Kansas, one of whom covered Oklahoma, and it had an affiliation with a real estate agent in Colorado and was recruiting affiliates in Nebraska, Iowa, and Missouri. As of the end of 2006, Rose's company had racked up more than 480 sales, about one-fourth in real estate with the balance in salvage vehicles. It had acquired a United Country Real Estate franchise, linking Rose's business to nearly 600 offices nationwide. On an average day in 2006, Rose had twenty-six active real estate listings on eBay, most in Kansas but with others in neighboring states. Typical was a listing for an apparently well-maintained 14,309-square-foot former grade school building in Hunter, in north-central Kansas, not far from Lucas and Tipton. The brick structure, which sits on four acres, carried a target price of $60,000, and by the end of October 2006, it had attracted seventeen bidders with two months remaining on the auction. The listing had forty-five high-resolution photographs and detailed information about the town of Hunter and its seventy-seven residents, the county, nearby attractions, and links to dozens of additional web sites with information about everything from hunting in the area to economic development incentives available to purchasers.

The company's web site listings receive an average of more than four million "hits," or visits, a month, and they come from eighty-five different countries. The Salina headquarters of Midwest eServices still is very much a family affair, including Rose's wife and two sons, but the growth of the business created a need for more space. Not surprisingly, Rose chose to expand by buying an abandoned school building in Salina, which he is converting into offices and loft apartments.

Part 3

POLICY OPTIONS FOR
RURAL AMERICA

The history of rural America suggests that the prospects for the survival or growth of a community tend to be highly idiosyncratic. Towns with seemingly similar prospects can follow quite dissimilar paths depending on circumstances that are often beyond their control, such as where a highway or a reservoir or a state prison is placed. Likewise, local leadership varies from town to town. The qualities of leadership that give hope to tiny places such as Palco or Tipton may be lacking in other communities that suffer from a lack of vision, or from local jealousies, small-mindedness, or from the unwillingness of people to reinvest in their community.

Politicians, academicians, and policy visionaries tend to see the issues facing rural America in a wider context and to develop broad-based plans that address those issues, directly or indirectly, on a far larger scale than an individual town or county. By their nature, such initiatives are often slow to be approved or implemented, if indeed they ever are, suggesting that if rural America were to sit back and wait for salvation from a federal or state program or a sweeping plan to change agricultural or ranching practices, time may run out. Fortunately, most rural Americans are innately skeptical of broad policy proposals or big federal programs, even as many of them collect U.S. Department of Agriculture payments. As the stories in this book suggest, many communities are willing to accept responsibility for their own future. Nevertheless, there are situations in which individual or community efforts simply can't suffice or are not appropriate. Many of the policy options for rural America affect communities across large areas of the country or require regional cooperation or federal direction and funding.

There is also one unpredictable factor that may affect agriculture and rural communities everywhere, and it requires broad—even international—policy responses. This wild card is global warming. Assessing the potential impact of it on rural economies is difficult, if not impossible, because there is no consensus on the causes, the timing, or the extent of global warming or even on whether it would be a good or a bad thing—or a little of both—for agriculture. Potential pluses include more rainfall and a longer growing season, while minuses include the likelihood of more insects and diseases, flooding of some coastal croplands, the possibility of more severe weather disturbances, and perhaps more soil erosion. Governments and researchers at many levels are trying to understand more about global warming and its potential effect on agriculture. The U.S. Global Change Research Information Office has published "Potential Impacts of Climate Change on Agriculture and Food Supply," and there are many such studies available, but as yet there is no broad agreement on either the extent of the threat or possible solutions and countermeasures that might be taken.[1]

13
The Federal Government's Role

In the 1960s the inner cities of America were widely believed to be falling apart owing to physical decay, political unrest, street violence, and the failings of an earlier generation of government programs that had created bleak, crime-ridden, low-income housing projects. The federal government sprang into action with newer and more expensive programs to help ensure a "Great Society," including the Demonstration Cities and Metropolitan Development Act of 1966, better known as "Model Cities," and designed to revitalize urban America.

Model Cities, which has been termed "America's worst urban program" by Steven Malanga, senior fellow at the Manhattan Institute, officially ended in 1974, but sizable remnants of it have, in fact, continued in one block-grant form or another to this day. Along the way it has spent over "$100 billion in thousands of communities, with little to show for the effort. Local officials squandered the billions by financing unworkable projects that often went bust, investing in new businesses that couldn't survive in depressed neighborhoods, and funding social programs with little idea of how they might actually strengthen their communities."[1] As Malanga points out, at least the original sponsors of the program were motivated by idealism and the conviction—misguided though it may have been—that it would help urban communities. The program has long since become just another convenient way for Congress to funnel pork-barrel money to congressional districts. There have been efforts by both Democratic and Republican administrations to reform or end the block-grant programs, efforts that have been resisted—successfully thus far—by Congress. However, bipartisan efforts have succeeded in creating some more effective programs, including the Low Income Housing Tax Credit, created by the Tax Reform Act of 1986, and the New Markets Initiative, a bipartisan pet project of former President Bill Clinton and former House Speaker Dennis Hastert. The programs provide tax credits for housing and business investments made within the targeted communities.[2]

Although rural Americans are far outnumbered by urban Americans, they have always enjoyed political power that is out of proportion to their raw numbers, a reality that can be traced all the way back to the negotiations and compromises that secured approval of the U.S. Constitution in 1787. North Dakota, which is one of the most rural states by any measure, has two powerful and effective members of the U.S. Senate: Byron Dorgan, who has been in Congress since 1980, and Kent Conrad, who has been in Congress since 1986 and is chairman of the Senate Budget Committee. Both are Democrats, which at first seems unusual since North Dakota almost always votes Republican in presidential elections. But North Dakota is an independent-minded state politically. It is the only state in the union that does not have voter registration, and it was home to the Nonpartisan League, which supported candidates of both major parties, lobbied for commodity price supports and other farmers' benefits, and influenced politics in several Midwestern and Western states in the 1910s and 1920s.[3]

For Dorgan, who was born in 1942 in Regent, North Dakota, population 211, trying to help small towns in rural America has been a priority throughout his career. In 2003 he and nine other senators, including Conrad, introduced a bill called the New Homestead Act, which specifically targeted communities with declining populations. The sponsors said, "We want to rekindle the spirit of the Homestead Act of 1862 . . . and to enact policies that offer hope and opportunity to the Heartland once again, [including] incentives to buy a home, pay for college, and get the financing [needed] to launch or expand a business."[4] The proposal incorporated similar incentives and credits to those found in the low-income housing and New Markets bills that were aimed at urban areas—and it avoided the controversial approach of the block-grant programs.

For individuals the bill offered repayment of up to $10,000 of college loans for people who live and work in rural America for at least five years, a $5,000 tax credit for people who buy homes in rural America, and created individual homestead accounts, which would be similar to individual retirement accounts. For businesses in high out-migration counties, the bill provided rural investment tax credits that would allocate a million dollars to each county and a New Homestead Venture

Capital Fund to invest $3 billion over ten years in businesses in those counties. Two-thirds of the money for the venture fund would come from the federal government, one-third from state and private sources.

Dorgan argued that his bill was not special-interest legislation and that "America needs a new Homestead Act as much as the Heartland does." [5] America didn't agree. Dorgan was able to get only sixteen cosponsors for his bill, all from states with large rural populations, and the 2003 bill died, as did a 2005 version. Perhaps Dorgan should have tried an approach favored by Robert Day, author of *The Last Cattle Drive*, who proposed a scholar and artist homestead act under which abandoned buildings and entire ghost towns would be given to people such as potters, musicians, and writers who needed a little seclusion to complete their works.[6]

Although the failure of targeted legislation such as the New Homestead Act may be frustrating to Dorgan and other rural Americans who have seen so much federal largess going to urban America, there is a legitimate public policy argument against such efforts. While everyone would agree that federal policy in the nineteenth century overpopulated a lot of rural areas west of the Appalachians, some people question whether the solution is to keep propping up areas that are inevitably going to decline. Indeed, one skeptic is North Dakota newspaper editor Jack Zaleski. When asked about federal programs such as the New Homestead Act, which would try to stimulate migration to rural areas, Zaleski was blunt: "Any effort to repopulate North Dakota is a fool's errand."[7] A majority of Congress apparently agree.

Norm Coleman, Republican senator from Minnesota and a cosponsor of the New Homestead Act, has a markedly different background from North Dakota's Dorgan. Coleman was born in 1949 into a large Jewish family in Brooklyn, New York, attended college on Long Island where he led antiwar and pro–civil rights protests, and then received a law degree from the University of Iowa. He went to work in the Minnesota Attorney General's Office and was elected mayor of Saint Paul in 1993, as a Democrat. But in 1996 he changed parties, having become disillusioned with the Democrats' positions on crime, education, and job growth, and was elected to the U.S. Senate in 2002, defeating former Vice-President Walter Mondale.

In 2005 Coleman and Arkansas Senator Mark Pryor introduced the

Rural Renaissance Act. Coleman's bill addressed deficiencies in the infrastructure of rural America and would have allocated $50 billion in grants and loans for such things as water and wastewater plants, telecommunications, police and fire facilities, hospitals and nursing homes, and renewable fuels projects. Funding for Coleman's bill would have come from issuing federal bonds, and the program was to be administered by a new Rural Renaissance Corporation. As was the case with the New Homestead Act, the Rural Renaissance Act had a rough reception in Congress in 2005, and in 2006 even a greatly watered-down version of the legislation (reducing the amount from $50 billion to $200 million) eventually went down to defeat.

It may be no great loss; $200 million in bonds "seems like a lot of money, but nationwide it is a drop in the bucket," said Lynn Hokanson, city administrator of Watkins, Minnesota, which itself needs $8 million to rebuild its aging infrastructure.[8] Watkins and others in local government in rural America endorse the Rural Renaissance concept but admit that $200 million wouldn't meet the needs of rural communities in Minnesota alone, let alone the entire country. Although the New Homestead and Rural Renaissance legislative efforts can only be described as modest in scope, and they steered clear of the examples of massive block grants and federal giveaways, they failed to gain broad support, particularly among legislators from urban America.

Looking back to see what opened up the federal coffers for urban communities, to the tune of many billions of dollars since the 1960s, it seems clear that rural America has not grabbed the public's attention the way urban America did in the days when rioting and massive and violent political protests filled the news. It was a time when society seemed to be coming apart. It was characterized by the assassinations of Martin Luther King Jr., John F. Kennedy, Robert F. Kennedy, and Malcolm X; cities were aflame—indeed, neighborhoods just a few blocks from the White House and the Capitol Building were literally on fire and under martial law—and the scene of the 1968 Democratic Convention in Chicago erupted into something like urban warfare. The flames were fanned by extremist and radical groups of every conceivable type, including the Black Panthers, the Weather Underground (which in 1970 declared a state of war against the United States), white supremacist groups in the south, antiwar protesters, and even the Gray Panthers, an organization of elderly, angry people which sprang into existence in 1970 when one of their number was forced to retire from her job against her will. The situation was highly volatile, and most Americans were scared. Partly as a result, the 1972 "law-and-order" presidential candidacy of the segregationist Alabama governor George Wallace was very credible until—in an attack characteristic of the era—he was gravely wounded by a would-be assassin's bullet.

Rural America offers no such fireworks. There have been occasional farmers' marches here and there and some dumping of commodities, but these have been aimed at federal farm policies, not at society or even the government as a whole. The closest most people can come to recalling anything like a rural uprising occurred 220 years ago when farmers in western Massachusetts took up arms against high taxes and crushing debt in Shays' Rebellion, which was defeated by the Massachusetts militia within a few months. In the more than two centuries since then, there have been many protest marches on Washington involving almost every conceivable interest group, including veterans, the unemployed, women's rights advocates, antiabortion activists, proabortion activists, gays and lesbians, the Ku Klux Klan, civil rights supporters, and antiwar groups. But not farmers.

Rural America, sparsely settled, highly independent, and inherently patriotic, is unlikely ever to be able to *force* the country to pay attention. For its part, Congress prefers to address rural issues, including those that have little or nothing to do with farming, within the context of its omnibus five-year farm bills, and it has been reluctant to accept proposals by Senators Dorgan and Coleman, and others, that don't fit within the farm-bill framework. As John Allen, former director of the University of Nebraska's Center for Applied Rural Innovation, said on PBS's *Nightly Business Report*: "If you think about it, in the United States we've correlated rural policy and ag policy. We've basically taken public dollars and funneled those into agriculture with the idea that if ag did well, rural would do well. That hasn't been the case for some time."[9]

Federal farm policy can be divided into two distinct eras: before and after 1933. Farm legislation as we have come to know it—providing aid to farmers through price and income supports—began in earnest during the New Deal with the Agricultural Adjustment Act of 1933, although there had been some modest subsidies during World War I and in the

1920s. Prior to that time, the federal government's involvement in farmers' finances consisted primarily of monetary controls, with farmers supporting an inflationary "easy money" policy. Although the United States was originally an agrarian economy, the U.S. Department of Agriculture (USDA) was not even created until 1862 and did not achieve cabinet status until 1889. In its early years the USDA concentrated on agricultural research, creation of land-grant colleges to provide agricultural education, and establishing the USDA Extension Service.

The Great Depression, and the droughts and dust-bowl conditions that coincided with it, led to significant and long-lasting changes in the role of the federal government in agriculture and rural America. In 1936, the USDA began its involvement in soil conservation and rural electrification; in 1946, the Farmers Home Administration was created; in 1949, Congress made price supports permanent; and in 1970, rural development was included in the farm bill for the first time.

Farm bills do change from time to time and reflect political perceptions and—to some extent—political reality; a look at USDA programs over the years is a pretty good indicator of what is going on in society at large. In the 1960s, the USDA supported the broader "War on Poverty" bandwagon by creating the Food Stamp Program, and in later years it would address such issues as environmental controls, energy, food safety, and civil rights. The Department of Agriculture officially became the lead agency for conducting federal policy in rural development when Congress passed the Rural Development Act of 1972, which stated: "The Congress commits itself to a sound balance between rural and urban America. The Congress considers this balance so essential to the peace, prosperity, and welfare of all our citizens that the highest priority must be given to the revitalization and development of rural areas."[10] This was the first broad statement of such a government policy, perhaps reflecting the fact that the previous year saw the birth of the first rural policy lobbying organization that was not agriculture oriented: the 80-55 Coalition for Rural America. When President Carter signed the 1980 version of the Rural Development Act, he said, "Rural and small town America has suffered a heavy loss of population and seen a decline in the number of family farms. Today rural America is entering a new era of opportunity for growth and progress."[11] By 2006 the second goal of the USDA's five-point strategic plan had become "Support Increased Economic Opportunities and Improved Quality of Life in Rural America." Unfortunately, and despite the federal government's emphasis on rural development for the last forty years, growth and progress have been in short supply in small-town rural America, at least if it is measured in terms of population trends.

In 2006 the USDA's total budget was just under $95 billion, of which only 2 percent went for rural development. However, if rural development is measured as a part of what the USDA considers its *discretionary* budget of $20 billion, the share increases to about 10 percent. The big— and in many cases nondiscretionary—items in the USDA budget were, and are likely to remain, food and nutrition (58 percent), which includes food stamps and childhood nutrition programs, and the Farm Service Agency (30 percent), which handles loans and income-support payments to farmers.[12] Of course, federal dollars also find their way to rural America through other government departments, including Housing and Urban Development, Health and Human Services, the Department of Transportation, the Department of Education, and the Department of Commerce. In fact, a study of overall federal funding in 2000 by the Economic Research Service indicates that total federal spending in rural America may be as much as three times greater than USDA spending alone.[13]

The 2007 Farm Bill, as proposed by the USDA, has been called by some a "tweaking" of the prior bill, keeping expenditures for rural development and other programs over the next five years close to 2006 levels, although there are some significant increases in funding for biofuels— notably cellulosic ethanol—which may well benefit rural America. Specific rural programs in the 2007 bill include $1.6 billion in guaranteed loans to complete the rehabilitation of more than 1,200 rural Critical Access Hospitals and $500 million for rural infrastructure projects such as water, waste disposal, and telecommunications. The bill would also consolidate and coordinate various rural economic development programs, totaling perhaps $200 million annually, and created by other legislation. Such programs include Rural Business Opportunity Grants and Rural Economic Development Loans and Grants. The infrastructure funding in the 2007 Farm Bill is similar to some portions of Senator Coleman's Rural Renaissance Act, although the amounts proposed are smaller. While the 2007 bill did not adopt the approach of the New Homestead

Act of specifically trying to attract people to depopulating rural areas, it did propose a potentially important program to provide additional support for beginning farmers and ranchers, in recognition of both the high cost of farm land and capital equipment and the average age of the current generation of farmers.[14] The federal program would add substantially to several existing smaller-scale efforts to help new farmers that are offered through some of the land-grant universities and the Farm Beginnings program of the nonprofit Land Stewardship Project, which offers courses and mentoring programs.[15] The 2007 Farm Bill stalled late in the year due to differences between the House and Senate versions and differences among several farm state senators, including North Dakota's Conrad, Iowa's Tom Harkin, and Montana's Max Baucus, over issues including conservation, rural development, budgeting, and commodity support policy. The stalemate increased the likelihood that the 2007 bill would emerge with few major differences from the 2002 bill, and the possibility loomed that Congress might simply vote to extend some existing farm programs if a deal couldn't be struck before the end of the year.[16]

Almost all discussion of government policy for rural America centers on the federal government, partly because state policy is so diffused but also because, as Willie Sutton was supposed to have said when asked why he had chosen a career as a bank robber, "That's where the money is."

It is true that since the New Deal there has been an increasing flow of money and power from the state to the federal level. But much of the federal money allocated for rural America is managed and distributed by the states. Two states, Oregon and Kansas, have taken the first steps to try to address rural issues and manage rural programs in a comprehensive fashion rather than have rural policy conducted coincidentally by many different agencies and departments. In 2004 Governor Ted Kulongoski created the Oregon Office of Rural Policy to coordinate rural policy and act as liaison with the legislature. Three years later, in her 2007 State of the State address, Kansas Governor Kathleen Sebelius said, "There is no reason for the future of rural Kansas to be one of faded signs and empty storefronts. The challenges faced by these communities require cooperation between families, businesses, government and organizations that focus on rural areas. To spur this cooperation, I'm proposing the Office of Rural Opportunity." Sebelius asked the office to establish Rural Opportunity Zones to provide tax incentives to employers creating jobs, and she singled out two rural Kansas companies, Cobalt Boats in Neodesha and ABZ Valves and Controls in Madison, as businesses showing that "there's no reason the next global leader in technology, energy or biosciences can't be founded in rural Kansas."[17]

As of 2007, Kansas and Oregon were the only states to have started dedicated rural development offices independent of the existing governmental structure. Such initiatives may increase the visibility of rural communities, help them to establish their identities, and better enable them to have their needs considered in a broader context than simply as extensions of a state's agricultural policies.

14
Back to the Future: Sustainable Agriculture and Its Effect on Rural America

Much as the industrial revolution transformed manufacturing and cities, industrial farming and ranching has transformed agriculture and rural communities. Traditionally, and up until the mid-twentieth century, most agriculture was multidimensional. Farms were small and labor intensive and usually combined a variety of crops with a variety of animals. Indeed, because of their isolation, many farms were—and had to be—largely self-sustaining. But as industrial tools and inexpensive fossil fuels and chemicals entered the picture, things changed. Multidimensional traditional agriculture gave way to specialization and to one-dimensional agriculture. Integrated crop/livestock systems—a fancy name for traditional farms with a few crops and a few animals—have almost disappeared, notes Frederick Kirschenmann, former director of the Leopold Center for Sustainable Agriculture at Iowa State University.[1]

The U.S. Department of Agriculture (USDA) describes most agriculture today—often called "conventional" or "corporate" agriculture—as characterized by "large-scale farms, single crops/row crops grown continuously over many seasons; uniform high-yield hybrid crops; extensive use of pesticides, fertilizers, and external energy inputs; high labor efficiency; and dependency on agribusiness. In the case of livestock, most production comes from confined, concentrated systems."[2]

This kind of agriculture has some unfortunate ecological consequences, including pollution and depletion of water supplies, soil erosion and compaction, and the potential to accelerate the spread of disease (avian flu, mad cow disease, etc.). Concerns about the effects of conventional agriculture have led to strong interest in what has come to be called "sustainable agriculture," a term with no clearly agreed-upon definition.

In a general sense, and in terminology used by the USDA, sustainable agriculture involves such concepts as "a way of practicing agriculture which seeks to optimize skills and technology to achieve long term stability of the agricultural enterprise, environmental protection, and consumer safety," and "a whole-systems approach to [agricultural] production that balances environmental soundness, social equity, and economic viability," relies on minimal artificial inputs, both for nutrients and for managing pests and disease, and reduces the deterioration of the soil and the depletion of the resources needed for production.[3] There are, of course, those who prefer different definitions or who argue that the term is so vague as to be meaningless. In addition, the term "sustainable agriculture" is a loaded one since it carries with it the implication that present-day conventional agriculture is not sustainable. Perhaps the simplest, and most elegant, definition of sustainability is that coined by the World Commission on Environment and Development (the Brundtland Commission): *Meeting present needs without compromising the ability of future generations to meet their own.*[4] Much of the problem and confusion with the term lies in one's definition of the word "sustainable," for, as one author and professor of agronomy noted, "After all, who would knowingly advocate a 'non-sustainable' agriculture?"[5]

While the debate over sustainable agriculture is an interesting and important one, its importance to rural communities is uncertain. The impact of conventional agriculture on such communities, however, is clear. Whatever its other costs and problems, conventional agriculture has transformed both agricultural productivity and the rural communities that support it. Today, one farmer produces more than five farmers in 1940, and the number of farmers in the country has dropped almost 80 percent from 14 million in 1910, on the eve of the conventional agricultural revolution, to about 3 million. Likewise, the number of farms has plummeted, from over 6 million in 1910 to about 2 million today.[6]

These economic and social realities are behind the depopulation of rural communities that has been described at length in this book. By one estimate, when one farmer is forced to leave a community, there is an economic loss in the neighborhood of $720,000.[7] Many of the proponents of sustainable agriculture argue that one result of its adoption would be to strengthen rural economies and to "maintain stable rural communities and quality of life."[8] That may be true, particularly if sustainable agriculture takes the "natural systems" approach proposed by people like Wes Jackson, founder of the Land Institute, in which manual labor is likely to replace much of the mechanization of farming. But there is nothing inherent in the concept of sustainable agriculture to require a *major* increase in labor-intensive agricultural practices. Still, to the extent that sustainable agriculture connotes a movement to smaller farms, characterized by things such as crop rotation and free-range livestock, it probably will require more farmers than conventional agriculture, and that would represent a favorable development for rural communities.

While sustainable agriculture is just a tiny part of agriculture today, it is a robust and growing one. The USDA funds a program called Sustainable Agriculture Research and Education, which promotes sustainable agriculture in a variety of ways and publishes information about sustainable farming in books such as *The New American Farmer: Profiles in Agricultural Innovation*. The most recent edition profiles 62 farmers and ranchers who are practicing sustainable agriculture, from Exeter, Maine (potatoes, barley, corn, and rye) to Pleasant Grove, California (rice, popcorn, and almonds) and from Montague, Michigan (dairy products, alfalfa, corn, oats, and wheat) to the Virgin Islands (vegetables, tropical fruits, and herbs).[9]

Organizations such as Iowa State's Leopold Center are quietly, but effectively, helping farmers and ranchers improve the sustainability of their operations. The center provides a wide variety of services—primarily to Iowa farmers—in three broad areas: ecology, marketing, and public policy. Some of the center's recent projects include running a training program to teach small farmers about marketing and business planning, assessing the potential for new products such as goat meat and wines, helping producers of organic and grass-fed meats to develop effective marketing programs and learn how to deal with large food distributors like the SYSCO Corporation, and developing potatoes with greater natural resistance to potato beetles.

As the people at the Leopold Center have found, sustainable farming is being driven to a large extent by customer demand, and the challenge often is to educate farmers about how best to fulfill that demand. Most of the people profiled in the USDA's *New American Farmer* are able to sell all of the products they can raise in local or regional markets, and at good prices. Consumer awareness of issues relating to the food supply has increased significantly over the last decade or two, as reflected in USDA and Food and Drug Administration policies regarding such things as food content and labeling, the rapid growth of farmers markets, companies such as Whole Foods and the entry into the "natural" foods business of mainstream companies such as Safeway and Wal-Mart. Farmers and ranchers in rural America have noticed this trend and in many regions are organizing local co-ops and other marketing organizations to try to serve the growing demand for such food.

Wes Jackson: Native to This Place

Perhaps the most visionary approach to sustainable agriculture, and one that holds out great promise for rural communities, may be the kind that is being championed by people such as Wes Jackson. Jackson is the founder of the Land Institute, a leader in developing "natural systems agriculture" and also home to one of the intellectual and creative centers of rural America.

Of all the people looking at rural life, few are as close to it as Jackson. In 1976 he was a forty-year-old professor of environmental studies at California State University in Sacramento. He had received his B.A. in biology at Kansas Wesleyan University, an M.A. in botany from the University of Kansas, and a Ph.D. in genetics from North Carolina State. Having lived through the turbulent 1960s on college campuses, he had also become comfortable with radical ideas and unconventional thinking.

This mixture of biology, botany, genetics, and radicalism led Jackson to abandon traditional academia and move to the outskirts of Salina, Kansas, to start the Land Institute, a school and research facility dedicated to developing perennial food crops through natural systems agriculture, which is a version of "sustainable agriculture," a term which Jackson feels has been overused and is nearly meaningless.

In an agricultural world dominated by high-yielding, resource-intensive annual crops, the Land Institute is seeking answers to some basic questions: Can perennial crops produce commercially adequate yields? Can a viable agricultural system be based largely on mimicking the native prairie? Can such systems be self-sustainable in terms of fertility and pest and disease control? The answers to these questions are still unclear, but in more than the three decades following the founding of the Land Institute, Jackson has earned a worldwide reputation as one of the most important and innovative thinkers of the era, becoming a Pew Conservation Scholar and a MacArthur Fellow. He has been named one of thirty-five "Innovators of Our Time" by *Smithsonian Magazine,* joining people such as Bill Gates, Yo-Yo Ma, Robert Moses, Richard Leakey, and Steven Spielberg.[10]

Jackson walked away from a promising and secure career to start an initiative that he almost certainly will never see reach a commercial, or even practical, stage. He once told an interviewer, "If you're workin' on something that you can finish in your lifetime, you're not thinkin' big enough!"[11] Jackson's dream of creating a fundamental change in agriculture would seem to be big enough: developing natural systems agriculture turns out to be an undertaking in which progress and results are measured in decades. "It's like watching paint dry," Jackson remarked as he walked through one of the institute's greenhouse laboratories. Actually, it's a lot worse than watching paint dry. Now over thirty years into its existence, Jackson expects it may be another fifty years before seeds are created that are "farmer ready" and that accomplish the goal of being able to provide bountiful food from perennial crops using naturally available water, soils, and fertilizer.[12]

The belief of Jackson and others in the value of perennial food crops is gaining some support within the broader agricultural community, including the USDA, which has a Sustainable Perennial Crops Laboratory, and in academia. "Given the challenges that will likely face us as a result of climate change, putting more perennials on many parts of our agricultural landscapes will become mandatory if we are to hold soils and nutrients in place," said the head of Iowa State's Leopold Center.[13] Research into sustainable agriculture and perennial food crops, however, remains a minuscule part of the money being spent on research to develop new seed products for conventional farming. The annual budgets for the Land Institute and the Leopold Center together are about $4 million, or less than 1 percent of the $500 million Monsanto spends on seed research alone. Interestingly, one new source of funds for both the Land Institute and the Leopold Center is the fast-growing Chipotle Mexican Grill restaurant chain, which uses ingredients that are "sustainably grown and naturally raised" whenever possible.[14] Even at the USDA, the main focus of its sustainable agriculture efforts is not on developing perennial food crops but on research such as "Molecular Characterization and Diversity Assessment of Cocoa Germplasm in the Americas." A team at the University of Minnesota working on perennial sunflowers and flax, and Steve Jones at Washington State University, who has been trying to develop perennial winter wheat, face ongoing funding uncertainties.[15]

That leaves the Land Institute, itself facing continual fund-raising requirements, as the center of such research. Actually, the institute has two products. The first is seed varieties that meet its criteria and that only can be developed slowly by, for example, crossing shallow-rooted annual plants such as wheat and sunflowers with deep-rooted, perennial wild legume and grass species such as bluestem grasses that can produce roots 8 feet deep. The second product of the institute is people, including graduates from its fellowship program who carry on the institute's work in other places.

If Jackson's dream ever becomes reality, the future will see polycultural perennial agriculture replacing, or more likely supplementing, conventional monocultural annual agriculture. The world will see crops that do not deplete natural soil nutrients, do not consume the dwindling supplies of water and oil as rapidly as conventional agriculture, and— since the crops won't require much, if any, cultivating—don't destroy the topsoil. The benefits of reducing or eliminating cultivating alone would justify developing perennial crops, as erosion is a major environmental problem. It is estimated that 2 billion tons of topsoil are lost through erosion in the United States each year, pouring chemical residue and dirt into rivers, streams, and reservoirs throughout the country and costing $40 billion to try to control it.[16]

But it is a race against time. Jackson believes conventional agriculture already is running on borrowed time and dwindling resources. He estimates that at least 80 percent of all the identified fossil fuel reserves have been used up in his lifetime—a lot of it supporting conventional agriculture. Although no one knows how much oil exists, even the oil companies recognize that cost-effective oil production has limits, and demand is increasing faster than new supply. As Chevron put it in one of a remarkably frank series of ads, "It took us 125 years to use the first trillion barrels of oil—We'll use the next trillion in 30."[17] And the demands on fossil fuels are only increasing, perhaps doubling over the next half-century, again according to Chevron. Even many of the fossil fuel alternatives are not "free lunches." Hydrogen production requires an energy source, commonly natural gas, but perhaps some day nuclear power. And ethanol is not created in a fossil-fuel-free process. It requires oil products for fertilizing, harvesting, and processing and heat—usually from coal or natural gas—for converting the crops to fuel. In short, ethanol production may not significantly reduce the use of fossil fuels.[18] Water—also needed for ethanol and hydrogen production—is getting scarce in many farming areas including the Great Plains states, and much of the water in sources such as the huge Ogallala Aquifer is already gone.[19]

What happens when these resources run out—or more likely become prohibitively expensive—before there is something there to replace them? What happens if the world's fossil-fuel-based agricultural system has no practical access to fossil fuels? What happens, in short, if something like perennial crop agriculture doesn't arrive in time? "Social upheaval!" Jackson says, adding, sadly, that even if natural systems agriculture works as he hopes, it may have "only a slight impact" on the situation. In Jackson's view, the world has been on an "energy binge," primarily based on substances created millions and billions of years ago, for most of the last two centuries. Yet most of the world views it not as a binge, or "a blip in human history" in Jackson's words, but as part of a natural and normal gift from nature to us.[20]

The quest for sustainable agriculture may have only a modest impact on rural population, although if the kind of agriculture favored by the Land Institute ever becomes reality, it *will* be likely to have an impact because it is more labor intensive than conventional agriculture. While repopulating rural America is not the motivation behind the Land Institute, or other sustainable agriculture efforts, Jackson and others are far from oblivious to the decline and depopulation of rural communities and the impact conventional agriculture has had.

But Jackson sees something a lot more fundamental, and a little more sinister, than simply the inexorable march of progress brought on by mechanization and the availability of fossil fuels. The subject excites his interest, taking him beyond his job as a researcher and into another of his roles, as a philosopher and historian. Citing Wendell Berry's *The Unsettling of America: Culture and Agriculture*,[21] Jackson views European conquest and settlement of America as turning Native Americans into "redskins." And "from the moment these natives became 'redskins' they became surplus people. . . . We established a precedent [and] in due time the descendants of [European] settlers also became surplus people—the new redskins, so to speak. The old farm families were removed and their rural communities destroyed as the industrial revolution infiltrated agriculture."[22] As a result, Jackson believes, neither the new nor the original "redskins" were able to show us how "to live harmoniously on the land. . . . They never really had a chance. They were moved too abruptly off the farm, out of small towns, into the cities."[23] Jackson sees the turning point occurring around 1880—the point of no return for being able to realize "a kind of pastoral commons on the Great Plains."[24]

Settlement was massive and unstoppable, and by 1900 nearly every quarter section was occupied. Land that had been unbroken since the glaciers began retreating 20,000 years ago was being fenced, plowed, and—often—irrigated. The previous farming economy was being replaced by a new one and a way of life that, whatever else one might say of it, increasingly was characterized by "alienation from nature."[25] Indeed, it was for many people an acknowledged part of the hubris of the industrial agricultural revolution that nature was now something to be conquered, not accommodated.

If, as Jackson contends, the inevitable decline of rural communities was set in motion by 1900, the movement didn't reach its peak until the 1940s:

> The "get big or get out" era following World War II was likely the consequence as much of the introduction of fossil fuel subsidies into the agricultural system as of economics. . . . In other words, farm policy originating in Washington may have been less responsible for the reduction in rural life than the disruption due to the fossil fuel subsidy. . . . In energy language, systems powered by contemporary sunlight [horses, mules, people] could not compete with systems powered by anciently stored energy [tractors, combines].[26]

Although Jackson believes it would be desirable "to repopulate much of the countryside and most of the rural communities," he isn't an advocate of doing so at any cost. "Locals and most rural sociologists alike believe the answer lies in jobs, any jobs so long as they don't pollute too much, . . . Rural America does not need jobs that depend on the extractive economy. We need a way to arrest consumerism. We need a different form of accounting so that both sufficiency and efficiency have standing in our minds."[27]

Jackson tries to avoid being seen as a nostalgic romanticist or a technological troglodyte (although he does confess to the belief that the airplane was "a bad idea," an opinion that many harried, cramped, and fearful travelers in the twenty-first century may share). Indeed, far from trying to recreate the nineteenth century, Jackson says that "if there is any lesson from what we understand about the nature of the universe . . . change is the rule . . . and though we may give tribute to a time past by something like the restoration of the likeness of Colonial Williamsburg, Williamsburg is as extinct as the dinosaurs [and] the restoration is like plaster over the bones of a museum dinosaur."[28]

"When we think about the revitalization of small towns and rural communities worldwide," Jackson says, "rather than insisting that we go back I am instead insisting that we be careful as we go forward to avoid several impulses" including the temptation to "gentrify the small places . . . and replace every piece of picket fence that existed a hundred years ago," or to try to create an ecologically sound future for such communities based on an extractive and unsustainable economy, whether it be oil and gas wells, energy-dependent crops, or—the new religion—energy-dependent biofuels such as ethanol. Rather, Jackson maintains, what is needed is a commitment simply to "provide the context for community to happen and live in ways that will keep it healthy," which, essentially, means to Jackson the need to adhere to a nature-based, ecologically sound agenda.[29]

In a world short on fossil fuels or any viable replacement for them, Jackson foresees the possibility—indeed, the necessity—of "resettling the countryside": "To gather dispersed sunlight in the form of chemical energy [i.e., food] in a fossil-free world will require a sufficiency of people spread across our broad landscape."[30] If Jackson is right, rural communities throughout the world would need to fill up again just to feed the 6.5 billion people alive today, much less the 10 billion or so that are expected by the year 2050.

Jackson tries to avoid being labeled as one who is antiprogress or who lives in the past. He espouses the inevitability and benefits of change and even suggests that the sun-powered future will be improved by "modern technological equipment."[31] Yet his vision of agriculture in a fossil-fuel-free world can look a bit like a movie being played backward. It is difficult not to imagine cars, trains, and planes reversing their paths and emptying millions of people back into rural communities where, once again, it will require five or more sun-powered people to do the work of one fossil-fuel-powered farmer.

There is one area in which Jackson most definitely sees the need for change if rural communities are to regain their vitality: education. Jackson believes universities have—perhaps unwittingly—contributed to rural decline and depopulation. "The universities now offer only one serious major: upward mobility. Little attention is paid to educating the young to return home and contribute to their communities. There is no such thing as a 'homecoming' major," by which Jackson means "home" in at least two contexts: the rural communities from which many people come—and to which most never return, and home as "a coherent community that is in turn embedded in the ecological realities of its surrounding landscape." "We educate kids to take tests," Jackson says, but "teachers don't even know how to talk about community responsibility."[32] In a general sense Jackson is probably correct. Most colleges devote little time to such issues. But there are some exceptions, including Iowa State University, which has a broad-based rural and agricultural agenda in addition to housing the Leopold Center. In Kansas, the state's land-grant school, Kansas State University, offers dozens of undergraduate and graduate programs in agriculture, veterinary science, and rural issues. Even the University of Kansas, which has a decidedly more urban orientation, is getting in the act. Since 1997 it has been taking faculty members on a popular "Wheat State Whirlwind Tour" of rural Kansas every May, including such towns as Palco, Lucas, and Cottonwood Falls.[33]

Still, Jackson may have a point, even when it comes to the land-grant schools. His concerns are echoed by the Center for Rural Affairs in Nebraska, which believes the land-grant schools have devoted too much time and money to courses and research that benefits large-scale conventional agriculture at the expense of family farming and that the universities' extension services should be doing more for rural economic development.[34]

A similar perspective was the subject of author Jacqueline Edmondson's study of Prairie Town, Minnesota. The citizens of Prairie Town were concerned that so many of their children moved away permanently after high school, and some of them came to the conclusion that their school was—like the colleges that Wes Jackson criticized—putting too much emphasis on "upward mobility" and encouraging students to leave the area "because it inculcated them with urban values and goals."[35] This led to an effort to alter the curriculum and begin looking for what Edmondson called "a new rural literacy" and a new cultural model for rural life that included education about the community and "some long-standing traditional values" that people felt were being lost.[36]

Jackson's own belief in the value of community—and the smaller the community the better—underlies his suspicion and distrust of grand plans and grand planners. "Although we have told one another on bumper stickers and at environmental conferences that we must 'think globally and act locally,' we introduce new terms such as 'sustainable' to apply to any perceived solution that catches our fancy. Instead of looking to community, we look to public policy. We hold a global conference in Rio."[37] One of the things that makes it difficult, if not impossible, to apply any "movement" label to Jackson is his stubborn habit of adhering uncompromisingly to his beliefs and his scorn for what he sees as halfway measures and ultimately unworkable compromises. His disdain includes events such as "Earth Summits," beginning with the United Nations Rio conference in 1992, which are so dear to the ranks of environmental activists. Jackson dismisses such conferences as essentially a waste of time, particularly their focus on "sustainable development," which Jackson calls "almost a contradiction in terms."[38]

Jackson parts company with mainstream environmentalists in other areas as well. He rejects the value of such "feel-good" developments ("Mother Teresa's" in Jackson's terms) as the ethanol craze and hybrid cars. They are, he feels, not only just Band-Aids but actually even worse because they lull people into thinking that solutions for things such as energy shortages are just around the corner, and well within our technological capabilities. "Things like the [hybrid Toyota] Prius fall under the Jevons' Paradox," Jackson says, referring to a theory advanced by the Victorian English economist William Stanley Jevons, who in 1865 wrote *The Coal Question*, about the fact that England was thought to be running out of coal. Although such concerns were premature, and England's coal decline didn't occur until the 1930s, Jevons introduced the theory that bears his name and that surprised him, hence the "paradox." It states that as technology improves the efficiency of using a given resource, the result is likely to be that overall consumption of the resource will increase, not decrease, and that in any event consumption is more likely to be influenced by other economic considerations than by the efficiency with which the product is consumed.[39]

Jackson also decries the effects of what he calls "fundamentalism" in agriculture. Not religious fundamentalism, but technological fundamentalism: the unholy trinity of government, business, and academic researchers operating through such entities as the USDA, companies like Cargill, Archer Daniels Midland, and Monsanto, and the land-grant universities. Sometimes what he seems to be targeting is capitalism, although a better term might be "unenlightened," or corporate capitalism, yet he also has little regard for communism, dismissing the former Soviet Union as just an example of "state capitalism." In fact, Jackson doesn't appear to give much thought to rival economic systems, other than the extent to which they *all* have produced something he does regard as an evil: conventional agriculture.

It is easy to dismiss Jackson as a dreamer or an idealist, yet it is difficult for anyone to dismiss the value, and potential benefits, of sustainable agriculture in general and the appeal of Jackson's natural systems agriculture in particular. Even if the odds are that Jackson is wrong, it cannot be ignored that if he is right the potential exists for widespread upheaval and unrest on a scale unknown in history. Many of Jackson's critics, and those with great faith in technology, might argue that he is unrealistically pessimistic. The Energy Future Coalition, a high-power establishment group with such heavyweights as billionaire businessmen Richard Branson and Ted Turner, former White House chief of staff John Podesta (for President Bill Clinton), and former Senate Majority Leader Tom Daschle on the steering committee, are urging the United States to "lead the way in the development and distribution of new energy technologies." The coalition takes a positive, hopeful view, saying "innovation is what America does best, and the creation and implementation of new technologies, such as the Smart Grid, advanced automobiles, and biofuels, will stimulate economic growth. In the process of bringing these new energy technologies to market, millions of jobs will be created."[40] Jim Woolsey, director of the Central Intelligence Agency during the Clinton administration and also on the advisory council of the Energy Future Coalition, predicts that already available technologies can soon result in cars getting from 100 to 500 miles per gallon.[41] And even if fossil fuels are exhausted someday, technological optimists point to other sources of energy: nuclear, hydrogen, sunlight, wind, and tides, to name but a few.

Unfortunately, there are gaps—unknowns—in the plans for potential fossil fuel replacements, such that either individually or taken together there is not yet a clear path from our present energy economy to a future one. It brings to mind a wonderful old cartoon that showed two scientists standing before a blackboard with complex equations on the left and right, connected in the middle by the words "THEN A MIRACLE OCCURS." One of the scientists is pointing to those words and saying to the other, "I think you should be more explicit here in step two."[42] So it is with all the "new" energy sources. They all have potential, they all have merit, but before they can replace fossil fuels at a reasonable cost and risk they all need to bridge those nagging gaps a little more explicitly. If they can't, and if no miracle occurs, Jackson's thesis suddenly becomes much more relevant.

But if those gaps are bridged, and if a new energy economy does emerge, it is likely that even as Jackson concedes the point, he will make two points in return. First, a practical one: that just because a new energy source bailed us out this time does not mean that such will always be the case. And second, a philosophical one, that, even if inexhaustible, inexpensive, abundant, and nonpolluting energy sources *were* forthcoming, people would still be better off morally, mentally, and spiritually, and would enjoy a more fulfilled and meaningful life, if they lived in a manner that was "native to this place" or, as Aldo Leopold put it, in "a state of harmony between man and the land."[43] And, of course, he might add that if one of the resources running out happens to be water, as is the case in many farming regions, there may be no practical solution on the horizon short of developing the kinds of broad-rooted, deep-rooted, drought-resistant perennials that are being studied at the Land Institute.

Sustainable Livestock

The industrial revolution in farming has had its counterpart in raising livestock, and it has also produced some controversial results.[44]

In many ways, of course, the two agricultural disciplines are linked. Massive feedlots for cattle, and similar facilities for hogs and poultry, became possible when farm productivity produced an abundance of corn and other grains to feed livestock in closely controlled environments. The cornucopia for livestock may become less bountiful, and more expensive, because of the increasing demand for grains for use in ethanol production. As of 2007 there were more than 114 ethanol plants operating in the United States, with 80 more under construction. In Kansas and Nebraska alone there were 19 plants producing 790 million gallons of ethanol a year, and at least 20 plants under construction and expected to add well over a billion gallons annually.[45] Ethanol's appetite for corn has created the biggest bull market for the grain since the 1970s, and in 2007 ethanol production consumed about 20 percent of the nation's annual corn crop. It has been estimated that to eliminate the need for imports from the Middle East it would be necessary to produce 50 billion gallons of ethanol annually—which would require that half the country's usable farmland would need to be devoted to corn, resulting in significant and politically unpopular increases in food prices.[46]

For a variety of reasons, corn is likely to remain the primary source of food and livestock feed, not biofuels, for the foreseeable future. First, farmers can increase their yields somewhat and curtail sales to other countries. Second, it is possible that other grains and raw materials, including corn stalks and grasses, can be used to produce ethanol. And finally, inherent in the corn-to-ethanol process itself is the production of a by-product called DDGS (corn distillers dried grains with solubles), which in effect recycles about a third of the corn used in making ethanol and is a good nutrient for feedlot cattle and perhaps for other livestock.[47]

Commercial poultry farming is a relatively recent development, dating to the early 1900s.[48] Well into the 1930s, most chickens were raised on family farms, primarily for their eggs, and their meat was considered something of a treat—hence the rural tradition of Sunday chicken dinners. Mechanized feeding, selective breeding, and factory farms with tens of thousands of chickens raised indoors changed all that, and the per capita consumption of chicken meat increased at least ten times between the 1940s and today. One result of the industrialization of the poultry business is that such traditional breeds as Rhode Island Reds and White Leghorns have been replaced with more efficient birds with less euphonious names, such as K-27's. The genetically engineered hens can lay about an egg a day for about a year, in close confinement, after which they're likely to be "picked up, slammed into a large truck, and delivered for Campbell's soups."[49]

Likewise with hogs. There was a time when most family farms had a hog pen and raised a few hogs primarily for their own consumption. Today, hog producers typically have from 2,000 to tens of thousands of animals on hand at any one time, usually in close confinement. According to Farm Sanctuary, an organization that monitors living conditions for livestock, the USDA now defines a "small" hog operation as one having fewer than 5,000 animals.[50]

Industrial livestock has cut both ways in rural communities. Large feedlots and slaughterhouses were once a part of the urban landscape in cities such as Chicago, Kansas City, and Denver. Environmental and aesthetic concerns, along with labor issues, led to their dispersal throughout the country, particularly to the rural areas of Iowa, Kansas, Nebraska, and Colorado.[51] Large feedlots—some capable of feeding as many as 70,000 cattle each—have generated jobs for many workers in rural communities. Liberal, Kansas, for example, has grown from about 400 people in 1900 to almost 20,000 today, and much of the growth can be attributed to its three large feedlots and the National Beef Packing plant, which slaughters and processes cattle.[52]

The creation of jobs on the livestock processing end have been offset by job losses in ranching, where industrial practices have had the same effect as on farming: productivity has increased on the ranches themselves, and much of the labor associated with raising cattle has shifted from pastures to feedlots. As with farms, the result has been larger ranches employing fewer workers per acre.

Yet as is the case with sustainable farming, sustainable ranching is growing rapidly—in part because of consumer demand for natural meat products, including beef from cattle that have spent all or most of their lives grazing on renewable grasslands rather than consuming chemical-laced grains produced by conventional monocultural farms or feedlots. Sustainable ranching practices focus on such things as controlled grazing, low-stress livestock handling, matching animals to the environmental conditions of the land, controlling livestock waste, and using biological controls to minimize disease.[53] Sustainable cattle ranching, which relies primarily on grassland grazing as opposed to corn feeding, may also get a boost from the increase in corn prices as a result of the growth of the ethanol industry.

Sustainable ranching may not create as many total jobs in rural America as quickly as the massive feedlots and slaughterhouses have done, but there is evidence that the jobs it does create—or saves—may be more beneficial to rural communities in the long run. According to the Corporation for the Northern Rockies, "The economic benefits common with sustainable management also help producers keep their land in production instead of selling parcels to developers. This not only helps family ranchers stay in business, it also maintains the economic diversity of rural communities and important public benefits such as open space."[54] The University of California's Sustainable Agriculture research program believes that "rural communities in California are currently characterized by economic and environmental deterioration. Many are among the poorest locations in the nation. The reasons for the decline are complex, but changes in farm structure have played a significant role. Sustainable agriculture presents an opportunity to rethink the importance of family farms and rural communities. Economic development policies are needed that encourage more diversified agricultural production on family farms as a foundation for healthy economies in rural communities."[55]

In 1986 a rancher in Texas, Joe Maddox, converted his traditional ranch near Colorado City to a version of sustainable ranching called holistic resource management, developed by Allen Savory, an animal biologist, in 1984. Holistic resource management combines elements such as planned grazing and the need to balance the needs of the herds and the land with the goal of increasing both the productivity and profitability of the business.[56]

By the 1990s the Maddox ranch that had been economically burdensome and personally unrewarding using conventional ranching techniques had become "resoundingly successful economically as well as environmentally." More important for rural America, the sustainable techniques employed on the Maddox ranch not only have enabled it to survive and prosper but to provide more jobs. "The ranch has become more labor intensive for us to manage," Joe Maddox says, "but less so in terms of livestock care."[57] The ranch that had barely supported four people and two families in 1986 using conventional ranching practices ended up supporting fourteen people and five families using sustainable techniques.[58]

There are actually many such success stories in rural America. Dick and Sharon Thompson have been running a 300-acre sustainable, traditional farm in Boone County, Iowa, since 1968. They use ridge tilling (planting on the ridges formed by past cultivation, which minimizes disturbing the soil), a crop-rotation plan of corn, soybeans, oats, and rye, and fertilizing with manure from their animals and biosolids from a nearby wastewater treatment plant. These methods have enabled them to double the amount of organic matter in their soil, cut soil loss in half, and achieve enviable net income per acre. The small farm easily supports two families, without requiring anyone to work off the farm and without receiving any government subsidies. By contrast, in an average year federal payments make up as much as half the operating income of conventional corn farmers in places such as Iowa and Minnesota, a situation that may change if corn prices continue to rise thanks to ethanol and export demand.[59] The Thompson farm also raises livestock, usually about seventy-five head of cattle and seventy-five hogs, which are considered "natural" and command high prices. It has been estimated that as many as 9,000 people have visited the Thompson farm, including other farmers who are seeking advice on moving to a more sustainable model.[60]

A little bigger, and a lot better known, is the Salatin family's Polyface Farm in western Virginia. The 800-acre farm has been in business since 1961, sustainably producing many products, including beef, chicken, rabbit, pork, and turkeys. All the animals are pasture raised, and the Salatins have developed an effective, but labor-intensive, system of moving them every day or two to fresh pastures. The reputation of Polyface Farms is so good that everything the farm can produce is quickly sold to their several thousand individual customers and some thirty restaurants in the area, including the Equinox in Washington, just across Lafayette Park from the White House. Joel Salatin, representing the third generation of Salatins at the farm, is also a tireless evangelist for natural and sustainable agriculture. He travels the world lecturing, has written several books including *You Can Farm* and *Holy Cows and Hog Heaven*, and he and Polyface Farm were featured in Michael Pollan's best-selling 2006 book *The Omnivore's Dilemma*.[61]

Sustainable agriculture appears to have the potential to be a net benefit to rural communities in many ways. First, it seems likely to be capable of increasing both the quantity and quality of rural jobs. Many conventional farms require only a few months of actual labor a year, much of it fairly specialized, mechanized, and repetitive. On traditional and sustainable farms such as Joel Salatin's, farming is pretty much a year-round, sunup-to-sunset job, often requiring some ingenuity and creativity. Second, there is evidence that sustainable agriculture may increase agricultural profitability, bringing more money into rural communities. And finally, it seems likely to increase the environmental and ecological health, and the attractiveness, of rural communities. An example of some of these ancillary benefits occurred on Joe Maddox's ranch. After he introduced sustainable practices on his property, some long-dry springs began to flow again, the environment became more lush, and the deer population increased enough to enable him to earn "substantial added income" from hunting fees and guided hunts during deer season.[62]

15
Ethanol and Alternative Energy: Rural America's Saviors?

The word "ethanol" appears at least fifty times in this book. Had it been written just a few years ago, it is unlikely that ethanol, or any other connection between alternative energy and rural America, would have been given much attention. Yet by 2006 ethanol was well on its way to becoming the buzzword of the decade, symbolizing a worldwide "green" fuels trend, and the U.S. ethanol industry was said to be the fastest-growing energy industry in the world, having increased production from 1.3 billion gallons in 1997 to over 5 billion gallons in 2006 and a forecast of over 11 billion by 2008.[1]

The ethanol phenomenon is a remarkable one and is being promoted by an impressive coalition that includes President George W. Bush and a bipartisan congress (led by "ethanolics" from Midwestern farm country).[2] Also pushing ethanol are companies such as Archer Daniels Midland and Monsanto, and 25×'25, a coalition for renewable energy that wants alternative fuels to account for 25 percent of energy use by the year 2025 and includes such strange bedfellows as the National Wildlife Federation and General Motors.[3] There is even a biofuels mascot: Corn Cob Bob (of the Canadian Renewable Fuels Association). Bill Gates is investing in alternative energy, and former Microsoft executive Martin Tobias heads Imperium Renewables, a new West Coast biodiesel provider. Venture capital investment in alternative energy companies almost doubled from $1.5 billion in 2005 to $2.9 billion in 2006. Silicon Valley's Kleiner-Perkins, one of the most prominent technology venture capital firms has hired environmental activist Al Gore and shifted its focus to "green energy" opportunities, including biofuels, which it thinks could be even bigger than computer technology and the Internet—yesterday's buzzwords.[4]

It may surprise most people, but neither ethanol—nor its potential role as a savior of rural America—is anything new. Ethanol is, simply, alcohol (grain alcohol, ethyl alcohol, ETOH) made by fermenting and distilling almost any growing biomass high in carbohydrates—from corn and potatoes to sugarcane, pasture grasses, and even trees. The history of ethanol's use is as old as man—older, perhaps: chimpanzees, for example, eat rotting fruit, apparently to get at the fermenting juice therein. Ethanol can substitute for gasoline, although it is less efficient, producing about one-third less energy than gasoline.

So-called "flex fuel" vehicles are being introduced to run on either gasoline or ethanol, yet that idea, too, is over a century old. Henry Ford's first car, in 1896, was designed to run on ethanol, and some of the early Ford Model T's could be adjusted to run on either gasoline or ethanol.

The first rural ethanol boom occurred in the 1930s, when thousands of Midwestern gas stations sold "gasohol," a blend of ethanol and gasoline. World War II put an end to much of the use of ethanol and gasoline for personal use as the fuels were allocated to the war effort, and following the war cheap oil pretty much drove gasohol from the market. The second ethanol boom began in the mid-1970s, when ethanol began to replace lead as an octane booster in gasoline. Helped by high oil prices, and government grants and subsidies, gasohol reappeared by 1979. The number of ethanol plants jumped from 10 in 1980 to 163 in 1984, but then oil prices dropped again, and the demand for ethanol slowed. By the late 1980s the overcapacity in the ethanol industry forced many plants to close. Government subsidies helped to keep the ethanol industry alive, as did concerns about pollution, and ethanol production grew moderately in the 1990s, primarily as a result of its use as an oxygenate to reduce carbon monoxide emissions.

By 2006, sharply rising oil prices, coupled with concerns about the reliability of some of the sources providing approximately 60 percent of the United States' oil needs (notably the Middle East and Venezuela), had resulted in a rush to ethanol. In his 2007 State of the Union speech, President Bush called for significant reductions in the country's use of oil-based gasoline—most of which comes from foreign sources.[5] The reduction would be accomplished by a combination of increasing the fuel efficiency of vehicles and greatly expanding the production of alternative fuels, primarily ethanol. The Bush proposals would require production of as much as 35 billion gallons of such fuels by 2017, an increase of 600 percent from 2006.[6]

Aware, perhaps, of concerns about the skyrocketing price of corn, the Bush plan estimates that *only* 15 billion gallons of the 2017 requirement need come from corn, with the balance from a yet-to-be-finalized commercial production process for cellulosic ethanol, a process that proponents believe can turn plentiful, native, perennial plants, which contain cellulose—switchgrass, for example—into ethanol. Estimates for when a commercially viable process will be developed to transform cellulosic materials into fuel range from a couple of years to more than a decade. Vinod Khosla, a cofounder of Sun Microsystems and now a venture capital investor in biofuels, believes cellulosic fuels will cost $1.25 a gallon or less by 2010.[7] But in fact, no one knows, and no one will know until the production process is perfected and the cost of the conversion process is known. Most people expect that the switchgrass conversion process will be more expensive than the corn conversion process, but any additional expense may well be more than offset by the significantly lower cost of the switchgrass itself. Similar developments are under way in India where attention is focused on jatropha, a heretofore largely ignored wild-growing, weedlike shrub that happens to have seeds that jatropha proponents feel have the potential "to save humanity" if they can be economically converted into biodiesel. [8]

The appeal of switchgrass is strong. It is a common North American prairie grass, and some type of switchgrass grows natively in most states. It does particularly well in the Midwest. Switchgrass is something that few had ever heard of until the latest ethanol boom, but it is becoming a rival with ethanol itself as the buzzword for the decade. Its Latin name, *Panicum virgatum,* sounds appropriate for a plant that finds itself in the midst of a near-panic to find ways to transform switchgrass into fuel.

If the switchgrass laboratory efforts don't produce the desired solutions, or don't produce them soon enough, the results could be dramatic. If most of the country's ethanol has to come from corn, the price of the commodity—on which so much food, including livestock, depends—might rise so high that "soaring food prices could cause urban riots in scores of low-income countries that rely on grain imports," including Nigeria, Mexico, and Indonesia, according to Lester Brown, founder and president of the Earth Policy Institute.[9] Brown's prediction came true much earlier than he had anticipated when tens of thousands of Mexicans took to the streets in early 2007 to protest the high cost of corn tortillas and demanded that Mexico "end its dependence on imports of American corn." Mexico imports about a fourth of its corn from the United States, and "most analysts agree that the main cause of the increase has been a spike in corn prices in the United States, as the demand for corn to produce ethanol has jumped."[10] The ramifications of high corn prices also began to be felt domestically by 2007 as Coca-Cola Enterprises, the largest bottler of Coca-Cola soft drinks, announced it was cutting 3,500 jobs because of rising prices for commodities, including corn syrup. "There has been a fundamental change in the sweetener market driven by corn, ultimately driven by the corn used in ethanol," said the company's chief financial officer.[11] High corn prices have also contributed to higher land prices, and in some corn-producing areas of Illinois, Nebraska, Iowa, and Indiana, prices almost doubled from 2005 to 2007.[12]

For rural America, and particularly the grain-producing areas of rural America, the alternative fuels policy debate is overshadowed by the fact that an alternative fuels energy boom already is in full swing and that rural America is reaping the harvest in terms of new plants, jobs, and higher commodity prices. Even switchgrass—should that ever materialize as a fuel source—will benefit rural America because the plant is found predominantly in rural areas.

The race to develop cellulosic and other forms of ethanol from substances other than corn is already looking like something of an economic bonanza for rural America. In 2007 the U.S. Department of Energy announced plans to pump hundreds of millions of dollars into at least six developmental production facilities. Although one of the plants—to make ethanol out of "selected garbage"—will be in the small city of Corona, California, the other five will be squarely in rural America. Emmetsburg, Iowa (population 3,958), will get a plant to convert corn cobs and corn stalks; Hugoton, Kansas (population 3,708), corn stalks and wheat straw; LaBelle, Florida (population 3,400), orange peels and wood waste; Shelly, Idaho (population 3,813), wheat and barley straw; and Soperton, Georgia (population 2,824), will get a plant to turn a variety of forest wastes into ethanol.[13] As *New York Times* reporter

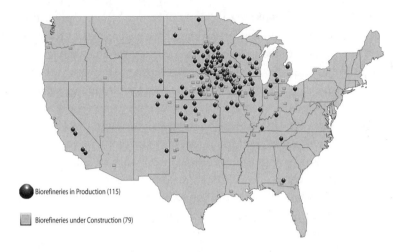

Biorefineries in Production (115)

Biorefineries under Construction (79)

Figure 5. Ethanol Biorefinery Locations
Source: Renewable Fuels Association, 2007.

Timothy Egan found when he traveled through rural America in early 2007, "in barren counties with shuttered stores on Main Street, people see a renaissance. They see a biorefinery every 50 miles or so, turning out American fuel for American drivers from American crops. And, once the technology moves from corn to cellulose they see the essential stuffing of the scarecrow from *The Wizard of Oz* providing a sustainable economy that also offers some answers for global warming."[14] The enthusiasm of the rural ethanol forces was summed up by Read Smith, a farmer in eastern Washington, who said, "We're going to revitalize rural America, we're going to pull the plywood off the windows. We're going to create a $700 billion per year industry that is not here today."[15]

Smith is certainly not alone. The ethanol boom is contributing to a widespread feeling that it may be the salvation of much of rural America, and indeed of corn-growing regions from Canada to Argentina. "Energy Bill Brings Prosperity to Rural America" was the headline of a 2006 press release from the U.S. Senate Committee on Energy and Natural Resources, patting itself on the back for the Energy Policy Act of 2005 and saying, "We can already see a remarkable revitalization of rural America."[16] The headline on a 2007 Associated Press story said: "Latin Corn Farmers See Gold in Ethanol," the *Denver Post* reported in the spring of

2007 that Colorado farmers were planting their largest corn crop since the 1930s, and a *Wall Street Journal* front-page headline proclaimed: "Energy Boom Lifts Small-Town Hope on Northern Plains," and added "Population Skid on Hold."[17]

The *Wall Street Journal* story describes Washburn, a town of 1,250 in central North Dakota, where the mayor, Al Christianson, proclaimed, "We've got the best future we've ever had."[18] A new ethanol plant brought 400 construction jobs and 40 permanent jobs to Washburn, and other small towns across the state are hoping to duplicate what's happening in Washburn. They may have good reason to hope. North Dakota—which has significant oil and coal deposits—is at the center of a great deal of energy activity, including five new ethanol plants, three biodiesel plants, five wind farms, and planning for possible coal-to-liquid fuels projects.

The question for Washburn, and similar towns, is how many of those workers can be enticed to stay in the area once the plant is completed in 2009, a similar challenge to that which faced Wilson, Kansas, when the Wilson Lake Dam project brought hundreds of workers to the community in the 1960s. Washburn has experienced that situation before. When a coal-fired power plant was built near town in the mid-1970s, Washburn's population grew to about 2,000. But few of the construction workers stayed—they were turned off by a harsh climate and a lack of housing and other amenities. An effort was made in Washburn to build housing, but most of the workers left, anyway, and as the population declined by about 35 percent over the next few years, the city ended up having to take possession of several undeveloped lots.

A similar effort is being made today in connection with the new Blue Flint ethanol plant near Washburn. The city sold a developer thirty lots for $1,000 each, and thirty homes are planned, many in the $150,000 range, with front porches and three-car garages. Other local developers plan to build a hotel and as many as fifty more new houses, and still more may be on the way as developers from outside the area try to determine whether Washburn's boom is for real.

It's a fair question. Although a lot of new housing is being created, and the local school's enrollment actually increased—by one student—in 2006, there's not much that can be done about the climate and the town's remoteness, although it is less than an hour from the capital,

Bismarck, which is a growing city of more than 57,000. At least one effort to improve Washburn's amenities ran into the all-too-common road-block that can happen when local interests are seen as being threatened. A planned new restaurant's application for a liquor license ran into opposition from local bars, resulting in a drawn-out city council fight that ended up with a citywide referendum. Irked at the delays, the restaurateur decided to open a restaurant in Bismarck, instead.

In neighboring Minnesota, a locally owned ethanol plant was built in 1996 in rural Benson, and although it has contributed significantly to the town's economy it has not stemmed the population loss, although supporters of the project are probably correct in saying that the loss would have been more severe had the plant not been built.[19]

The challenges of providing restaurants and other amenities may not, however, be the greatest problem facing rural American towns as they try to capitalize on the alternative fuels boom. More important is the extent to which the ownership of alternative fuels production is local, and the economic case for alternative fuels is a sound one. Archer Daniels Midland, the largest ethanol producer in the United States, with a market capitalization of $21 billion in 2007, produces about 20 percent of the country's ethanol. Other large national companies are expanding their ethanol investments. According to the Renewable Fuels Association, about 40 percent of existing ethanol plants, and only four out of thirty-three plants under construction, are majority locally owned.[20] There is evidence that locally owned plants (which generally means that they are owned by local corn farmers) contribute more to the local community. An Iowa State University study in 2006 found that the greater the percentage of local ownership, the more jobs were created within the community.[21] The reason for this is that when profits from the plant go into the pocketbooks of local investors—rather than to distant corporations and their owners—more money finds its way back to the community in return for goods and services, which eventually creates local jobs.

The results of the Iowa State study were echoed in a report by the National Corn Growers Association, which found that locally owned plants contributed as much as 50 percent more to the local economy than absentee-owned plants,[22] and a study by David Morris of the Institute for Local Self-Reliance suggests that a high amount of local ownership of biorefineries could "utterly transform rural America" and urges

Congress to make sure that alternative fuels legislation favors local ownership.[23]

Farmer ownership is not without potential pitfalls. Inherent in such ownership is the potential for conflict between farmers-as-farmers trying to get the highest prices for their crops and farmers-as-ethanol-plant-owners trying to obtain commodities at the lowest possible cost. And, mindful of past energy booms and busts in rural America, the Iowa State study warned: "It is important to remember, however, that the econometrics in these modeling studies work in reverse. Losses in plants that are locally owned resulting in sharply reduced or no payments to investors will be felt as job losses in regional economies, and those losses will be greater in areas with higher local ownership."[24]

To those who believe the future of alternative fuels is all but assured, such warnings may seem to be unnecessary. After all, oil is running out, many of the sources for it are unreliable, and there appear to be vast, renewable sources of energy right in our own backyard. So what could go wrong? Perhaps nothing, but as the ethanol bubble was inflating to unheard-of dimensions and farmers were buying new equipment at near-record levels, there were voices of caution: voices that rural America—having been stung before—might want to ponder. One is reminded of the long-running gag in Charles Shultz's *Peanuts* comic strip—the one in which every autumn Lucy Van Pelt offers to hold a football so Charlie Brown can try a field goal. Of course, Lucy always pulls the ball away just before Charlie gets there, causing him to fly into the air and collapse onto the ground. But the next year, reassured by Lucy's latest and most sincere promises, Charlie agrees to give it a try, and every year Charlie winds up flat on his back. Even as small towns were building houses and expanding schools to accommodate their imminent ethanol-induced prosperity, and farmers were investing in ethanol plants and expanding corn production, there was this ominous headline from a Reuters story about the changing economic landscape: "U.S. Ethanol Firms May Scrap Plants as Margins Fall."[25] The combination of a 60 percent rise in the price of corn and a 30 percent drop in the price of oil from mid-2006 to early 2007 raised questions about the economic viability of ethanol—*even with a $0.51 cent-per-gallon subsidy and a $0.54 cent-per-gallon high tariff on foreign ethanol imports*. The *Wall Street Journal*, in a story headlined "Ethanol Boom Is Running Out of Gas," warned that the combination of high commodity prices, the rising cost of ethanol plant construction, and low ethanol prices threatened the ethanol industry, particularly the smaller—often farmer-owned—ethanol plants. One industry observer remarked that by October 2007, some ethanol companies were "under deathwatch," and the *Journal* story noted that one publicly traded biofuels company had filed a warning with the Securities and Exchange Commission "about its ability to continue as a going concern."[26]

According to the investment bank Credit Suisse the commodity price changes over the second half of 2006 and into 2007 have reduced the expected returns on ethanol production from about 35–40 percent to 5–13 percent, which "should cause some cancellations and deferments" in plant construction. Should oil prices drop below $50, ethanol production at new plants would likely become uneconomical, according to Mark Flannery of the Credit Suisse Global Oil Team.[27] The price of natural gas, which is used to supply the heat for most ethanol plants, presents another variable in the ethanol equation, and during 2006 it fluctuated from $4 to $10 per one million British thermal units.

One result of the price changes has been that ethanol companies that went public in 2006 have had a rough ride. VeraSun Energy Corporation dropped from almost $30 a share in 2006 to under $11 by late 2007, and Aventine Renewable Energy dropped from $40 to less than $10. Companies such as Global Ethanol Holdings in Australia and Hawkeye Renewables in Iowa postponed their plans for public offerings.[28]

With all these variables, it is not surprising that a chart showing the price of ethanol itself looks like a roller coaster—going from about $1.80 at the beginning of 2006, to a high of $3.60 in July of that year, $1.90 in January 2007, and less than $1.60 by late 2007. The price swings all but wiped out the commodity's profitability, which, despite near-record-high oil prices, dropped from over $2.50 a gallon in 2006 to just a few pennies by November 2007.[29] Ethanol is volatile in more ways than one and is dependent on what happens with other commodity prices that are notoriously difficult to predict, as rural America *may* have learned from its experiences with ethanol, oil, and natural gas in the 1970s and 1980s. If it didn't learn, it may face the same fate that awaits Charlie Brown every football season.

Ethanol may well bounce back. Oil prices may rise. Corn prices may drop. Rural America may, indeed, benefit. The problem is that there are too many "mays" for anyone to know for certain what will happen or when, and it is clear that if ethanol and other biofuels don't pan out, rural America will be hard hit, again. Unless, of course, Congress accedes to demands by the ethanol lobby essentially to insulate ethanol producers from market risk by increasing the ethanol subsidy if oil prices fall.[30]

Costs aside, there are also a lot of other concerns about ethanol. Environmentalists complain that ethanol consumes about as much energy to make as it produces and that ethanol plants deplete aquifers, cause air pollution, and pollute water supplies. Protests against ethanol plants have occurred in Indiana, Illinois, Missouri, Nebraska, Kansas, and Wisconsin.[31] The journal *Foreign Affairs* devoted parts of two issues in 2007 to a debate about the likelihood that, because of the increased demand for ethanol, corn prices would rise high enough, and for a long enough time, to raise food prices out of the reach of the poor.[32] Concerns about grain prices have also come from groups such as the National Cattlemen's Beef Association, the National Turkey Federation, and the National Chicken Council—all potent interest groups—that are beginning to challenge the economics of the ethanol bandwagon. [33] Advocates of sustainable agriculture and conservation fear that the demand for corn will cause farmers to forgo crop rotation and will tempt farmers and the U.S. Department of Agriculture to remove land from the conservation reserve program and devote it to corn production—often in areas where the water supply is questionable. Some question the use of subsidies and tariffs, arguing that, if ethanol is as good a deal as its proponents claim, it should be able to survive without government aid. The tariffs are also something of an embarrassment, as President George W. Bush found in early 2007 when he visited Brazil—a major ethanol producer—and was reminded by Brazilian President Luiz Inácio Lula da Silva that the United States "talks a lot about free trade but they like to protect their own products."[34] And there is the problem of storing bumper crops of corn and getting ethanol to where it's needed. By the 2007 harvest, stories began appearing about the shortage of silos to store the corn and the fact that existing oil and gas pipelines aren't designed to handle ethanol, raising concerns that it will take a lot of time and money to build ethanol-capable pipelines to get the fuel from the sparsely populated producing areas of the country to the big urban markets.[35] Railroads could provide at least an interim solution, but most are already operating at or near capacity carrying grain, coal, and containers. While rail-roads are adding capacity, they, too, are aware of the dangers of overin-vesting in ethanol. "We are going to do what it takes to move it," said the chief executive officer of Iowa Interstate Railroad, "but you just don't bet the farm on something that is volatile and controlled by many different forces."[36]

For the time being, rural America is enjoying the attention and the boost it is getting from ethanol, and it is likely that in one form or an-other rural communities eventually *will* benefit significantly from alter-native fuels production. The energy lesson for them is that the road can be a bumpy one and that the headlines proclaiming that the salvation of rural America is at hand need to be balanced by an understanding of both history and economics.

16

Reinventing Rural America: The Buffalo Commons and Other Regional Metaphors

A trip to the Great Plains in 1985 by a college professor from New Jersey and his wife helped lead to a new way of looking at rural communities and, ultimately, some urban ones as well.[1] In August of that year, Frank Popper, his wife Deborah, and their two young children were exploring the northern Great Plains in their aging mustard yellow Toyota Corolla station wagon, which did not survive the trip. Popper was a professor at Rutgers who had studied the American frontier and written an article for the *Yale Review* in which he argued that much of the American western frontier, which many historians had considered essentially closed by about 1900, was still open and was likely to remain so.[2] Both Popper and his wife, who was studying geography and the environment, were struck by the many small, failing farm communities they encountered. They also found a lot of land that had been plowed but lacked adequate water. It wasn't well suited for farming and was in danger of creating the conditions for another dust bowl like the one that had decimated the plains in the 1930s. In 1987, the Poppers published what *Planning Magazine* called "a daring proposal for dealing with inevitable disaster." The article, "The Great Plains: From Dust to Dust," introduced the term "Buffalo Commons" and created enormous controversy. The Poppers recommended, in essence, returning large parts of ten states from New Mexico and Texas in the south to Montana and North Dakota in the north to "their pre-white condition" through the creation of an enormous historical preservation and soil conservation project that, they believed, had the potential ultimately to become the world's largest national park.[3] The Great Plains area begins in the east near the 98th meridian, "Where the West Begins," according to many, including the late Texas historian Walter Prescott Webb who wrote that the 98th meridian—roughly a line running north from near San Antonio through Oklahoma City and Wichita to a point just west of Fargo, North Dakota—marked the place where "eastern civilization based on land, water, and timber broke down. People who moved west of the line, where water and timber became scarce, had to reinvent civilization to survive."[4] From the 98th meridian, the Great Plains stretch several hundred miles westward to the Rocky Mountains.[5]

The land in question is characterized by short grasses, very few trees, and aridity—averaging less than 20 inches of precipitation a year. The Poppers called it "America's steppes, [with] the nation's hottest summers and coldest winters, greatest temperature swings, worst hail and locusts and range fires, fiercest droughts and blizzards, and therefore its shortest growing season." The settling of the area and attempts to farm much of it, as the Poppers saw it, were "the result of the largest, longest-running agricultural and environmental miscalculation in American history."[6] The Poppers believed that, for the reasons they had identified, the region would continue to lose population, as it has.

But the Poppers had a remedy, or at least an intriguing conceptual suggestion. Their Buffalo Commons idea received wide attention in national publications and spawned a variety of efforts large and small, public and private, to turn the land over to the buffalo and other native animals and to stop plowing and irrigation. It also produced a quick, defensive reaction by people in the areas that would be affected. Many of them still felt that better days were just around the corner, and they scoffed at the notion that a couple of urban academics could understand life on the plains. The Poppers received threatening and abusive letters, and on more than one occasion they required a police escort when they appeared at meetings in the area. In the 1930s a similar reaction greeted U.S. Department of Agriculture officials such as Lewis Gray and Rexford Tugwell, who saw the devastation of the dust-bowl years and floated the idea that farming in the plains be abandoned in favor of grasslands. Gray proposed that the government buy 75 million acres of "submarginal" land and convert it to a controlled grazing management plan. Tugwell and his colleagues were lambasted as part of a "Washington nuthouse of college professors," and it was suggested that Tugwell be deported to Russia.[7]

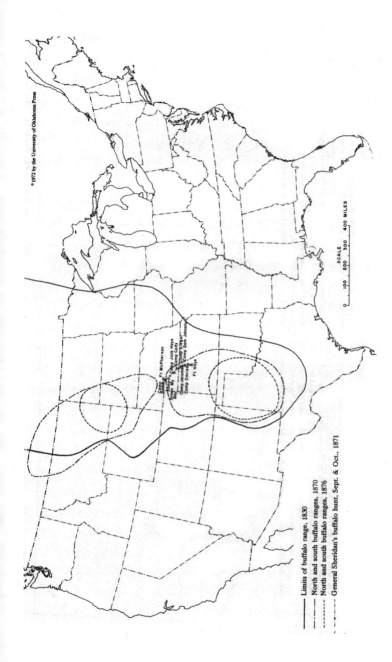

Figure 6. Buffalo Range

Source: Homer E. Socolofsky and Huber Self, *Historical Atlas of Kansas*, 2nd ed. (Norman: University of Oklahoma Press, 1988), Plate 35.

Copyright © 1972, 1988 by the University of Oklahoma Press.

But throughout the 1990s, the plains' population continued to drop, as did the water levels in wells and aquifers, and by the twenty-first century people were starting to warm to the Buffalo Commons idea, including former Kansas governor Mike Hayden. When the Poppers first published their Buffalo Commons idea Hayden, who had been born near Atwood in the heart of the Great Plains, was the Kansas governor. He rejected the Buffalo Commons idea. "Tell the Poppers that America's Great Plains do not equal the Sahara," he said, adding later that the idea "made about as much sense as suggesting we seal off our declining urban areas and preserve them as a museum of twentieth century architecture," an idea which may not have been as absurd as Hayden thought (it appeared later in slightly different form as part of an actual urban commons idea for Detroit).[8]

By 2004, Hayden, then Kansas's secretary of wildlife and parks, had changed his mind. He had seen his home county, Rawlins, lose 15 percent of its population in the decade of the 1990s, and his family farm that had once supported sixteen people was supporting only four by 2000, and three of those were over the age of 80. "The truth is, I was wrong," Hayden said. "The Poppers ended up being somewhat conservative in their estimates of the out migration from the Plains. The losses have actually exceeded most of the Poppers' projections."[9]

Part of the problem with the Buffalo Commons idea was that people feared it would lead to a massive public land grab, a conclusion that was not illogical since the Poppers had written in their original article of the need "for the federal government to step in and buy the land" and that "the federal government's commanding task on the Plains for the next century will be to recreate the nineteenth century."[10] Yet in the years since the article was written, the Poppers and others realized that the term "Buffalo Commons" was not a concrete land-use plan but more a metaphor and "an appeal for rethinking possibilities on the Plains— falling somewhere between conventional agriculture and pure wilderness."[11] Although the federal government has created twenty National Grasslands, and operates several soil conservation programs, there has been no land grab, nor has a unified and comprehensive plan for implementing Buffalo Commons throughout the plains been developed.

One of the most intriguing features of the Poppers' idea, and the one with particular relevance to the survival of rural communities, is their notion that a commons such as the one they envisioned would become a major regional amenity and international tourist attraction. Earlier chapters have referred to the relatively bright prospects for those rural areas with amenities such as large bodies of water or mountains. In the conventional view, the Great Plains suffers from an "amenity deficiency," yet perhaps something like the Buffalo Commons can create the amenity, and the kind of positive identity, that the Great Plains has lacked since it was settled. The Poppers foresaw a day when many rural communities throughout the commons—"islands in a shortgrass sea"—would support new kinds of commerce, including hunting and fishing stores and outfitters, taxidermists, and high-end restaurants and lodging.[12]

There is evidence to support the Poppers' hopes for a commons, particularly for its potential as a tourist attraction. In the Flint Hills of eastern Kansas, a tallgrass prairie "commons" has emerged as a successful tourist attraction. It has a strong local tourism coalition, a national scenic byway, an abundance of hunting—including deer, ducks, quail, and turkey—and well-preserved and restored towns such as Cottonwood Falls, Council Grove, and Strong City: towns whose populations are stable or have been increasing. In addition, the area has several popular annual events, including the Land Institute's Prairie Festival, dramatic prairie burns that attract tens of thousands of people, and the Symphony in the Flint Hills (with the Kansas City Symphony)—a concert that every year sells out almost immediately. In addition, there have been many books written about the flora, fauna, and people of the region. The jewel of the Flint Hills is the 10,000-acre Tallgrass Prairie National Preserve, created in 1996. It is the largest remaining example of an ecosystem that once covered some 400,000 square miles in the United States, an area that was more than twice the size of California. It may not be unrealistic to expect that a Buffalo Commons, potentially extending over a million square miles, could surpass the success of the Flint Hills.

As the Poppers and others continued to study the Buffalo Commons idea, they realized that because it was more a metaphor or a concept for land use than an actual plan its very ambiguity helped create and sustain the ongoing public dialog that followed. Twelve years after the publication of their 1987 proposal, the Poppers updated it in an article titled "The Buffalo Commons: Metaphor as Method," in which they explained the "metaphor" concept and expanded the idea to other parts of the country.

The Buffalo Commons proposal had been interpreted in many different ways. Some saw it as requiring federal leadership, while others pushed for state and private action. Some saw it as only about buffalo, others thought it could include cattle, and many wanted it expanded to include all kinds of wildlife, including wolves and antelope. In 2005 a group of ecologists and conservationists published an article in the journal *Nature* urging that a U.S. ecological history park be created in the plains.[13] "The park, where large and sometimes dangerous predators would roam free, could be an economic boon to depressed farming regions that humans are fleeing from anyway," wrote LiveScience managing editor Robert Roy Britt.[14] The Buffalo Commons concept also is flexible in other ways. It "does not rule out . . . better irrigation methods, alternative crops, or more telecommuting; instead it coexists with them [and] can coexist with other metaphors including those yet to emerge."[15]

As a result, the Buffalo Commons idea has taken on an evolving life of its own. The Poppers believe that "the question is no longer why or whether the Buffalo Commons will occur, but how."[16] Today, even absent unified leadership, pieces of the Buffalo Commons are emerging from a variety of sources, including the National Forest Service and the U.S. Department of Agriculture, the Nature Conservancy, the Sierra Club, the Great Plains Restoration Council, the World Wildlife Fund, state governments, Native Americans (some of whom must be smiling—or perhaps weeping—at the irony inherent in Buffalo Commons), and private parties including Ted Turner, who owns almost 2 million acres spread across fifteen ranches in seven states. Many of his ranches are raising buffalo with sustainable and ecologically sound livestock management practices, and eight of them also offer commercial hunting and fishing, including properties where people are willing to spend several thousand dollars a week hunting buffalo, elk, and other game.[17] While Turner's is certainly the largest such operation, there are hundreds of smaller ranches throughout the plains where buffalo have replaced cattle or croplands. Buffalo are on the rebound. It is estimated there are about 450,000 buffalo in the United States and Canada (about 10 percent of which are owned by Turner), compared to fewer than a thousand in the late nineteenth century after they had been hunted to near-extinction from a peak population of perhaps 30 million.[18] By comparison, there are estimated to be almost 100 million head of cattle in the United States, including 35 million head of beef cattle.[19] The market for buffalo, which for a century has been considered an exotic rarity, is growing and now can be found in some supermarkets and on restaurant menus, as well as through specialty mail-order suppliers. As is the case with grass-fed cattle, buffalo's appeal for consumers stems in part from its free-range image and a lower fat content.

In addition to buffalo and bigger game animals, the Great Plains has seen a boom in bird hunting, which began in the 1990s, thanks in large part to the opening up of millions of acres of former croplands that the federal government has removed from cultivation through its Conservation Reserve Program. It is estimated that as much as 36 million acres—an area larger than the state of Illinois—is in the Conservation Reserve Program and is returning to the kinds of pasture and grasslands that can support large bird populations. Farmers like LeRoy "Frenchy" Authier in Vivian, South Dakota, have abandoned raising wheat and cattle in favor of operating hunting lodges. His family's Medicine Creek Pheasant Ranch can "gross six times what the farm did."[20] "Pheasant hunting is a good way to keep the farm in the family and the family on the farm," said Authier's wife, Katherine.[21] Similar hunting successes have occurred throughout the plains. The Conservation Reserve Program, which began in the 1980s, is reversing a sharp decline in hunting that occurred after World War II as industrial farming gobbled up grasslands to grow commercial grains, greatly reducing bird populations. The pheasant population in North Dakota, for example, got so low that pheasant hunting was abolished altogether in 1965, but today the state has a busy three-month season for both pheasant and turkeys.[22]

Yet in rural economics there is no such thing as a free lunch. Resources are limited, and rural economies are interrelated and interdependent. As a result, there is the potential—indeed the likelihood—for tension between promising rural initiatives such as the hunting and the ethanol booms that have both contributed significantly to steady increases in the price of farmland from 2001 through 2007. The biggest threat to hunting in rural areas comes from the demand for corn to fuel the many ethanol production facilities in rural America. Some want the Conservation Reserve Program scaled back to allow more farming and more corn, while others oppose it and fear the potential for an ethanol collapse similar to the oil price collapse in the 1980s that ruined many rural economies. The agricultural economist Dan Basse predicts that someday soon "there will be a food fight between the livestock industry and this biofuels or ethanol industry."[23] Such tensions may test the flexibility of the Buffalo Commons concept, although, according to its authors, it is sufficiently flexible that it should be able to coexist with other land uses and "does not rule out . . . better irrigation methods [or] alternative crops."[24]

The flexibility of the Buffalo Commons concept is just one of its unforeseen merits. The other is that it has become evident that such metaphors are useful on a broad scale and in a variety of environments. The Great Plains is not the only region that faces issues such as depopulation and unemployment related to economics, technology, and the environment. Many farming, mining, logging, and small manufacturing communities have suffered as their economies have weakened, the Poppers note, and they suggest that regional metaphors may help such communities and regions rethink their identity and plan for their future. Among the regions they have identified are the Lower Mississippi Delta, central Appalachia, the Upper Midwest, northern New England, and the Pacific Northwest.

Most such areas are rural, but urban areas also may benefit from a new identity from time to time. The Poppers cite the example of Chicago, which in 1900 was widely seen as a sprawling mass of unsightly industry and often-contentious ethnic and racial groups. By the 1950s Chicago had been repackaged by *Chicago Tribune* publisher Robert McCormick into something called "Chicagoland," which was touted as "a kind of ultra normal, common-sense alternative to the excesses of the East and West coasts. . . . A place apart, a calm heartland of bedrock American values."[25] Today, more than eighty years after McCormick introduced the term in his newspaper, Chicagoland—connoting a vibrant, world-class megalopolis—has achieved ubiquity, including adoption by McCormick's rival, the *Chicago Sun-Times*.

The use of one animal, buffalo, as part of a metaphor for an entire region is being duplicated in the Northwest, where endangered salmon species have become a symbol for many initiatives including revitalizing logging areas and controlling urban growth. Calling this metaphor the "Salmon Return," the Poppers believe that "like buffalo on the Plains the salmon offers its region simultaneous commercial, wildlife, and mythic possibilities."[26] There turn out to be many similarities between buffalo and salmon: both have the potential to improve the region's attractiveness and amenity rating; both are strong and positive symbols, yet are sufficiently ambiguous and flexible to support a variety of interests; both are potentially lucrative; and both appeal to Native Americans. Already one Native American leader had advocated a Buffalo-Salmon Summit.[27]

Other potential regional metaphors include Silicon Valley, the Sunbelt, the New South, America's Breadbasket, and the Everglades, which has served as a symbol and an example for land-use planning in all of Florida and for resistance to the further spread of airports, casinos, highways, malls, and subdivisions. In addition, regional metaphors can coexist with subregional metaphors. For example, within the multistate Buffalo Commons region are struggling areas such as northwest Kansas, which might benefit from adopting a subregional identity that would be more appealing to prospective newcomers, businesses, and tourists alike.

One day, northwest Kansas might be transformed from a disjointed grouping of small and shrinking counties in the High Plains, best known as "flyover country" or "America's steppes," into something a little more colorful and marketable. Perhaps it would become a twelve-county High Plains region or, recognizing the Indians who once called the area home, a Cheyenne region. The new entity would have about 50,000 people, perhaps with its nominal capital at Colby, and with at least one first-class airport, several attractive hotels and motels, a variety of annual events from car racing to rodeos to agricultural conventions, a four-year college, a Cheyenne regional historical and art museum, a major hospital with satellite facilities, a regional theater, a planning and economic development agency, and a Cheyenne regional trade and tourism office, promoting the Cheyenne "brand" and strengths to the world. The subregional metaphor could go well beyond being just a vehicle for preserving and promoting cultural, historical and geographic identities. The subregion's counties might explore ways to share services across the region, avoiding unnecessary duplication and providing a greater range of resources than any single county could provide on its own.

Such an entity would improve the chances that more of the 12,000 cars a day that speed through northwestern Kansas would stop and explore the area, and businesses looking at places to locate would be able to find many more of their needs met in a Cheyenne region than would have been possible if they were dealing with an individual county or town within the region.

The Cheyenne region also would be able to consolidate efforts to seek federal, state, and private funding for the area. Such funding sources would not have to deal with twelve different counties and dozens of towns and small cities or with the accompanying duplication of paperwork and priorities. The region would be better positioned to have its interests understood by the state government in Topeka and better equipped to represent the area in regional and interstate negotiations regarding such things as water and energy. Similar regions could be duplicated throughout much of the rest of the state, and in other states, and while such regionalization may be unnecessary in metropolitan areas, it would provide the more rural areas of the country an opportunity to reinvent and reposition themselves for the twenty-first century.

Kansas Governor Kathleen Sebelius may have opened the door for state support of initiatives such as subregions when she said in her 2007 State of the State speech that she was appointing her lieutenant governor to lead a budget review "to cut additional waste and find *new ways to provide services more efficiently*" (emphasis added).[28] The time may be at hand when rural America can improve its chances for growth and survival by taking a fresh and critical look at how it views itself and how it defines itself as a community—much as some of the communities profiled in this book have done in efforts to promote tourism and economic development.

The idea of regional metaphors that the Poppers came up with in 1987 offers both urban and rural America that rarest of gifts: a second chance to reinvent themselves and help preserve what is best in their past while also offering an opportunity to influence and shape their future.

Afterword

The question that kept coming up while I was writing *Survival of Rural America* was, in one form or another, "So, what *is* going to happen to rural America?" Well, small-town rural America faces enormous challenges in the twenty-first century. It's a numbers game. If populations continue to decline, more schools and stores will close, and more communities will wither and die. It's as simple as that.

Whether rural American populations grow or shrink depends, primarily, on two things: jobs and lifestyle. Of the two, jobs may be the easiest to create. Perhaps such favorable developments as the growth of the alternative fuels industry, advances in telecommunications and the internet, and the demand for natural foods produced using sustainable methods will spark a meaningful rural employment revival. Perhaps states will help rural communities to restructure and redefine themselves, achieving economic efficiencies, improving services, and gaining critical mass while also building strong local identities based on a new kind of "community."

Yet as many communities have found out, jobs are not a panacea. A job can be relatively easy to create, but a desirable rural lifestyle can be—and has been—difficult to bring about. Although it is often said that young people leave their rural homes because there aren't enough good jobs, it is also true that many are enticed away by the lure of urban life and its material and social amenities. At some point during the twentieth century, rural living seemed to have lost whatever cachet or status it ever had and began to lose its lifestyle battle with urban America. This has been going on for a long time, certainly since well before the decline of the family farm eliminated so many jobs in rural America. It even inspired its own song, "How 'Ya Gonna Keep 'Em down on the Farm (after They've Seen Paree)?", written during World War I, when hundreds of thousands of rural soldiers had gone off to war in Europe.

"Reuben, Reuben, I've been thinking,"
Said his wifey dear;
"Now that all is peaceful and calm,
The boys will soon be back on the farm;"
Mister Reuben, started wink-ing,
And slowly rubbed his chin;
He pulled his chair up close to mother,
And he asked her with a grin:

CHORUS

How 'ya gonna keep 'em, down on the farm,
After they've seen Pa-ree?
How 'ya gonna keep 'em away from Broad-way;
Jazzin' a-round,
And paintin' the town?
How 'ya gonna keep 'em away from harm?
That's a mistery;
They'll never want to see a rake or plow,
And who the deuce can parleyvous a cow?
How 'ya gonna keep 'em down on the farm,
After they've seen Paree?[1]

Today the attraction is more likely to be going to college than to Broadway or Paree. A lot of rural students get good secondary school educations and go on to college, where the education they receive (often majoring in "upward mobility," as Wes Jackson put it) is more likely to aim them toward urban America than back to rural communities.

There were two things I found I could count on everywhere in rural America. First, nearly everyone waved at me if I was driving through town, or nodded and said hello if I was walking, often inquiring if they could be of assistance. These were not perfunctory kinds of greetings. As best I could tell they really *were* glad to see me. The second was that almost everyone I met believed, correctly, that their towns suffered from a deficit in material amenities when compared to urban America. People would talk with varying degrees of confidence about jobs and economic development, but express frustration about their community's need for a clothing store, a health club, a restaurant or two—even a coffee shop:

the kinds of things that people in cities take for granted, even joke about. The satirical newspaper the *Onion* reported that Starbucks had announced it was opening a new Starbucks in the bathroom of an existing Starbucks.[2] Funny to those in cities who wonder why there are so many of them, but anyone suffering from a Starbucks overdose need just spend some time in a small rural town to see what life is like without one.

Rural America will never be able to compete with urban America in the material (retail and service) amenity category. Yet rural America has its own charm and its own kinds of amenities. Rather than Starbucks or Morton's Steakhouse or the Sharper Image, the amenities tend to be things like a low crime rate, affordable housing, open space, recreational opportunities, and good schools. There is also one aspect to rural life that may be a plus or a minus, depending on one's perspective. Rural communities necessarily involve a high degree of closeness, of intimacy. In cities, many people go about their business anonymously, for the most part. But not so in a small rural town. A trip to the bank, the post office, or a local bar, is likely to involve seeing people you know. This can be appealing to some, including perhaps the lonely, the elderly, the very young, and also community-oriented families, while others—teenagers come to mind—prefer to keep their distance and their anonymity. Perhaps that's one of the reasons so many young people move away from their small hometowns.

Unlike urban areas, rural amenities and attractions tend to be things that aren't advertised in neon signs or on television: a trout stream or a pheasant hunting spot near town, a local farmer who sells fresh goat cheese from his house, breathtaking sunsets across fields of wheat or corn, or an unhurried chat with a child's teacher or the town's mayor. Often, rural amenities are so understated that they're not even what urban Americans think of as amenities at all. One of my favorites is the subject of the book *From the Garden Club: Rural Women Writing Community,* by Charlotte Hogg, who teaches English and writing at Texas Christian University.[3] She writes about Paxton, Nebraska, population 614 and dropping, where her grandmother lived and who, together with some other older Paxton women, devoted much of her time to employing her love of literacy in service to the community. The Paxton Garden Club women wrote news articles and local histories and memoirs, volunteered at the library and the University of Nebraska Extension Service, and helped both to create and preserve their rural culture. Not a big deal, perhaps. "Only women's work," some would, and did, say.

The Paxton, Nebraska, Garden Club, the Lucas, Kansas, grassroots arts scene, the Fairfield, Iowa, transcendental meditation community. It is these kinds of little things, unexpected things, that make rural America so appealing, at least to me, and that may represent the kinds of subtle attractions that will enable rural communities to hold their own against the malls and merchandising of metropolitan America.

Time will tell.

Notes

INTRODUCTION. RURAL AMERICA: OUR FIELD OF DREAMS

[1] Thomas Frank, *What's the Matter with Kansas?* (New York: Metropolitan Books, 2004).

[2] David Danbom, "Why Americans Value Rural Life," *Rural Development Perspectives* 12, 1 (1996): 18 (Washington, D.C.: U.S. Department of Agriculture, Economic Research Service).

CHAPTER 1. TRANSITION: THE DEPOPULATION OF RURAL AMERICA

There is an abundance of sources of information about rural America, and many of them are referenced in the text or the endnotes. The country's three major national newspapers, *Wall Street Journal, New York Times,* and *USA Today* all provide coverage of rural issues, and both the *Journal* and the *Times* do so with some regularity, and in some depth. There is also a wealth of information available at the U.S. Department of Agriculture's web site.

[1] Max Borders and H. Sterling Burnett, "Farm Subsidies: Devastating the World's Poor and the Environment," Brief Analysis, no. 547, National Center for Policy Analysis, March 24, 2006, http://www.ncpa.org/pub/ba/ba547/.

[2] R. D. Kaplan, *An Empire Wilderness* (New York: Random House, 1998), 23.

[3] Florida, Arizona, and Nevada were the leading in-migration states. See Marc J. Perry, "Domestic Net Migration in the United States: 2000 to 2004," *Population Estimates and Projections,* Current Population Reports, April 2006, http://www.census.gov/prod/2006pubs/p25-1135.pdf.

[4] United Nations Human Settlements Programme, Tools and Statistics Unit: Europe, http://ww2.unhabitat.org/habrdd/trends/europe.html.

[5] Joel E. Cohen, "Human Population: The Next Half Century," *State of the Planet,* November 14–December 5, 2003, www.rockefeller.edu/labheads/cohenje/PDFs/309SciencePopulationNextHalf.pdf.

[6] Daniel Fitzgerald, *Ghost Towns of Kansas* (Lawrence: University Press of Kansas, 1988), ix.

[7] Ibid.

[8] Thomas Frank, *What's the Matter with Kansas?* (New York: Metropolitan Books, 2004), 59.

[9] U.S. Census Bureau, State and County Quick Facts, Buffalo County, South Dakota, http://quickfacts.census.gov/qfd/states/46/46017.html.

[10] Frank, *What's the Matter with Kansas?* 62.

[11] William Allen White, "What's the Matter with Kansas?" *Emporia Gazette*, August 15, 1896, http://www.h-net.org/~shgape/internet/kansas.html.

[12] Ibid.

[13] Jack Coffman and George Anthan, "Sweeping out the Plains," *APF Reporter* 21, 2, http://www.aliciapatterson.org/APF2102/Coffman_Anthan/Coffman_Anthan.html.

[14] Michael Judge, "Iowa's Job Thieves," *Wall Street Journal*, March 17–18, 2007; William Kandel and John Cromartie, "New Patterns of Hispanic Settlement in Rural America," USDA Economic Research Service, Rural Development Research Report no. 99, May 2004.

[15] Coffman and Anthan, "Sweeping out the Plains."

[16] Kellogg Foundation, "The State of 21st Century Rural America: Implications for Policy and Practice," Proceedings Summary, March 20–22, 2005, Kellogg Foundation Seminar Series, http://www.wkkf.org/DesktopModules/WKF_DmaItem/ViewDoc.aspx?CID=297&ListID=28&ItemID=2970045&fld=PDFFile. The private contribution to rural development is little better than the federal, amounting to just $100 million of the $30 billion in annual charitable grants.

[17] Ibid.

[18] Quoted in Coffman and Anthan, "Sweeping out the Plains."

[19] Ibid.

[20] Thomas A. Lyson, "What Does a School Mean to a Community? Assessing the Social and Economic Benefits of Schools to Rural Villages in New York," *Journal of Research in Rural Education* 17, 3 (Winter 2002): 133.

[21] New York Senator Hillary Rodham Clinton: Speeches and Columns, "Remarks of Senator Hillary Rodham Clinton Calling for a Rural Renaissance to Restore the Promise and Prosperity of Main Streets and Rural Communities," July 31, 2006, http://clinton.senate.gov/news/statements/details.cfm?id=260431&&.

[22] Thomas A. Lyson and William W. Falk, *Forgotten Places: Uneven Development in Rural America* (Lawrence: University Press of Kansas, 1993).

[23] Ibid.

[24] Quoted in Richard K. Kolb, "For the Men Who 'Do the Dying': American Deaths in Iraq Continue to Mount. Here Is Who and How They Are Dying—War in Iraq," *VFW Magazine*, August 2003.

[25] Walter Prescott Webb, *The Great Frontier* (1952), as quoted in Frank J. Popper, "The Strange Case of the Contemporary American Frontier," *Yale Review* 76 (Autumn 1986): 101–121.

CHAPTER 2. PROSPECTS FOR A RURAL REVIVAL

[1] See, e.g., "The Coming Rural Renaissance," an audio interview of University of Missouri professor John Ikerd, at "Rural People, Rural Policy," W.K. Kellogg Foundation Website, at http://www.wkkf.org/default.aspx?tabid=94&CID=274& ItemID=2740437&NID=85&LanguageID=0, 2003.

[2] K. M. Johnson and C. L. Beale, "The Rural Rebound," *Wilson Quarterly* 22 (Spring 1998): 16–27.

[3] M. Rich and D. Leonhardt, "Saying Goodbye California Sun, Hello Midwest," *New York Times,* November 7, 2005, http://www.nytimes.com/2005/11/07/ business/07move.html?pagewanted=2&ei=5070&en=e0b8f01deaa79a28&ex= 1134622800.

[4] Nola Kelsey, *Bitch Unleashed: The Harsh Realities of Goin' Country* (Bloomington, Ind.: Authorhouse, 2005); Marilyn Heimberg Ross and Tom Ross, *Country Bound: Trading Your Business Suit Blues for Blue Jean Dreams* (Chicago: Upstart Publishing Co., 1997).

[5] Joel Kotkin, "The Great Plains," *Wall Street Journal,* August 31, 2006. Kotkin is a senior fellow at the New America Foundation.

[6] Johnson and Beale, "The Rural Rebound."

[7] Douglas County, Colo., Assessor, "Historic Abstracts of Assessment," http:// www.douglas.co.us/assessor/Historic_Abstracts_of_Assessment.html.

[8] Johnson and Beale, "The Rural Rebound."

[9] Timothy Aeppel, "Still Made in the USA," *Wall Street Journal,* October 26, 2006.

[10] Johnson and Beale, "The Rural Rebound."

[11] Roger Fillion, "Doing Homework," *Rocky Mountain News,* February 6, 2006.

[12] Johnson and Beale, "The Rural Rebound."

[13] James R. Shortridge, *The Middle West: Its Meaning in American Culture* (Lawrence: University Press of Kansas, 1989), 138.

[14] Ibid.

[15] As cited in ibid.

[16] Neal Peirce and Curtis Johnson, "Six States? Growth, Hope and Despair," New England Futures, Montpelier, Vt., January 2006, http://www.newengland futures.org/issues/growth/sidebar2/.

[17] Noel Perrin, *Best Person Rural: Essays of a Sometime Farmer* (Boston: David R Godine, 2006); Perrin's quote is taken from Bill Kaufman, Bookmarks Review of "Best Person Rural," *Wall Street Journal*, November 24, 2006.

[18] Ibid.

[19] Shortridge, *The Middle West*, 143.

[20] "Minnesota: A State That Works," *Time* (August 13, 1973), 35.

[21] http://www.morganquitno.com.

[22] U.S. Census Bureau, Population Division, Interim State Population Projections, 2005, http://www.census.gov/population/www/projections/projections agesex.html. The states expected to achieve the greatest gains include: Arizona, Florida, North Carolina and Texas.

[23] David E. Brown and Louis E. Swanson, *Challenges for Rural America in the Twenty-First Century* (University Park: Pennsylvania State University Press: 2003), 404.

[24] Dean Joliffe, "Rural Poverty at a Glance," U.S. Department of Agriculture, Economic Research Service, July 2004, http://www.ers.usda.gov/publications/rdrr100/rdrr100.pdf.

[25] Dean Joliffe, "The Cost of Living and the Geographic Distribution of Poverty," U.S. Department of Agriculture, Economic Research Service, September 2006, http://www.ers.usda.gov/publications/err26/err26.pdf.

CHAPTER 3. KANSAS: THE ESSENCE OF RURAL AMERICA

[1] Mark Preston, "The Most Representative State: Wisconsin," *CNN.com*, July 27, 2006, http://www.cnn.com/2006/POLITICS/07/27/mg.thu/. Least representative were New York, West Virginia, and Mississippi.

[2] Homer E. Socolofsky and Huber Self, *Historical Atlas of Kansas*, 2nd ed. (Norman: University of Oklahoma Press, 1988), 53.

[3] I was born in Kansas City, Missouri, a couple of miles from the Kansas border, and attended college at the University of Kansas. Both of my parents were born in small Kansas towns, and they owned some ranch land and farmland in the state. My father's job in the grain business took me to many small Kansas towns and introduced me to many small-town Kansans. Since my father wrote a weekly grain market commentary for his firm and was a trader at the Kansas City Board of Trade's wheat futures market, he also introduced me to subjects such as agricultural price supports, and he kept a close eye on the weather and on foreign trade.

[4] "Native American Tribes of Kansas," http://www.native-languages.org/kansas.htm.

[5] Daniel Henniger, "Truman Capote's Dark Visitation to a Red State," *Wall Street Journal*, November 4, 2005. *In Cold Blood* was originally published by Random House in 1965.

[6] David E. Brown and Louis E. Swanson, *Challenges for Rural America in the Twenty-First Century* (University Park: Pennsylvania State University Press, 2003), 397.

[7] "What's Right with Kansas," house editorial, *New York Times*, November 15, 2006, http://www.nytimes.com/2006/11/15/opinion/15wed4.html?_r=1&oref=slogin.

[8] George S. Will, "Democrats vs. Wal-Mart," *Washington Post*, September 14, 2006.

[9] Bob Hemenway, chancellor, "Evolution Statement," Monday Messages, University of Kansas, Office of the Chancellor, September 26, 2005, www.chancellor.ku.edu/messages/2005/september2605.shtml?M.

[10] Monica Davey, "Fight over Evolution Shifts in Kansas School Board Vote," *New York Times*, August 3, 2006; "Kansas Restores Evolution Standards for Science Classes," *CNN.com*, February 14, 2001, http://archives.cnn.com/2001/US/02/14/kansas.evolution.02/.

[11] U.S. Census Bureau, "Persons 25 Years Old and over with a Bachelor's Degree or More, 2005," State Rankings—Statistical Abstract of the United States, http://www.census.gov/compendia/statab/ranks/rank19.htm.

[12] Robert W. Baughman, *Kansas in Maps* (Topeka: Kansas State Historical Society, 1961), 54.

[13] Ibid.

[14] Thomas Frank, *What's the Matter with Kansas?* (New York: Metropolitan Books, 2004), 28.

[15] Ibid., 30.

[16] L. Frank Baum, *The Wonderful Wizard of Oz* (Chicago: George M. Hill, 1900).

[17] [Philip Wedge and Thomas Averill], Independent Study Course Preview, ENGL 570: "Kansas Literature," University of Kansas Continuing Education, n.d., www.kuce.org/isc/previews/engl/engl570_pref.html.

[18] Frank, *What's the Matter with Kansas?* 29.

[19] Quoted from a reprint, L. Frank Baum, *The Wizard of Oz* (New York: Ballantine, 1979), 1–2.

[20] William Inge, *Picnic* (1953; New York: Dramatists Play Service, 1981), 5–7.

[21] Ronald Reagan, "Remarks at Kansas State University at the Alfred M. Landon Lecture Series on Public Issues," September 9, 1982, American Presidency

Project, http://www.presidency.ucsb.edu/ws/index.php?pid=42945, and quoted in James R. Shortridge, *The Middle West: Its Meaning in American Culture* (Lawrence: University Press of Kansas, 1989), 141.

[22] David D. Danbom, "Why Americans Value Rural Life," *Rural Development Perspectives* 12, 1 (n.d.): 15–18, U.S. Department of Agriculture Economic Research Service, http://www.ers.usda.gov/publications/rdp/rdp1096/rdp1096d.pdf.

CHAPTER 4. RURAL COMMUNITIES AT RISK

[1] Stephen Moore, "300,000,000," *Wall Street Journal*, October 3, 2006.

[2] Richard Rubin, "Not Far from Forsaken," *New York Times Magazine*, April 6, 2006.

[3] Ibid.

[4] Leonard Hall, *A Journal of the Seasons on an Ozark Farm* (Columbia: University of Missouri Press, 1980), 192.

[5] Ibid., "Preface to New Edition."

[6] Dave Ranney, "Small Kansas Farms Falling by the Wayside," *Lawrence Journal-World*, June 22, 2005.

[7] James R. Shortridge, "A Cry for Help: KansasFreeLand.com," *Geographical Review* 94, 4 (October 2004): 530–541.

[8] Peter T. Kilborn, "Bit by Bit, Tiny Morland, Kan., Fades Away," *New York Times*, May 10, 2001.

[9] U.S. Census Bureau, State and County Quick Facts, Phillips County, Kansas, http://quickfacts.census.gov/qfd/states/20/20147.html. By 2005 the population had dropped another 8 percent.

[10] Timothy Egan, "Amid Dying Towns of Rural Plains, One Makes a Stand," *New York Times*, December 1, 2003.

[11] U.S. Census Bureau, State and County Quick Facts, Kansas, http://quickfacts.census.gov/qfd/states/20000.html.

[12] Dave Ranney, "Schools Shrink as Kansans Pull Up Stakes," *Lawrence Journal-World*, July 30, 2006, http://www2.ljworld.com/news/2006/jul/30/schools_shrink_kansans_pull_stakes/.

[13] Ibid.

[14] Robert Sanchez, "A New Game Plan," *Denver Post*, September 3, 2006.

[15] Ibid.

[16] Alain Jehlen and Cynthia Kopkowski, "Is Smaller Better?" *NEA Today*, February 2006, at http://www.nea.org/neatoday/0602/coverstory.html.

[17] Diane Weaver Dunne, "Are Smaller Schools Better Schools?" *Education World*, July 20, 2000, http://www.education-world.com/a_issues/issues108.shtml.

[18] Wenfan Yan, "Is Bigger Better?" (Center for Rural Pennsylvania, Harrisburg, September 2006), http://www.ruralpa.org/rural_school_consolidation.pdf.

[19] Thomas A. Lyson, "What Does a School Mean to a Community? Assessing the Social and Economic Benefits of Schools to Rural Villages in New York," *Journal of Research in Rural Education* 17, 3 (Winter 2002): 131.

[20] Seth Godin, *Purple Cow: Transform Your Business by Being Remarkable* (New York: Portfolio Hardcover, 2003).

[21] Gary Lee, "Om on the Grange," *Washington Post*, November 12, 2006.

[22] Cornelia Butler Flora, Jan L. Flora, and Susan Fey, *Rural Communities: Legacy and Change* (Boulder, Colo.: Westview Press, 2004). Cornelia Butler Flora is the director of the North Central Regional Center for Rural Development and the Charles F. Curtiss Distinguished Professor of Agriculture and Sociology at Iowa State University. The first chapter of this book describes and explains different approaches to determining what is rural and the difficulty posed by the varied nature of rural communities.

[23] Roger Martin, "Just a Hop, Skip and Jump," *Catalyst*, University of Kansas Endowment Association, Lawrence, Spring 2003. See also Alexei Barrionuevo, "Taking the Taxi to Higher Heights," *New York Times*, July 26, 2006; and Kathy Barnstorff, "The Small Aircraft Transportation System (SATS) 2005 Technology Demonstration," report, National Aeronautics and Space Administration, Langley Research Center, January 13, 2005, http://www.nasa.gov/vision/earth/improving flight/sats_2005_demo65374_prt.htm.

CHAPTER 5. "WELCOME HOME" AND THE "FREE LAND" MOVEMENT

[1] Daniel Kadlec, "The Land of the Free," *Time*, July 11, 2005, 40.

[2] Robert W. Baughman, *Kansas in Maps* (Topeka: Kansas State Historical Society, 1961), 68. Most of the ads were paid for by railroad companies.

[3] Pacific Railroad Act of 1862, "Pacific Railroad Acts," Central Pacific Railroad Photographic History Museum, http://www.cprr.org/Museum/Pacific_Railroad_Acts.html.

[4] Ibid.; and "State by State Numbers," Homestead National Monument Association, nps.gov/home/historyculture/statenumbers.htm. April 24, 2007.

[5] Nicholas D. Kristof, "Make Way for Buffalo," *New York Times*, October 29, 2003.

[6] Timothy Egan, "Amid Dying Towns of Rural Plains, One Makes a Stand," *New York Times*, December 1, 2003.

[7] Dennis Darrow, "Plant Closures in Ark Valley Temper News of Job Gains," *Pueblo Chieftain*, November 23, 2005.

[8] Kadlec, "The Land of the Free," 42.

[9] Jeffrey Zaslow, "You Can Go Home Again: Buffalo Tries to Reclaim Its Native Sons and Daughters," *Wall Street Journal,* August 17, 2006.

[10] John Cyr, interviewed by author, October 2005, Beloit, Kansas. All quotations from Cyr are taken from this interview.

[11] James R. Shortridge, "A Cry for Help: KansasFreeLand.com," *Geographical Review* 94, 4 (October 2004): 530–541.

[12] Including *Time, USA Today,* the *Wall Street Journal,* the *New York Times, Kiplinger's Personal Finance* magazine, and many television programs.

[13] Kadlec, "The Land of the Free," 42.

[14] John Ritter, "Towns Offer Free Land to Newcomers," *USA Today,* August 30, 2005.

[15] Anita Hoffhines, interviewed by author, October 2005 and February 2006, Ellsworth, Kansas. All quotations from Hoffhines in the book are taken from these interviews.

[16] William Spain, "Yes in My Backyard: Tiny Sauget, Illinois, Likes Business Misfits," *Wall Street Journal,* October 3, 2006.

[17] Ibid.

[18] Zaslow, "You Can Go Home Again."

[19] Timothy Aeppel, "As Its Population Declines, Youngstown Thinks Small," *Wall Street Journal,* May 3, 2007, 1.

[20] "Shrinking Cities Institute Kicks off This Fall with Charrette and Forum," *CUDC Quarterly* (Cleveland Urban Institute Collaborative) 4, 2 (Summer 2005), http://www.cudc.kent.edu/e-cudc-Quarterly/news/shrinkintro.html.

CHAPTER 6. PLAINVILLE AND ROOKS COUNTY: HIGH PLAINS, HIGH STYLE

[1] "Rooks County U.S. Census (1880–1930)," Genealogy Today Directory, n.d., http://dir.genealogytoday.com/usa/ks/rooks/census.html.

[2] Richard L. Forstall, "Kansas: Population of Counties by Decennial Census: 1900 to 1990," U.S. Bureau of the Census, Population Division, n.d., http://www.census.gov/population/cencounts/ks190090.txt.

[3] Candace Rachel, personal communication, March 3, 2006. The K-18 Baseball Tournament in northwest Kansas is for children 12–15; it is named after the K-18 Highway, which goes through Plainville.

[4] Candace Rachel, interviewed by author, at her office at the *Plainville Times,* February 9, 2006.

[5] Ibid.

[6] Stacy Downs, "Plainsman Crafts a Simple, Sublime Vision," *Kansas City Star*, August 21, 2005; Chuck Comeau, interviewed by author, October 11, 2005. All quotes from Comeau not attributed to Downs or other sources are taken from this interview.

[7] Ibid.

[8] Ibid.

[9] Eric W. Norris, "Business Booming for Plainville Store," *Hays Daily News*, October 7, 2004, http://www.rookscounty.net/business_booming.htm.

[10] Downs, "Plainsman Crafts a Simple, Sublime Vision."

[11] Bobby White, "Tech's Cutting Edge? Try a Tiny Town," *Wall Street Journal*, July 27, 2006.

[12] Richard Rubin, "Not Far from Forsaken," *New York Times Magazine*, April 9, 2006. At last report, the company, SEO Precision, Inc., was still in business and still in Divide County.

[13] See Chapter 4 for an explanation of the purple-cow theory.

[14] Christina Binkley, "Hot Wheels Keep on Turning," *Wall Street Journal*, August 26, 2006.

[15] Mylene Mangalindan, "Buzz in West Texas Is about Jeff Bezos and His Launch Site," *Wall Street Journal*, November 10, 2006.

[16] Fortuitously, at least for the present, Chuck Comeau's eldest son works in the family business, and his younger siblings—still in school—may follow similar careers.

[17] Most of the information about Palco was provided by Monte Keller, from privately printed sources and from members of the Palco Community Economic Development group during interviews in 2005 and 2006. Information from the author is available on request.

[18] With the dramatic jump in energy prices in 2005, Rooks County's valuation increased 53 percent (ibid.).

[19] Named after the Palco High School mascot, the rooster.

[20] Monte Keller, interviewed by author, October 14, 2005, and October 12, 2006.

[21] For information on meth labs in rural America, see Mary Reinertson-Sand, "Methamphetamine Frequently Asked Questions," Rural Assistance Center, revised June 4, 2007, http://www.raconline.org/info_guides/meth/methfaq.php.

[22] Rubin, "Not Far from Forsaken."

[23] "Weather Almanac for May 2006: Three Strikes on Codell," *Weather Doctor*, http://www.islandnet.com/~see/weather/almanac/arc2006/alm06may.htm.

[24] Mentioned in "History of Rooks County: Codell," http://www.rookscounty.net/rooks_county_history.htm#Codell.

CHAPTER 7. ATWOOD AND RAWLINS COUNTY: SURVIVING IN THE GREAT AMERICAN DESERT

[1] Richard L. Forstall, "Kansas: Population of Counties by Decennial Census: 1900 to 1990," U.S. Bureau of the Census, Population Division, n.d., http://www.census.gov/population/cencounts/ks190090.txt.

[2] "Spotlight on Atwood," *McCook Daily Gazette,* August 25, 2005, 4.

[3] Rex Buchanan and Robert Buddemeier, "The High Plains Aquifer," Public Information Circular 18, Kansas Geological Survey, Lawrence, Kansas, October 2001, http://www.kgs.ku.edu/Publications/pic18/pic18_1.html.

[4] Unless otherwise indicated, all information about Atwood and Rawlins County was obtained during interviews with Chris Sramek and others in Atwood in February 2006. Information is available on request from the author.

[5] Forstall, "Population of Counties by Decennial Census: 1900 to 1990."

[6] Kansas usually ranks high in studies of states that are good for new businesses and entrepreneurs, placing first in a study featured in *Forbes.com* in 2004. See Lawrence J. McQuillan, "Live Free or Move," Forbes.com, May 24, 2004, http://www.forbes.com/free_forbes/2004/0524/164.html.

[7] "About WIRE," Women in Rural Enterprise, http://www.wireuk.org/about.aspx.

[8] Jo Josephson, ed., "Telling Their Stories: Women Business Owners in Western Maine," Western Mountains Alliance and the University of Maine (Wiscasset, Maine: Coastal Enterprises, 2006), http://www.westernmountainsalliance.org/publication-attachments/PDFTellTheirStories.pdf.

[9] "HomeTown Competitiveness: A Come-Back/Give-Back Approach to Rural Community Building," http://www.htccommunity.org/.

[10] The centers are located throughout the state, which is divided into eight regions for purposes of administration, and offers counseling, business planning, and educational support.

[11] "Jobs and Economic Opportunities!" Rawlins County, Kansas, http://www.rawlinscounty.info/CommunityFuturesSummary.pdf.

[12] Ogallala Commons, http://www.ogallalacommons.org.

CHAPTER 8. TIPTON: THE TOWN THAT REFUSED TO DIE

[1] Richard L. Forstall, "Kansas: Population of Counties by Decennial Census: 1900 to 1990," U.S. Bureau of the Census, Population Division, http://www.census.gov/population/cencounts/ks190090.txt.

[2] Kansas itself averages 32 people per square mile, Kansas City almost 1,000, and New York City more than 25,000, according to the U.S. Census Bureau's

"Quick Facts" data for the year 2000 (U.S. Census Bureau, State and County Quick Facts, Kansas, http://quickfacts.census.gov/qfd/states/20000.html).

³ Leon Streit, "Tipton: The Town" (private manuscript, Tipton, Kans., March 2000), made available through the courtesy of Sandy Hake, secretary at the Tipton Christian School.

⁴ Sources for Tipton include interviews with Gary Hake, Sandy Hake, and Tipton Christian School staff and parents in February 2006; Mark Ahlseen, "A Lesson from the Plains," *Freeman,* May 2005; and Terry Bailey, "Against the Grain: Saving the Small Town School," *Tipton Times,* March 2004.

⁵ See the Tipton Academy web site at http://www.tiptonacademy.com/index. php.

⁶ Rich Tosches, "Meet Maggie and Mercedes, the Student Body at a Wyo. School," *Denver Post,* September 20, 2006.

CHAPTER 9. OTTAWA COUNTY: THE CHALLENGES OF BECOMING A RURAL BEDROOM COMMUNITY

¹ Richard L. Forstall, "Kansas: Population of Counties by Decennial Census: 1900 to 1990," U.S. Bureau of the Census, Population Division, n.d., http://www. census.gov/population/cencounts/ks190090.txt.

² HomeGain, "Ottawa Kansas Real Estate," n.d., http://www.homegain.com/ local_real_estate/KS/ottawa.html.

³ Mark Freel, interviewed by author, Minneapolis, Kansas, October, 2005, 2006.

⁴ "A New Life for the Country: The Report of the President's Task Force on Rural Poverty" (Washington, D.C.: Government Printing Office, 1970), 2, available through the Education Resources Information Center at http://eric.ed.gov/ ERICWebPortal/custom/portlets/recordDetails/detailmini.jsp?_nfpb=true&_& ERICExtSearch_SearchValue_0=ED054906&ERICExtSearch_SearchType_0= eric_accno&accno=ED054906.

⁵ Clayton L. Hogg, "Delphos, Kansas: Pride of Solomon Valley," n.d., http:// www.geocities.com/Clay_Hogg/DelphosKS1.html.

⁶ Ibid.

⁷ Tom McGavran, interviewed by author, Minneapolis, Kansas, October 2005.

⁸ See Dave Rose and Midwest eServices, Chapter 12.

⁹ John Cyr, interviewed by author, October 2005, Beloit, Kansas. All quotations from Cyr are taken from this interview.

¹⁰ Cornelia Flora, personal communication; March–May 2007. Jan Flora and Cornelia Flora, "Local Economic Development Projects: Key Factors," Depart-

ments of Agricultural Economics and Sociology, Virginia Polytechnic Institute and State University, Blacksburg, 1991. The Oberlin/Decatur County web site is at http://www.oberlinkansas.org/.

[11] See Chapter 12.

[12] See the Rural Assistance Center, "Health and Human Services Information for Rural America," http://www.raconline.org/.

[13] Barnaby J. Feder, "Remote Control for Health Care," *New York Times,* September 9, 2006, http://www.nytimes.com/2006/09/09/business/09node.html?ex=1185422400&en=1a9a07eee49377bf&ei=5070.

CHAPTER 10. "THE AMAZING 100 MILES": TOURISM IN RURAL AMERICA

[1] "Colorado's Central Plains" is part of the Prairie Development Corporation, http://www.prairiedevelopment.com/.

[2] The Amazing 100 Miles Tourism Coalition, "Drive and Explore the Amazing 100 Miles," http://www.amazing100miles.com/.

[3] Eastern Colorado, which is indistinguishable from western Kansas, also gets the "flyover" and "drive-through" treatment. "If only they would get off the highway and see the vastness," a resident of tiny Stratton, Colorado, told a reporter. Dana Coffield, "A New View of the High Plains," *Denver Post,* July 23, 2006, p. A-27.

[4] Richard L. Forstall, "Kansas: Population of Counties by Decennial Census: 1900 to 1990," U.S. Bureau of the Census, Population Division, http://www.census.gov/population/cencounts/ks190090.txt.

[5] "The Midland Hotel—100+ Years of History," Wilson, Kans., http://www.midland-hotel.com/aboutHotel.php.

[6] Lindsborg, in McPherson County, has assiduously cultivated and preserved its Swedish heritage and has eleven restaurants, five lodging choices, and scores of shops—many with a distinctly Swedish flavor.

[7] Steve Eschbaugh, interviewed by author, Wilson, Kansas, February 2006.

[8] Information about Wilson and the Wilson Foundation was taken from interviews with Steve Eschbaugh, Anita Hoffhines, Larry Ptacek, and other members of the Wilson Foundation in October 2005 and February and October 2006.

[9] This was stated by a member of the Wilson Development group who insisted on remaining anonymous.

[10] Kansas State Historical Society, "Samuel P. Dinsmoor: A Kansas Portrait," n.d., http://www.kshs.org/portraits/dinsmoor_samuel_p.htm.

[11] Information about Lucas and its art tradition was obtained by interviews with Rosslyn Schultz and Lynn Schneider in Lucas in October 2005, and in articles such as Phyllis J. Zorn, "Expect the Unexpected When Visiting Lucas," Hays Daily News, May 7, 2006.

[12] See the "World's Largest Collection of World's Smallest Versions of World's Largest Things," http://www.worldslargestthings.com/.

[13] The Kansas Explorers Club web site is at http://www.explorekansas.org/.

CHAPTER 11. SEDAN:
COMMUNITY BUILDING FROM THE TOP DOWN

[1] Nita Jones and Bill Kurtis, interviewed by author, Sedan, Kans., October 2006.

[2] Leopold Center for Sustainable Agriculture, "Mexican Restaurant Calendar Sales to Support Leopold Center," news release, January 22, 2007, Iowa State University, http://www.leopold.iastate.edu/news/newsreleases/2007/calendar_012207 .htm.

[3] See Michael Pollan, The Omnivore's Dilemma (New York: Penguin Press, 2006); Thousand Hills Cattle Company, "Interview with Todd Churchill," n.d., http://www.thousandhillscattleco.com/freshandnaturalinterview.html.

[4] See, e.g., Candy Sagon, "Grass-fed Beef Called Healthier," Washington Post, March 15, 2006, F1; and Jo Robinson, "Grass-Fed Basics," Eatwild.com, http:// eatwild.com/, 2006.

[5] Ibid.

[6] Bill Haw, interview, "Modern Meat," PBS Frontline, n.d., http://www. pbs.org/wgbh/pages/frontline/shows/meat/interviews/haw.html.

[7] Marian Burros, "eating well; There's More to Like about Grass-Fed Beef," New York Times, August 30, 2006, available at http://select.nytimes.com/gst/ abstract.html?res=F30F1EFB3A5A0C738FDDA10894DE404482&n=Top%2f Reference%2fTimes%20Topics%2fPeople%2fB%2fBurros%2c%20Marian.

CHAPTER 12. SELLING RURAL AMERICA: DAVE ROSE AND EBAY

[1] Dave Rose, Midwest eServices, Inc., interviewed by author, Salina, Kans., October 2006.

[2] Stephanie Simon, "Real Estate Hunters Go Old School," Los Angeles Times, December 22, 2004.

[3] Ibid.

[4] Oklahoma Department of Commerce, "Spotlight—Buffalo, OK: Buffalo

Uses a High-Tech Approach to Sell an Abandoned School, Create Jobs," n.d., http://www.okcommerce.gov/index.php?option=content&task=view&id=1372& Itemid=459.

[5] Timothy Aeppel, "Still Built on the Homefront," *Wall Street Journal,* October 24, 2006.

PART 3. POLICY OPTIONS FOR RURAL AMERICA

[1] Cynthia Rosenzweig and Daniel Hillel, "Potential Impacts of Climate Change on Agriculture and Food Supply," *Consequences* 1, 2 (Summer 1995), U.S. Global Change Research Information Office, http://www.gcrio.org/CONSEQUENCES/ summer95/agriculture.html; "Climate Change and Agriculture: Report of a Center for Rural Affairs Task Force," Center for Rural Affairs, March 26, 2007, cfra.org/ node/256.

CHAPTER 13. THE FEDERAL GOVERNMENT'S ROLE

[1] Steven Malanga, "America's Worst Urban Program," *City Journal,* Spring 2005, http://www.city-journal.org/html/15_2_urban_program.html.

[2] Kimberley Hendrickson, "Bush and the Cities," *Policy Review* (Hoover Institution), August–September 2004, http://www.policyreview.org/aug04/ hendrickson.html.

[3] Robert L. Morlan, *Political Prairie Fire* (Minneapolis: University of Minnesota Press, 1955).

[4] Senator Byron L. Dorgan (North Dakota), "Summary of S. 675" (Homestead Act), n.d., http://dorgan.senate.gov/issues/northdakota/homestead/summary .cfm.

[5] Byron L. Dorgan, "The Case for a New Homestead Act," n.d., http://dorgan .senate.gov/issues/northdakota/homestead/case.cfm.

[6] Robert Day, "The Scholar and Artist Homestead Act for 21st Century America," n.d., at http://www.landinstitute.org/vnews/display.v/ART/2002/04/24/ 3d10b853b0a0e. (Robert Day's novel, *The Last Cattle Drive,* was published by the University Press of Kansas, Lawrence, in 1987.)

[7] Quoted in Jack Coffman and George Anthan, "Sweeping out the Plains," *APF Reporter* 21, 2, http://www.aliciapatterson.org/APF2102/Coffman_Anthan/ Coffman_Anthan.html.

[8] Quoted in Juliana Thill, "Coleman Seeks Aid for Projects in Rural Communities," *Litchfield Independent Review,* December 15, 2005, reprinted at http:// coleman.senate.gov/index.cfm?FuseAction=Articles.View&Article_id=109& Month=10&Year=2006&IsPrint=True&IsPopUp=True.

⁹ Quoted in the *Nightly Business Report,* "'Farm Town Futures': The New Homestead Act," May 27, 2004, transcript available at http://www.pbs.org/nbr/site/onair/transcripts/040527/.

¹⁰ U.S. General Services Administration, 42 U.S.C. 3122: Rural Development Act of 1972, http://www.gsa.gov/Portal/gsa/ep/contentView.do?P=PMHP&contentId=12191&contentType=GSA_BASIC.

¹¹ Jimmy Carter, "Rural Development Policy Act of 1980 Statement on Signing S. 670 into Law," American Presidency Project, September 24, 1980, http://www.presidency.ucsb.edu/ws/index.php?pid=45128.

¹² U.S. Department of Agriculture, "USDA Budget Summary and Annual Performance Plan, 2006: Table of Contents," n.d., at http://www.usda.gov/agency/obpa/Budget-Summary/2006/FY06budsum.htm.

¹³ Faqir S. Bagi, Richard J. Reeder, and Samuel D. Calhoun, "Federal Funding in Appalachia and Its Three Subregions," *Rural America* 17, 4 (Winter 2002), http://www.ers.usda.gov/publications/ruralamerica/ra174/ra174d.pdf.

¹⁴ Mike Johanns, secretary of agriculture, "USDA 2007 Farm Bill Proposals," U.S. Department of Agriculture, http://www.usda.gov/documents/07finalfbp.pdf.

¹⁵ See the Farm Beginnings Program at the Land Stewardship Project at http://www.landstewardshipproject.org/programs_farmbeginnings.html.

¹⁶ David Rogers, "Farm Bill Withers in the Absence of a Strongman," *Wall Street Journal,* October 5, 2007, A6; and Mary Clare Jalonick, "Billions More Added to Farm Bill," Associated Press, October 4, 2007, http://www.washingtonpost.com/wp-dyn/content/article/2007/10/04/AR2007100402140.html.

¹⁷ Kansas Governor Kathleen Sebelius, "State of the State Address," January 10, 2007, http://www.governor.ks.gov/news/sp-stateofstate2007.htm.

CHAPTER 14. BACK TO THE FUTURE: SUSTAINABLE AGRICULTURE AND ITS EFFECT ON RURAL AMERICA

¹ Darcy Maulsby, "Fred Kirschenmann Addresses the Disappearing Middle," *New Farm* (Rodale Institute), December 17, 2003, http://www.newfarm.org/depts/talking_shop/1203/biodynamic2.shtml.

² Mary V. Gold, comp., "Sustainable Agriculture: Definitions and Terms," Special Reference Briefs Series no. SRB 99-02, Updates SRB 94-05, Alternative Farming Systems Information Center, U.S., Department of Agriculture, Beltsville, Md., September 1999, http://www.nal.usda.gov/afsic/AFSIC_pubs/srb9902.htm.

³ Ibid.

⁴ My emphasis. See Gro Harlem Brundtland, ed., *Our Common Future: The World Commission on Environment and Development* [the Brundtland Report]

(Oxford: Oxford University Press, 1987); Corporation for the Northern Rockies, "What Is Sustainability?" n.d., http://www.northrock.org/sustainability/what_is_ sustainability.shtml.

⁵ Charles A. Francis, "Sustainable Agriculture: Myths and Realities," *Journal of Sustainable Agriculture* 1 (1990): 97–106.

⁶ National Agricultural Statistical Service, "Farm Labor: Number of Farms and Workers by Decade, US" (1910–2000), chart, U.S. Department of Agriculture, http://www.nass.usda.gov/Charts_and_Maps/Farm_Labor/fl_frmwk.asp.

⁷ Frederick Kirschenmann, director, Leopold Center for Sustainable Agriculture, "A Revolution in Agriculture," presentation, May 3, 2002, at http://www. leopold.iastate.edu/pubs/speech/files/0502_glynwood.pdf.

⁸ Gold, comp., "Sustainable Agriculture."

⁹ Sustainable Agriculture Research and Education, *The New American Farmer: Profiles of Agricultural Innovation,* 2nd ed. (Washington, D.C.: Sustainable Agriculture Network, 2005), at http://www.sare.org/publications/naf2/ thompsond.htm.

¹⁰ Craig Canine, "35 Who Made a Difference: Wes Jackson," *Smithsonian Magazine,* November 2005, http://www.smithsonianmag.com/issues/2005/november/ jackson.php.

¹¹ Ted Landphair, "VOA News: Can Grains Keep Replenishing Themselves?" Voice of America, April 17, 2006, reprinted at http://www.allbusiness.com/ government/3652837-1.html.

¹² Wes Jackson, interviewed by author, Salina, Kansas, October 2006. Unless otherwise noted, all information about the Land Institute was obtained during this interview.

¹³ Kirschenmann, "A Revolution in Agriculture."

¹⁴ Chipotle Mexican Grill, "The Rooting and Foraging Continues to Pay Off: Chipotle Mexican Grill Announces More Naturally Raised Meats in Select Markets," press release, February 20, 2007, http://phx.corporate-ir.net/phoenix. zhtml?c=194775&p=irol-newsArticle&ID=964984&highlight=.

¹⁵ Robert Schubert, "Washington State Wheat Breeder Won't Sow Clearfield Seed, Borlaug Warns against Privatization of Public Breeding," Cropchoice.com, May 27, 2003, http://www.cropchoice.com/leadstry4a49.html?recid=1665; Burl Gilyard, "Endless Energy," University of Minnesota Alumni Association, May 11, 2004, http://www.alumni.umn.edu/Endless_Energy.html.

¹⁶ Scott Russell Sanders, "Lessons from the Land Institute," *Audubon,* March–April, 1999, reprinted at http://magazine.audubon.org/landinstitute.html.

[17] Chevron Corporation, advertisement for willyoujoinus.com, n.d., http://www.willyoujoinus.com/advertising/print/.

[18] Alexei Barrionuevo, "Boom in Ethanol Reshapes Economy of Heartland," *New York Times*, June 25, 2006, http://www.nytimes.com/2006/06/25/business/25 ethanol.html?ex=1308888000&en=3db79885d5ce7f34&ei=5088&partner=rssnyt& emc=rss.

[19] Mark Jaffe, "Pure Power," *Philadelphia Inquirer*, 1995, http://sln.fi.edu/inquirer/hydrocar.html.

[20] Wes Jackson, *Becoming Native to This Place* (New York: Counterpoint Press, 1994), 102.

[21] Wendell Berry, *The Unsettling of America: Culture and Agriculture*, 3rd ed. (1977; reprint, San Francisco: Sierra Club Books, 1996).

[22] Jackson, *Becoming Native to This Place*, 14.

[23] Ibid.

[24] Ibid., 18.

[25] Ibid., 20.

[26] Ibid., 80.

[27] Ibid.

[28] Ibid., 112.

[29] Ibid., 114–115.

[30] Ibid., 4.

[31] Ibid.

[32] Ibid., 3, 88.

[33] See the "Wheat State" tour web site at http://www.wheatstate.ku.edu/.

[34] Center for Rural Affairs, "Research and the 2007 Farm Bill," white paper, 2007, http://www.cfra.org/policy/2007/research/whitepaper.

[35] Jacqueline Edmondson, "Prairie Town: Rural Life and Literacies," *Journal of Research in Rural Education* 17, 1 (Spring 2001): 3–11.

[36] Ibid.

[37] Jackson, *Becoming Native to This Place*, 3.

[38] Ibid., 105.

[39] Horace Herring, "Jevon's Paradox," *The Encyclopedia of Earth*, November 30, 2007, http://www.eoearth.org/article/Jevon's_Paradox.

[40] Energy Future Coalition, "Frequently Asked Questions," n.d., http://www.energyfuturecoalition.org/preview.cfm?catID=39.

[41] R. James Woolsey, "Gentlemen, Start Your Plug-Ins," *Wall Street Journal*, December 30, 2006.

[42] S. Harris Math Cartoons, at "Science Cartoons Plus," n.d., http://www.sciencecartoonsplus.com/galmath2.htm#.

[43] Aldo Leopold was one of the founders of wildlife preservation, conservation, and environmentalism. His *Sand County Almanac* (1949; reprint, New York: Oxford University Press, 2001) has sold over 2 million copies and remains in print today; his influence is often compared to that of Henry David Thoreau and John Muir. The sustainable agriculture institute at Iowa State University is named for him.

[44] For purposes of this book, the term "livestock" is defined broadly and includes all domestic animals commonly raised for food.

[45] "Kansas Ethanol Fact Sheet," ksgrains.com, n.d., http://www.ksgrains.com/ethanol/kseth.html#Plantspercent20Underpercent20Construction; ksgrains.com is sponsored by the Kansas Corn Commission, the Kansas Grain Sorghum Commission, the Kansas Corn Growers Association, and the Kansas Grains Sorghum Producers Association. See also the Nebraska Ethanol Board, "Nebraska Ethanol Industry: Ethanol Plants in Nebraska," n.d., http://www.ne-ethanol.org/industry/ethplants.htm; and Lauren Etter and Bill Thompson, "Big Corn Crop May Not Curb Prices," *Wall Street Journal*, March 21, 2007.

[46] Barrionuevo, "Boom in Ethanol."

[47] Scott Kilman, "Corn Is Booming as Ethanol Heats Up," *Wall Street Journal*, November 4–5, 2006. Also see Iowa Corn, "Ethanol: Frequently Asked Questions about DDGS [Distillers Dried Grains with Solubles]," http://www.iowacorn.org/ethanol/ethanol_12.html#About. Iowa Corn is sponsored by the Iowa Corn Promotion Board and the Iowa Corn Growers Association. There is some indication that DDGS may not be as suitable for hogs or poultry as it is for cattle, and even as cattle feed it is subject to the same concerns that apply to other corn-based feed and their effects on animals that evolved primarily as grass eaters.

[48] M. T. Kidd, "Successful Broiler Production Depends on a Sound Feeding Program," Information Sheet 1609, n.d., Mississippi State University, Mississippi State, http://www.msstate.edu/dept/poultry/pubs/is1609.htm.

[49] Thomas Rowe Mastick, "Farming Pioneers to Pioneer Factory Farmers," *The Land Report*, no. 87, Land Institute, Salina, Kansas, Spring 2007, 6.

[50] Farm Sanctuary, "U.S. Hog Farms Get Bigger But Not Better," *Farm Sanctuary News*, Spring, 2002, http://www.farmsanctuary.org/newsletter/hog_farms.htm. Farm Sanctuary also sometimes engages in rescue missions for mistreated livestock, conducts education campaigns, and lobbies for government action, for example, opposing the practice of allowing ill or "downer" cattle to enter the food supply. The USDA banned such practices in 2003.

[51] CertifiedAngusBeef.com, "Map of CAB License Feedlots," n.d., http://www.cabpartners.com/feedlots/map.php.

[52] NationalBeef.com, "In the News: National Beef Acquires Vintage™ Natural Beef," August 1, 2006, http://www.nationalbeef.com/newsTrans.asp?ID=54. Interestingly, and something of a sign of the times, in addition to its primary products, National Beef—which processes more than three million cattle a year—has two lines of "natural" beef and recently bought California-based Vintage Natural Beef.

[53] Corporation for the Northern Rockies, "Sustainable Land Stewardship," n.d., http://www.northrock.org/sustainability/stewardship.shtml.

[54] Ibid.

[55] University of California, "What Is Sustainable Agriculture?" Sustainable Agriculture Research and Education Program, Davis, California, December 1997, http://www.sarep.ucdavis.edu/concept.htm.

[56] Holistic Management International, web site at http://www.holisticmanagement.org/. Holistic Management International is based in Albuquerque, New Mexico, and provides holistic management services to nonagricultural businesses and manufacturers.

[57] Greta Hunter Watson and Nessa Richman, "Dynamic Ranching, Texas Style," *Farm Stories,* Southern Sustainable Agriculture Working Group, January 1994, http://www.ssawg.org/maddox.html.

[58] R. H. Richardson, "Environmental Resilience and Sustainable Conservation," *Earthworks: An Online Journal of Geography from the University of Texas at Austin,* April 27, 1996, http://www.utexas.edu/depts/grg/eworks/proceedings/engeo/richardson/richardson.html.

[59] Michael Pollan, *The Omnivore's Dilemma* (New York, Penguin Press: 2006), 61. See also Ronald A. Wirtz, "A Fair Price for Whom?" *Fedgazette* (a publication of the Federal Reserve Bank of Minneapolis), March 2002, http://www.minneapolisfed.org/pubs/fedgaz/02-03/price.cfm.

[60] Sustainable Agriculture Research and Education, "Profile: Dick and Sharon Thompson and Family, Boone, Iowa," in *The New American Farmer.*

[61] The Polyface Farm web site is at http://www.polyfacefarms.com/.

[62] Watson and Richman, "Dynamic Ranching, Texas Style."

CHAPTER 15. ETHANOL AND ALTERNATIVE ENERGY: RURAL AMERICA'S SAVIORS?

[1] Mark Clayton, "New Prospects for U.S. Glut of Ethanol Plants," *Christian Science Monitor,* January 5, 2007, http://www.csmonitor.com/2007/0105/p01s04-wmgn.html.

[2] Alexei Barrionuevo, "Boom in Ethanol Reshapes Economy of Heartland," *New York Times,* June 25, 2006, http://www.nytimes.com/2006/06/25/business/25 ethanol.html?ex=1308888000&en=3db79885d5ce7f34&ei=5088&partner=rssnyt& emc=rss.

[3] See the 25×'25 web site at http://www.25x25.org/.

[4] Jim Carlton, "Kleiner's Green Investment Machine," *Wall Street Journal,* December 14, 2006.

[5] George W. Bush, "State of the Union," January 23, 2007, http://www. whitehouse.gov/stateoftheunion/2007/index.html.

[6] Nick Timiraos, "Inside Bush's Energy Proposals," *Wall Street Journal,* January 27, 2007.

[7] Vinod Khosla, "The War on Oil," *Wall Street Journal,* January 23, 2007.

[8] Patrick Barta, "Jatropha Plant Gains Steam in Global Race for Biofuels," *Wall Street Journal,* August 24, 2007.

[9] Lester Brown, quoted in Prasenjit Bhattacharya, "Ethanol Could Fuel Rise in Corn," *Wall Street Journal,* January 16, 2007.

[10] Elisabeth Malkin, "Thousands in Mexico City Protest Rising Food Prices," *New York Times,* February 1, 2007, http://www.nytimes.com/2007/02/01/world/ americas/01mexico.html?ex=1327986000&en=3e1fadc41a37e9e9&ei=5088& partner=rssnyt&emc=rss&pagewanted=print.

[11] Reuters, "Coke Bottler Plans to Cut 3,500 Jobs," February 14, 2007, http:// www.nytimes.com/2007/02/14/business/14coke.html?ex=1329109200&en= ddf9a0b55aa5c64b&ei=5088&partner=rssnyt&emc=rss.

[12] Ilan Brat and Thadeus Herrick, "Ethanol Boom Fuels Brisk Sales of Midwest Farmland," *Wall Street Journal,* March 7, 2006.

[13] John J. Fialka, "DOE Sets Ethanol-Fuel Effort," *Wall Street Journal,* March 1, 2007.

[14] Timothy Egan, "The Nation: Refueled: Life on the Ethanol Guzzling Prairie," *New York Times,* February 11, 1007, http://select.nytimes.com/gst/ abstract.html?res=F30D17F9355B0C728DDDAB0894DF404482&n=Top%2f Reference%2fTimes%20Topics%2fSubjects%2fE%2fEthanol.

[15] Ibid.

[16] U.S. Senate Committee on Energy and Natural Resources, "Energy Bill Brings Prosperity to Rural America," press release, June 14, 2006, http://energy. senate.gov/public/index.cfm?FuseAction=PressReleases.Detail&PressRelease_id =234992&Month=6&Year=2006.

[17] Julie Watson, "Latin Corn Farmers See Gold in Ethanol," *International Business Times,* February 19, 2007, http://www.ibtimes.com/articles/20070219/

mexico-corn-bonanza.htm; Bryan Gruley, "Energy Boom Lifts Small-Town Hope on Northern Plains," *Wall Street Journal,* December 1, 2006.; Steve Raabe, "The Newest Cash Crop: Ethanol," *Denver Post,* April 8, 2007.

[18] Gruley, "Energy Boom Lifts Small-Town Hope."

[19] Egan, "The Nation: Refueled: Life on the Ethanol Guzzling Prairie."

[20] Renewable Fuels Association, "Industry Statistics," n.d., http://www.ethanolrfa.org/industry/statistics/.

[21] Leopold Center for Sustainable Agriculture, "ISU Study Determines Regional Economic Values of Ethanol Production in Iowa," September 22, 2006, press release, http://www.leopold.iastate.edu/news/newsreleases/2006/ethanol_092206.htm.

[22] National Corn Growers Association, "Study: Farmer-Owned Ethanol Plants Contribute More to Local Economies," September 12, 2006, http://ncga.com//news/releases/2006/news091206.asp.

[23] David Morris, "Energizing Rural America: Local Ownership of Renewable Energy Production Is the Key," Center for American Progress, January 2007, http://www.americanprogress.org/issues/2007/01/pdf/rural_energy.pdf.

[24] Leopold Center for Sustainable Agriculture, "ISU Study Determines Regional Economic Values."

[25] Matthew Robinson, "U.S. Ethanol Firms May Scrap Plants as Margins Fall," Reuters, January 22, 2007, http://www.alertnet.org/thenews/newsdesk/N22604105.htm.

[26] Lauren Etter and Ilan Brat, "Ethanol Boom Is Running Out of Gas," *Wall Street Journal,* October 1, 2007, A2.

[27] Robinson, "U.S. Ethanol Firms May Scrap Plants"; and Marcus Balogh, "Ethanol Unlikely to Fully Solve US Oil Issues," Credit Suisse, June 23, 2006, http://emagazine.credit-suisse.com/app/article/index.cfm?fuseaction=OpenArticle&aoid=155644&lang=EN.

[28] Jonathan Fahey, "Ethanol: Payback Time," January 23, 2007, http://www.forbes.com/2007/01/23/ethanol-energy-conservation-biz-energy-cz_jf_0123ethanol.html.

[29] California Energy Commission, "Fuel Ethanol Terminal Market Price—18-Month History," November 2005–May 2007, http://www.energy.ca.gov/gasoline/graphs/ethanol_18-month.html; Chicago Board of Trade, October 2, 2007, http://www.cbot.com/cbot/pub/page/0,3181,1754,00.html; Lauren Etter, "Ethanol Craze Cools as Doubts Multiply," *Wall Street Journal,* November 28, 2007, A1.

[30] John J. Fialka, "Coalition Pushes Wider Ethanol Use," *Wall Street Journal,* February 28, 2007.

[31] Joe Barrett, "Ethanol Reaps a Backlash in Small Midwestern Towns," *Wall Street Journal,* March 23, 2007.

[32] C. Ford Runge and Benjamin Senauer, "How Biofuels Could Starve the Poor," *Foreign Affairs,* May/June 2007.

[33] Kimberley Strassel, "Ethanol's Bitter Taste," *Wall Street Journal,* May 18, 2007.

[34] Holman W. Jenkins, "Ethanol Liberation Movement," *Wall Street Journal,* March 14, 2007.

[35] Shelly Banjo, "Bumper Crops of Corn, Problems by the Bushel," *Wall Street Journal,* August 10, 2007.

[36] Ilan Brat and Daniel Machalara, "Can Ethanol Get a Ticket to Ride?" *Wall Street Journal,* February 1, 2007.

CHAPTER 16. REINVENTING RURAL AMERICA:
THE BUFFALO COMMONS AND OTHER REGIONAL METAPHORS

[1] Frank Popper and Deborah Popper, interviewed by author, New York City, August 4, 2006. Frank is still a professor at Rutgers, Deborah is now an associate professor at the College of Staten Island/City University of New York, and both are visiting professors at Princeton University. Quotes from the Poppers and references to their work, unless otherwise cited, came from the meeting with them and from subsequent correspondence.

[2] Frank J. Popper, "The Strange Case of the Contemporary American Frontier," *Yale Review* 76 (Autumn 1986): 101–121.

[3] Deborah Epstein Popper and Frank J. Popper, "The Great Plains: From Dust to Dust," *Planning Magazine,* December 1987. In fact, buffalo roamed across much of the United States and Canada, but they thrived on the prairie grasslands, their most recent home territory.

[4] Dr. Todd Kerstetter, "Where the West Begins," *Frog & Globe,* n.d., http://www.his.tcu.edu/Frog&Globe/SiteArchives/Kerstetter-West.htm.

[5] Walter Prescott Webb, *The Great Plains* (Boston: Ginn & Co., 1931), 3–36.

[6] Popper and Popper, "The Great Plains: From Dust to Dust."

[7] Craig Miner, *Next Year Country* (Lawrence: University Press of Kansas, 2006), 254.

[8] Dave Ranney, "Buffalo Commons Idea Gets Second Look," *Lawrence Journal-World,* February 9, 2004, http://www2.ljworld.com/news/2004/feb/09/buffalo_commons_idea/.

[9] Ibid.

[10] Popper and Popper, "The Great Plains: From Dust to Dust."

[11] Matt Moline, "Land Use Ideas Resurface: Forum at K-State to Discuss Controversial Buffalo Commons Research," *Topeka Capital-Journal,* March 21, 2004, http://www.cjonline.com/stories/020204/kan_landuse.shtml.

[12] Popper and Popper, "The Great Plains: From Dust to Dust."

[13] C. J. Donlan, H. W. Greene, J. Berger, C. E. Bock, J. H. Bock, D. A. Burney, J. A. Estes, D. Forman, P. S. Martin, G. W. Roemer, F. A. Smith, and M. E. Soulé, "Re-wilding North America," *Nature* 436 (August 18, 2005): 913–914.

[14] Robert Roy Britt, "Lions, Camels and Elephants, Oh My! Wild Kingdom Proposed for U.S.," LiveScience, August 17, 2005, http://www.livescience.com/animalworld/050817_big_animals.html.

[15] Frank Popper and Deborah Popper, "The Buffalo Commons: Metaphor as Method," *Geographical Review,* October 1999, 465.

[16] Ibid.

[17] Mark Gunther, "Ted Turner's Montana Adventure," *Fortune,* October 4, 2006, http://money.cnn.com/2006/10/03/news/economy/pluggedin_gunther_bison.fortune/index.htm.

[18] John Cloud, "Why the Buffalo Roam," *Time,* March 15, 2007, http://www.time.com/time/magazine/article/0,9171,1599697,00.html.

[19] National Agricultural Statistics Service, "U.S. Cattle Supplies and Disposition," March 24, 2006, U.S. Department of Agriculture, http://www.usda.gov/nass/PUBS/TODAYRPT/speca06.pdf.

[20] Joseph T. Hallinan, "A Pheasant Boom Lifts Farm Fortunes on Great Plains," *Wall Street Journal,* November 17, 2006.

[21] Ibid.

[22] North Dakota Game and Fish Department, "Small Game Hunting," n.d., http://gf.nd.gov/hunting/small-game.html.

[23] Alexei Barrionuevo, "Boom in Ethanol Reshapes Economy of Heartland," *New York Times,* June 25, 2006, http://www.nytimes.com/2006/06/25/business/25ethanol.html?ex=1308888000&en=3db79885d5ce7f34&ei=5088&partner=rssnyt&emc=rss.

[24] Popper and Popper, "The Buffalo Commons: Metaphor as Method," 501.

[25] Rick Lyman, "2 Commanding Publishers, 2 Powerful Empires," *New York Times,* March 14, 2000.

[26] Popper and Popper, "The Buffalo Commons: Metaphor as Method," 503.

[27] Ibid.

[28] Kansas Governor Kathleen Sebelius, "State of the State Address," January 10, 2007, http://www.governor.ks.gov/news/sp-stateofstate2007.htm.

AFTERWORD

[1] "How 'Ya Gonna Keep 'Em down on the Farm (after They've Seen Paree)?" lyrics by Joe Young and Sam M. Lewis with music by Walter Donaldson (1918); lyrics are posted at "How 'Ya Gonna Keep 'Em down on the Farm (after They've Seen Paree)," http://www.usgennet.org/usa/mo/county/stlouis/ww1-music/downonthefarm.htm.

[2] "New Starbucks Opens in Rest Room of Existing Starbucks," *Onion,* July 27, 1998, http://www.theonion.com/content/node/29030.

[3] Charlotte Hogg, *From the Garden Club: Rural Women Writing Community* (Lincoln: University of Nebraska Press, 2006).

Index